Social Theory and the Politics of Higher Education: Critical Perspectives on Institutional Research

Social Theory and Methodology in Education Research series
Edited by Mark Murphy

The Bloomsbury *Social Theory and Methodology in Education Research* series brings together books exploring various applications of social theory in educational research design. Each book provides a detailed account of how theory and method influence each other in specific educational research settings, such as schools, early childhood education, community education, further education colleges and universities. Books in the series represent the richness of topics explored in theory-driven education research, including leadership and governance, equity, teacher education, assessment, curriculum and policy studies. This innovative series provides a timely platform for highlighting the wealth of international work carried out in the field of social theory and education research, a field that has grown considerably in recent years and has made the likes of Pierre Bourdieu and Michel Foucault familiar names in educational discourse. Books in the *Social Theory and Methodology in Education Research* series offer an excellent resource for those who wish to use theoretical concepts in their research but are not sure how to do so, and who want to better understand how theory can be effectively applied in research contexts, in practically realisable ways.

Also available in the series

Education Governance and Social Theory, edited by Andrew Wilkins and Antonio Olmedo
Foucault and School Leadership Research, Denise Mifsud
Norbert Elias and the Sociology of Education, Eric Lybeck
Social Theory for Teacher Education Research, edited by Kathleen Nolan and Jennifer Tupper
The Future of Qualitative Research, edited by Matthew Thomas and Robin Bellingham

Forthcoming in the series

Education Research with Bourdieu, Shaun Rawolle
Poststructuralist Theory and Educational Research, Tim Jay

Social Theory and the Politics of Higher Education: Critical Perspectives on Institutional Research

Edited by
Mark Murphy, Ciaran Burke, Cristina Costa
and Rille Raaper

BLOOMSBURY ACADEMIC
LONDON • NEW YORK • OXFORD • NEW DELHI • SYDNEY

BLOOMSBURY ACADEMIC
Bloomsbury Publishing Plc
50 Bedford Square, London, WC1B 3DP, UK
1385 Broadway, New York, NY 10018, USA

BLOOMSBURY, BLOOMSBURY ACADEMIC and the Diana logo are trademarks
of Bloomsbury Publishing Plc

First published in Great Britain 2021

Series design by Louise Dugdale
Cover image © metamorworks / iStock

A catalogue record for this book is available from the British Library.

A catalog record for this book is available from the Library of Congress.

ISBN: HB: 978-1-3501-4155-1
        ePDF: 978-1-3501-4156-8
        eBook: 978-1-3501-4157-5

Series: Social Theory and Methodology in Education Research

Typeset by RefineCatch Limited, Bungay, Suffolk

To find out more about our authors and books visit www.bloomsbury.com
and sign up for our newsletters.

Contents

Contributors

Jen Azordegan has worked as a contract academic, researcher and project officer in Australian higher education for over a decade. She previously worked as an education policy researcher in the US in the not-for-profit sector. Jen recently completed her PhD, which explores the experience of an Australian school engaging parents from an Afghan refugee background. Guided by the work of Pierre Bourdieu, the study details the complexities involved in school/family relationships in a modern, multicultural Australia and considers the role of schools in perpetuating cycles of disadvantage. In 2019, Jen was appointed Evaluation and Strategic Projects Manager at the Australian Catholic University, where she evaluates and researches university-community engagement from the student, staff and community perspective. This is her first permanent role in an Australian university.

Ciaran Burke is an Associate Professor of Higher Education at the University of the West of England. His research largely draws on Bourdieu's theory of practice to examine social inequalities in higher education and the graduate labour market. Most recently his research has focused on graduate resilience and inequalities within cultural and creative industries. He is the co-founder and co-convenor of the British Sociological Association's "Bourdieu Study Group" and co-convenor of the Society for Research into Higher Education's "Employability, Enterprise and Work-Based Learning Network"

Fabian Cannizzo is a sociologist in Melbourne, Victoria, Australia. His research interests include the cultural sociology of academic life, careers in the creative industries, and the intersection between education and cultural production. His latest works include 'Tactical evaluations: Everyday neoliberalism in academia' (*Journal of Sociology*) and (with Nick Osbaldiston) *The Social Structures of Global Academia* (Routledge, 2019).

Kate Carruthers Thomas is a Senior Research Fellow and Project Manager for Athena SWAN at Birmingham City University, UK. Kate specialises in interdisciplinary enquiry into contemporary higher education, inequalities and gender. She has recently published research on rethinking student belonging (Routledge, 2018) and gender as a geography of power in the academy (Palgrave

Macmillan, 2019). Kate uses poetics and graphics as well as conventional academic formats to present and discuss her work.

Cristina Costa is an academic at Durham University, UK. She has a strong interest in exploring the intersection of education and emergent social phenomena through different social theory lenses. She has conducted research on digital literacies and digital inequalities, curriculum innovation, digital scholarship practices, and widening participation, with an emphasis on student estrangement in higher education.

Fiona Christie is a Senior Research Associate, Decent Work and Productivity Research Centre, Manchester Metropolitan University (MMU), UK. Fiona is a careers professional who has moved into a research career. Her professional life has included extensive advice and guidance, teaching and management in higher education (Universities of Manchester and Salford), having originally qualified and practised in the secondary/further education sector. In her research life she completed her part-time PhD in Educational Research (Higher Education) with Lancaster University in 2018. Her focus was on graduate transitions, careers and employability. She is currently the Director of Research and Knowledge for the Association of Graduate Careers Advisory Services (AGCAS). Her research interests include career studies, career development, education, employability, higher education, inequalities, professional identity, social justice, social learning theories, social mobility, and work.

Fiona Creaby is a Senior Lecturer at Manchester Metropolitan University (MMU) UK. She specialises in leadership development and business management drawing on many years spent in non-profit and public sector contexts, state schools, NGOs and social enterprise charities. Her research interests include identity studies, reflexivity and sociocultural theory and her doctoral research explored leadership identity through the lens of Figured Worlds.

Stephen Day is Head of the Division of Education at the University of the West of Scotland. His recent work focuses on Secondary and Primary science education and the development of higher education students' criticality.

Jess Harris is an Associate Professor at the University of Newcastle, New South Wales, Australia. Her research interests focus primarily on practices to change traditional structures in order to improve education for all students, both in Australia and internationally. She has a specific interest in qualitative research methods, using conversation analysis and methodology to analyse structures and patterns in social interactions in institutional settings. Jess worked in fixed-term, research-only positions for over a decade before, during and after her doctoral studies. She began an ongoing appointment at the University of Newcastle in 2016.

David Hodgson is Senior Lecturer in Social Work at Curtin University, Perth, Western Australia. David has conducted research in the areas of compulsory school leaving policy, school attrition, services for families and children, and social work curriculum. David is an Associate Editor for the journal *Australian Social Work*, and he has recently co-authored two books: *Key Concepts and Theory in Social Work* (Palgrave Macmillan, 2017) *and Social Justice Theory and Practice for Social Work: Critical and Philosophical Perspectives* (Springer, 2019).

Alexandra Jones is a Lecturer at the University of Newcastle, New South Wales, Australia. Her research interests include comparative education, cosmopolitan studies and globalised trends in educational policy. Sitting at the intersection of sociology and human geography, her own research draws upon feminist and post-humanist analytical frameworks to study the cosmopolitan and othering practices of teachers and students in a range of educational settings. Alexandra was employed as a casual researcher for seven years, during and after her doctoral studies. She is currently employed on contract at the University of Newcastle.

Tomás Koch is a faculty member at the Social Sciences Faculty, Playa Ancha University (Chile) and PhD student at the Centre for Social Theory of Ghent University (Belgium). His research interests include scholarly communication, the sociology of science and the sociology of higher education. Currently his research concerns the evolution of scholarly communication. He is also a member of Observatorio de Participación Social y Territorio (Playa Ancha University).

Julio Labraña is a researcher at the Center of Comparative Educational Polices, University Diego Portales (Chile) and PhD from the Universität Witten/Herdecke. His work focuses in particular on the changes in contemporary higher education systems and their impact on society as a whole, the sociology of higher education and the history of ideas. He is also a member of Núcleo de Estudios Sistémicos Transdisciplinarios (Universidad de Chile) and the Latin American Studies Association (LASA).

Eric Lybeck is a Presidential Academic Fellow at the Manchester Institute of Education at the University of Manchester, UK. Working in the emerging field of

Critical University Studies, his work draws on processual and civic approaches to social knowledge and practices to make new connections between the disciplines of sociology and education. This includes analysis contained in his forthcoming book, *The University Revolution*, to be published by Routledge, that interprets the rise of the modern university as equivalent in significance to the industrial and democratic revolutions. His doctoral research at Cambridge explored the history of the social and legal sciences during the late-nineteenth century transfer of university models from Germany to America, and his current postdoctoral research examined changes in student expectations in Britain. He is currently editor-in-chief of the journal *Civic Sociology*, published by University of California Press.

Mark Murphy is Reader in Education & Public Policy, School of Education, University of Glasgow. He has published widely in the field of social theory and applied research, with books including the forthcoming *Social Theory: A New Introduction* (Palgrave, 2021), *Habermas and Social Research: Between Theory and Method* (Routledge, 2017), *Theory as Method: On Bourdieu, Education and Society* (with C. Costa, Routledge, 2016) and *Bourdieu, Habitus and Social Research: The Art of Application* (with C. Costa, Palgrave, 2015). Mark is the editor of the book series *Social Theory and Methodology in Education Research* (Bloomsbury Press) and is co-editor of the multi-authored website www.socialtheoryapplied.com.

Anne Pirrie is a Reader in Education at the University of the West of Scotland. Her recent book *Virtue and the Quiet Art of Scholarship: Reclaiming the University* (Routledge, 2019) offers a fresh and unorthodox perspective on what it means to be a 'good knower' in a social and educational environment dominated by the market order.

Rille Raaper is Assistant Professor in the School of Education at Durham University. Rille's research interests and experience lie in the sociology of higher education. She is particularly interested in student experience and identity, related university policies and practices, and student politics. She has conducted numerous research projects on higher education policy and practice and its impact on students as learners, citizens as well as political agents. She has published widely in high impact journals such as the Journal of Education Policy, Critical Studies in Education, British Journal of Sociology of Education and Teaching in Higher Education. She is a member of the editorial board for the journals Critical Studies in Education, Teaching in Higher Education, and the Journal of Applied Social Theory.

James Rattenbury is a Senior Lecturer at Manchester Metropolitan University (MMU), UK. After graduating from Manchester Polytechnic in 1988, he worked in industry and local government before returning to lecture at MMU in 2002. He holds a Post Graduate Certificate in Education, a Masters in Research and a Masters in Professional Studies. He is a fellow of the Association of Chartered Certified Accountants (ACCA), and a former ACCA examination assessor. His research interests include social mobility and widening participation, professional identity and social theories of learning.

Diego A. Salazar-Morales is a doctoral candidate at King's College London. He has previously held research positions at the Hertie School of Governance, Berlin and the LSE where he completed his MSc in Public Policy and Administration. Diego has also professional experience in various positions of the Peruvian government, including: Ministry of Education, Superintendence of Higher Education and National Planning Centre. His research interests are in global politics, policy instruments, and implementation with a special focus on education, health and fiscal policies.

Nerida Spina is a Senior Lecturer at the Queensland University of Technology, Australia. Her research interests include everyday work and experiences of teacher, school leaders and pre-service teachers. She is also interested in teacher inquiry and social justice. Her research is situated within the sociology of education, with a particular interest in applying the method of inquiry known as institutional ethnography to reveal power relations and structures. Nerida was employed as a casual and contract researcher for a decade before, during and after her doctoral studies.

Cedomir Vuckovic is a PhD candidate at the University of Manchester, UK affiliated with both The Morgan Centre for Research into Everyday Lives, and Movements @ Manchester. Cedomir's PhD research focuses on the recent changes to English higher education, such as the 2012 tuition fee increase, and how these may have encouraged new strategies of resistance, protest and non-conformity. His approach involves working with participatory design methods alongside more traditional qualitative methods, to explore the more 'everyday' forms of resistance that students may engage in outside of formally organised protest, such as withdrawal, apathy and non-conforming identities.

Lynelle Watts is a Senior Lecturer at Curtin University, Perth, Western Australia. Lynelle has conducted research in the areas of teaching and learning in higher education, reflective practice and critical reflexivity in social work, social work curriculum, and assessment tools for carers of people with mental illness. Lynelle is the Associate Editor (Social Media) for the journal *Australian Social Work*. In addition to teaching and researching in social work, Lynelle is the co-author of two books: *Key Concepts and Theory in Social Work* (Palgrave Macmillan, 2017) and *Social Justice Theory and Practice for Social Work* (Springer, 2019).

Luísa Winter Pereira has a degree in Law from the Federal University of Paraná (Brazil) and an Erasmus Mundus Master's Degree in Women's and Gender Studies from the University of Łódź (Poland) and the University of Granada (Spain). She is the author of articles on gender-based violence and institutional violence within the academic context. Currently, as a geoepistemic migrant, she is writing her PhD between the University of Granada's 'Women's Studies, Gender Discourses and its Practices' programme and the Centre for Social Studies of the University of Coimbra's 'Postcolonialisms and Global Citizenship' programme amid precarious work and terrific academic enthusiasm. Her research focuses on the production of woman-scholar subjectivity and the material conditions of knowledge production.

Series Editor's Foreword

Mark Murphy

Education research has a long history of adapting ideas from social theory. While this has always been the case when it comes to educational foundations, in recent years there has been an enormous growth in the adoption of social theory in the field of educational research. The names of theorists such as Pierre Bourdieu, Jürgen Habermas, Judith Butler and Michel Foucault have become commonplace in the field, making social theory ever-more familiar to those who both conduct education research and utilise it in their teaching.

As its familiarity increases, so too does the desire to engage with social theory in more thoughtful and effective ways. There is currently a pressing desire to apply social theory in educational research contexts, which makes sense, as without theory, much education research can be overly descriptive and/or restricted by narrow definitions of professional practice. Social theory can assist in efforts to transcend the everyday taken-for-granted understandings of education, while also reflecting erstwhile concerns around power, control, social justice and transformation.

The issue then becomes one of applying theory to method, with the focus shifting to a growing interest in the art of application itself. This interest comes with a set of key questions attached:

- How best to apply concepts such as habitus, subjectivation and performativity in educational research contexts?
- What are the ways in which methodological concerns meet theoretical ones?
- In what ways does social theory shape the quality of research outcomes?

These questions require thoughtful responses and the purpose of this book series is to help provide solutions to these issues, while also helping to develop the capacity, in particular of post-graduate and early career researchers, to successfully put social theory to work in research. This is especially important as theory application in method is a challenging and daunting enterprise. The set of theories developed by the likes of Foucault, Jacques Derrida, Bourdieu *et al*, could never be described as 'simple' or easy to navigate. On top of that there are a variety of issues faced when applying such ideas in research contexts, a field of complex interwoven imperatives and practices in its own right. These challenges – epistemological, operational, analytical – inevitably impact on researchers and our attempts to make sense of research questions, whether these be questions of governance and political regulation, social reproduction, power, cultural or professional identities (among others). So care needs to be taken when applying a challenging set of ideas onto a challenging set of practices, incorporating a consideration for both intellectual arguments alongside the concerns of the professional researcher.

The series should hold a strong appeal to researchers who are keen to apply social theory in their research, as evidenced by the growing audience for the editor's own website www.socialtheoryapplied.com. It will offer an excellent resource for those who wish to begin using theoretical concepts in their research, and will also appeal to readers who have an interest in better understanding how theory can be effectively applied in research contexts, in practically realisable ways.

In terms of output, this series is designed to provide a collection of books exploring various applications of social theory in educational research design. Each book provides a detailed account of how theory and method influence each other in specific educational research settings, such as schools, early years, community education, further education colleges and universities. The series represents the richness of topics explored in theory-driven education research, including leadership and governance, equity, teacher education, assessment, curriculum and policy studies. It also provides a timely platform for highlighting the wealth of work done in the field of social theory and education research, a field that has grown considerably in recent years and has made the likes of Pierre Bourdieu and Michel Foucault familiar names in educational discourse.

Embedded in the design of the series is an explicit pedagogical component, with a focus on the 'how' of applying theory in research methodology and an emphasis on operationalising theory in research. This pedagogical remit is addressed explicitly in the texts in different ways – the responsibility of addressing this falls to the authors and editors, but can take the form of case studies, learning activities, 'focus' sections and glossaries detailing the key theoretical concepts utilised in the research.

This book, edited by myself, Ciaran Burke, Cristina Costa and Rille Raaper, is I hope a worthy addition to the book series. It critically engages with the politics of higher education from three perspectives – institutional, academic and student. This provides a more expansive picture of the higher education environment, delivering a richer account of the political pressures and struggles affecting academic life. A more rounded perspective is especially timely at this historical juncture. As the book goes to press, universities worldwide are having to grapple with the troubling impacts of Covid 19. These impacts provide an excellent illustration of the changing world of higher education, as senior management teams struggle to adjust to a radically altered financial environment, academics scramble to transfer their teaching online, and students wonder if a virtual university experience is adequate to their needs. Covid 19 has thrown into sharp relief so many of the political issues that confront the sector in the 21st century, not just the classic debate over institutional autonomy and control, but also troubling concerns over prestige and expertise, authority and legitimacy, as well as the quasi-market economics of academic supply and demand. On top of this, the most significant health crisis in a generation has reinforced the sense that universities have never been more important to society and the economy, while also indicating that the social value and position of higher education is built on precarious foundations.

This context of social utility and precarity is fertile ground for the politicised thrust of socio-theoretical investigation, which is strongly evident in the current book. The collection incorporates a wide variety of social theories to help deliver a critical examination of the politics of higher education, including those of Barbara Adam, Michel Foucault, Margaret Archer, Niklas Luhmann, Doreen Massey, Jürgen Habermas, Pierre Bourdieu, Hartmut Rosa, Norbert Elias and Donna Haraway. This intellectual wide-lens is especially welcome, as no one theorist has a monopoly over analysis of higher education. The diversity of research approaches is also well represented in the collection, each chapter offering a unique research perspective as well as adopting a level of critical reflexivity to their research design. This diversity and reflexivity is bolstered by the range of contributors, who hail from a variety of international contexts, including the UK, Australia as well as a number of countries in South America (Brazil, Peru, Chile). Diversity is also evident in the selection of topics as case studies, which range from gender and identity, casualisation, student satisfaction through to student protest.

The focus on diversity, reflexivity and social theory speaks to another politicised aspect of higher education, the politics of research. This collection is a contribution to knowledge in social theory and education research methodologies, one that can help develop skills and expertise in the application of theory in higher education research contexts. But I hope it also contributes to broader debates about the politics of education research, and in particular the role of theory in research methodologies. Theory work is vital to research design, as without it researchers find themselves without the tools to adequately interpret the data they have collected. But the role of theory is easily overshadowed in contexts such as the UK, where the pressure to evidence 'impact' is strong, as is the pressure to fall in line with politically-motivated ideas of what constitutes 'useful' research. Although the impact agenda is not a bad thing in itself, it can have the troubling effect of narrowing innovation and originality, theory relegated to the level of esoteric. 'Impact' is also a very powerful mechanism of control, governments using their financial resources to steer the interests and efforts of academic researchers towards their own political concerns.

This is dangerous territory as original and significant theory-driven research can be sidelined, and with it the freedom to interrogate the politics of the institutions that develop and supply 'useful' research for political purposes. It is also dangerous because social theory provides an innovative alternative to bogus conceptions of value-free social science, a decades-long hangover from the positivism debates of the 1960s. Social theory provides researchers with a different take on 'value-freeness', one where academics have the *freedom to value*, to theorise the social and institutional practices of interest to them (Murphy, forthcoming). This freedom needs to be nurtured and supported – how else do we encourage new theories to develop, ones that are adequate to the task of examining the university in the 21st century?

That said, theory needs the perspective of practice, provided by research data, via which it can interrogate itself and provide a 'critical perspective' on its own reaches and limitations. This form of academic rigour is a vital component of research methodologies and design, and reflects the importance also of extending the researcher's knowledge and understanding of theories and their relevance – the freedom to theorise is dependent on this. I'm pleased to say that both of these aspects, research rigour as well as the intellectual wide-lens of social theory, are well represented in this collection. Many thanks to Ciaran, Cristina and Rille and to all the chapter authors for their excellent contributions to the book.

References

Murphy, M. (forthcoming 2021). Publicness and intellectual work: Rethinking academic freedom in the age of impact. In M. Olssen, R. Watermeyer and R. Raaper (eds), *International Handbook on academic freedom*. Cheltenham: Edward Elgar press.

Introduction: Theorising the University in an Age of Uncertainty

Mark Murphy, Ciaran Burke, Cristina Costa and Rille Raaper

Introduction

The purpose of this book is to deliver a critical examination of the changing politics of higher education through the intellectual prism of social theory. For a long time academics have applied a wide variety of social theories to help understand the workings of power in social life. This book turns the focus around and instead shines a theoretical light on the politics of academic life. Social theory and its erstwhile concerns with power and knowledge, privilege and authority, autonomy and control, is the ideal toolkit through which to deliver such an examination, and the book combines the power of theory with a wide range of methodologies, case studies and research topics.

This book is significant for a number of reasons. The higher education sector is experiencing change at a rapid rate internationally, with universities in particular pushed and pulled in various policy directions and in some regions involved in real political turmoil. There have been dramatic changes in the financing and governing of universities; alongside this, institutions have witnessed protests from students about their experience and the quality of their courses. Consumerism and marketisation have become part of the fabric of institutional and academic life, and academics in many countries consider their work and profession to be under threat and changing beyond recognition.

Based on an ever-increasing evidence base, this is all true. It is also true that modern higher education provision has a lot to live up to – it is easy to forget that, alongside the pressures of accountability, regulation and competition, universities still answer to a set of other alternative demands and desires. For all the debate over consumerism and neoliberalism, the university is still expected to assist in creating generations of independent thinkers, which in turn are expected to provide a sound basis for a critically-reasoning public that can speak truth to power. It is also expected to act as an institutional powerhouse of ideas, a prized space within which the relation between theory and practice can test itself out across a wide range of disciplines. As well as these not insignificant expectations, the university, and higher education more generally, is still judged against the once-revolutionary ideals of democracy, reason, truth and justice, ideals which uphold the university as a publicly oriented institution. This public character for many represents the beating heart of the institution (Murphy 2011; Zumeta 2011), a publicness that positions the university as a trusted broker of political, economic and cultural life.

This collection of interlinked ideals represents the counter-argument to the prevailing tendencies of control and compliance, a normative grounding for a persistent critique that has never disappeared in the discourses over academic life. But these ideals are under threat from the forces of marketisation, competition and privatisation, with critics suggesting that these combined forces leave little room to breathe for alternative forms of governance to take hold. Social theory is the vessel through which this critique makes itself heard, itself a vehicle for the upholding of enlightenment values and the ideals of justice. It is a vital set of tools by which to 'test' the sector against its most cherished values. These factors, alongside the ongoing and often fractious debates over academic freedom and the legitimacy of expert knowledge, indicate that this collection is a timely one, as it aims to examine these and other issues conceptually and to make sense of them holistically.

The book explores these topics through a theoretical 'wide lens', putting to work the ideas of Michel Foucault, Niklas Luhmann, Barbara Adam, Doreen Massey, Margaret Archer, Jürgen Habermas, Pierre Bourdieu, Hartmut Rosa, Norbert Elias and Donna Haraway, among others. The collection incorporates a wide variety of social theories to help deliver a critical examination of the politics of higher education. Alongside this, the case study chapters draw on a range of approaches to research, and each chapter includes a set of critical reflections on how they have sought to relate social theory and research methodology. There are also a number of excellent examples of hybridised approaches to theoretical work, with one chapter, for example, exploring governance through the dual lens of Luhmann/Foucault.

In terms of contributors, the book draws on the expertise of researchers from a wide range of geographical contexts, including authors from the UK and Australia, as well as countries in South America (Brazil, Peru, Chile). The book includes a set of case studies of higher education from three different continents

(Europe, Australia, South America), thereby shining a light on the international context of higher education. Researchers from all career stages are represented, including a number of early career researchers who can talk to their experience of conducting PhD research. Diversity is also evident in the selection of topics as case studies, which range from gender and identity, casualisation, research performance through to student protest.

The book offers a close fit to the series in which it is published: *Social Theory and Methodology in Education Research*. One of the ways in which this fit is delivered is the requirement that every case study chapter includes a section entitled 'critical reflections on social theory and methodology'. This provides a space for contributors and readers to consider the ways in which the research evidence bridges the gap between theory and method – a key objective of this book and the series more generally.

Pedagogical features

The book has a strong pedagogical component, designed to assist the reader in understanding the relation between social theory and higher education research. This is reflected in the design of key aspects of the book, which include:

Context chapters: As well as this more general introduction to the book, each section has an opening chapter which provides an overview of some of the major political and theoretical issues that impact institutional governance, academic work and the student experience. This will offer the reader a strong basis from which to engage with the subsequent chapters in each section.

Focus on theory and method: Each case study chapter includes a section entitled 'critical reflections on social theory and methodology', which provides a space for contributors and readers to consider the ways in which the research evidence bridges the gap between theory and method – a key objective of the series in which this collection belongs.

Consistent focus: A consistent and recurring theme throughout the content is the ways in which a changing political landscape has impacted on institutional life, whether this be in relation to institutional governance, academic work or the student experience. This shared focus allows the reader to build connections between conceptual frameworks and to enhance their knowledge of the relationship between social theory and methodology across the research field.

Organisation and content of the book

The book is organised into three sections, preceded by an introduction. The three sections are:

1. Social theory and university governance
2. Social theory and the politics of academic work
3. Social theory and the politics of student experience

The content of the book covers three key areas: (1) institutional governance, with a specific focus on issues such as measurement, surveillance, accountability, regulation, performance and institutional reputation; (2) academic work, covering areas such as the changing nature of academic labour, neoliberalism and academic identity, and the role of gender and gender studies in university life; and (3) student experience, which includes case studies of student politics and protest, the impact of graduate debt and changing student identities. Each section begins with an introductory chapter, designed to 'set the scene' for the case studies that follow. With this structure, the book identifies how the changing politics of higher education has impacted on institutional governance, as well as the two main groups of people affected by these politics: academics and students. This offers a form of research triangulation, providing a privileged vantage point from which to assess the various ramifications of changing political imperatives. The structure also allows readers to compare and contrast different conceptual and research approaches within their own specialised research field.

Section 1: Social theory and university governance

The section on social theory and university governance introduces the reader to three pertinent ways of exploring the field of academic governance whilst applying different theoretical lenses. The works of Nobert Elias, Michel Foucault and Niklas Luhmann are put to work with the intention of promoting critical debate about different issues currently impacting the academy. These include: (1) a discussion of emerging managerial hierarchies as a by-product of increasing external and internal pressures placed on the academy; (2) the deconstruction of student satisfaction data as a key indicator of quality and governing strategies; and (3) an analysis of accountability mechanisms that foment a type of performativity that undermines the conventions associated with the university. All three chapters speak to key issues currently affecting academia internationally and all three chapters make use of social theory to emphasise the importance of these tools in fostering deeper understandings of the issues at hand. Two of the chapters in this section combine the work of different theorists in the search for new, original perspectives, thus breaking away from a monological approach to theorising to which the field of education research has grown accustomed. This is particularly visible in two of the chapters in this section (Chapters 4 and 5), as detailed below.

Chapter 2 sets the scene for the section, providing an introduction to key issues pertaining to the governance of universities. Mark Murphy opens the chapter with a succinct account of how university governance has changed in the last decades to embrace a business-oriented and marketised model. The 'traditional' collegial model of institutional governance, he argues, found itself marginalised in the face of managerial imperatives such as efficiency and performance, alongside heightened surveillance and disciplinary practices as adjustments and answers to what he calls an 'uber-competitive environment'. It is in this regard that Murphy asserts that university governance provides fertile ground for socio-theoretical explorations, as social theory has often found a home in governance studies, through the insights of different theorists such as Max Weber, Michel Foucault and Pierre Bourdieu; theorists that have been applied to modern-day academic governance by a range of academics.

In Chapter 3, Erik Lybeck explores changes in university administration and governance in the UK in relation to the works of Norbert Elias. He discusses the emergence of new hierarchies due to internal and external pressures, especially state and market interventions, which position vice chancellors at the centre of decision-making. From this perspective, Lybeck invites the reader to interpret the structure of university executive groups as a kind of court society, homologous to the absolutist courts Elias analysed in *The Court Society* and *The Civilizing Process*. In these contexts, etiquette and manners were binding norms that agents could not afford to challenge due to the threat of exclusion from these figurations. A parallel can be drawn with current academic figurations in that no manager has the power to challenge the structure. Making use of archival research techniques, Lybeck conducts his inquiry in the context of an elite university in the UK and, in comparison with other university charters, statutes and ordinances, applies Elias' work on 'game models' to contemporary phenomena, namely the UK academic union strikes of March 2018. He concludes that the strikes amounted to a popular revolt akin to the French Revolution, in which the authority of court was challenged by rank-and-file staff – even though the 'revolution' may have stalled. This suggests perhaps that reforms could re-establish balance in the wake of this otherwise unplanned, unintended, yet inefficient and unjust configuration.

Next, in Chapter 4, Stephen Day and Anne Pirrie explore how the Foucauldian concepts of governmentality, subjectification and technologies of self can be put to work in understanding how measures of student satisfaction have effects on the relationship between academics and students as well as working practices in the university. The authors assert that 'academics face major challenges when it comes to upholding the purposes and values of higher education within contemporary society'. They also propose that practices that commodify higher education are reductive in that they lack key understandings of the purpose of the university and therefore need to be challenged. It is here that Foucault's work is instrumental in providing a counter-narrative, a narrative that is more easily evidenced when Foucauldian concepts are translated and transformed into a methodological apparatus that aid such inquiry. In this first instance, the authors have drawn on document analysis, but upon reflection have arrived at the conclusion that this approach can be expanded into further empirical work. This has led them to consider future methodological proposals aimed at exploring the lived experience and working practices of academics to foster additional, critical understandings of academic governance. These understandings, as the authors remark, may also benefit from further lensification, as for example, that of Bourdieu's concept of habitus. Ultimately, what this chapter shows us is that research is processual and that opportunities for theory application present themselves not only conceptually but also operationally, i.e. the application of theory to complex research questions often leads to further problematisation of the issues at hand. An examination of how theories can stretch to do justice to the research phenomenon is one of the many steps of theory application. Thus, researchers are often left with the task of enlisting further theories – and theorists – when wanting to expand their inquiry. This not only allows for new perspectives, but also for further original contributions.

Koch and Labraña propose the exploration of governmentality through the conception of performativity in the context of Chilean higher education policies in Chapter 5. In so doing, they combine the works of Niklas Luhmann on organisational theory and Michel Foucault's discourse analysis to develop a theory-informed understanding of the consequences of adopting 'new' accountability mechanisms in higher education. They argue that higher education accountability systems create a regime of power and truth à la Foucault, that replaces traditional cultures, such as those based on prestige and reputation whilst deepening the technification of universities as decisional organisations. Chapter 5 also provides a pertinent reflection on the intrinsic relationship between theory and method, which the authors detail as requiring (1) a deep contextual knowledge of the reality researched to avoid the mechanisation of theory application, as well as (2) the understanding that the production of regimes of truth is inserted within a given social reality thus localising the use of theory, methods and data. Finally, the authors share the perspective that theoretically and empirically grounded reflections are essential to the exploration of higher education systems. If nothing else, they present an answer to how certain theories are often represented, idealised and/or elevated without deep consideration. Appreciating the role theory plays in the research process is essential in both developing critical understandings across the different stages of the research process as well as in laying the ground for new theoretical work.

Section 2: Social theory and the politics of academic work

Section 2 starts with an introductory chapter on how academic work and academic identities can be construed through different lenses. Focusing on how the politics of academic work shapes and informs academics' professional and intellectual selves, Cristina Costa provides a brief account of the impact of neoliberal policies on the scholarly practices and identity (trans)formation of academics. Chapter 6 is thus devoted to a discussion of how the role of the academic has been weakened in favour of marketisation goals and how different theoretical lenses can help us form critical perspectives of such phenomena. For example, Bourdieu's work shows how *Homo Economicus* is taking over from *Homo Academicus*, not only because of how knowledge practices, time and space are construed within academia, but also because of how these higher education power structures force academics to constantly re-evaluate their position and with it their sense of self. Here, a discussion of 'recognition' is important, Costa notes, not only through a perspective of how the dynamics of structure and agency (mis)attributes academics' social status in academia, but also how it intrudes on academics' sense of self-respect and self-esteem. To this latter approach a Honnethian perspective – which has been less prominent when representing the pathologies that currently affect academic selves – lends itself well. Problems regarding the casualisation of academic work are also briefly highlighted, pointing to the work of Georg Lukács and Norbert Elias as entry points for debates. This chapter ends by asserting that both the neoliberalisation of higher education and increasing political interventions targeted at higher education worldwide are in effect acts of depoliticisation of the academy. The purpose is to weaken the influence of intellectual power. Chapter 6 paves the way for the following chapters where some of these aspects are discussed not only in detail, but also through other complementary lenses, thus showing the multiplicity of approaches and intellectual journeys social theory can take us on.

In Chapter 7, Fabian Cannizzo draws on Barbara Adam's sociology of time to develop a time-sensitive perspective on academic identity and governance. Implicit in this approach is an invitation to a diachronical analysis of social life and socialised rhythms as opposed to a synchronic reading of the same reality. This, he argues, would allow academics to resist a reading of temporality through the power structure of managerial governance and engage in what Adam calls a perspectival framework that discards dualistic takes of time to adopt a relational perspective. Through this conceptual piece, Cannizzo shows how Adam's perspectival framework allows researchers to conceptualise time 'as a performative chronopolitics aimed at achieving control over areas of social life'. This relational perspective of time as a social construction is dependent on one's understanding of how academic work and academic life are organised. As Cannizzo points out, a relational approach to studying academic time will encounter methodological difficulties, but also promises innovations in academic labour studies when empirically exploring how academic identities can be explored through temporal perspectives. In this case, harnessing theory to excavate a relational understanding of reality through method becomes key to the project of critical analysis.

In Chapter 8, David Hodgson and Lynelle Watts pose the question: 'What has being an academic come to mean in the neoliberal spaces of the modern university?' This leads them on an exploration of a reflexive methodology to discuss their practice as academics in relation to the contemporary conditions present in the academy. Guided by existential and stoic traditions that encourage deliberative thinking, they embark on a dialogical journey of meaning-making, using these theoretical understandings to foreground their reflections. They also use them to think differently and 'think with' as part of dialogues turned into research instruments aimed at unearthing the impact of the neoliberal university on felt experiences. In the context of this chapter, the theoretical contribution of existentialism implies navigating the ambiguity inherent in life as a form of personal liberation and of locating meaning and purpose. The contribution of stoicism, on the other hand, lies in the use of reflection as a tool of 'mastery of the self'. In the words of the authors, engagements with such theoretical underpinnings (as method) can have a liberating effect in that one's introspective work of developing relational and intersubjective knowledge becomes key to the development of one's sense of identity. In short, Chapter 8 presents an excellent and clear example of the application of stoic and existentialist theories to research practice in the context of academia. In doing so, it ends up unveiling an additional role of theory: that of fostering self-knowledge, which in this particular case seems to be implicit in deliberative practices hinting at self-care, a theme that is becoming more and more prominent in today's academia, as further discussed in Chapter 10 (see below).

Next, in Chapter 9, Kate Carruthers Thomas explores the application of Doreen Massey's socio-spatial concepts to a contemporary investigation of gender and intersectional factors and their impact on experiences of the workplace and careers in a post-1992 UK university. More concretely, Thomas – influenced by Massey's work – is compelled to explore how gender operates as a geography of power in the context of academia. Massey's theoretical concepts worked dialectically to shape both the research questions and the methodology of her projects. Thomas goes on to reflect how the dynamics established between conceptualising and operationalising the research led to the development of what she has called 'spatial storytelling', a methodology that combines two interdependent research instruments: narrative enquiry interview and visual mapping to 'capture the psychosocial dimensions of the interactions between individual and institution and to uncover and explore spaces between organisational rhetoric and lived/living experience'. Again, a theme that has developed – even if in implicit ways – around this edited collection and which also features in Thomas' chapter is that of demonstrating the capacity of social theory for 'relational' explorations of reality. This is evident in the chapter through the way Thomas relates space(s) to power to theorise gender as a geography of power within the university and through which understandings of belonging can emerge. What Thomas also illustrates is that understandings of education practices is not and should not be limited to disciplinary boundaries, which in itself could be deemed a geography of power. She evidences this eloquently through her application of Massey's work in her research.

In Chapter, 10 Luísa Winter Pereira speaks to a newly formed term, 'caringzenship' – translated from the Spanish *cuidadanía*. It is a play on words meaning care (*cuida*) and citizenship (*ciudadanía*) to explore the possibilities of university experience beyond a neoliberal and Westernising logic of organising and producing academic knowledge. She starts by enlisting the works of Gayatri Spivak to explore current conditions of knowledge production and questions if the subaltern can produce knowledge. Spivak's work is used here as a way to start unpacking the normativity that exists in the construction and production of knowledge and which Winter Pereira names *epistemonormativity*: a set of rules that defines the boundaries of proper and improper knowledge that seem to affect women academics in particular. She elaborates on such epistemic injustices by drawing on personal examples and concerns herself with critical reflections on social theory as a way to think about the material conditions of construction of her academic subjectivity within the unequal structures of academia. This emphasis on the use of social theory as a way to explore her own location within academia compels Winter Pereira to draw on different theories that comprise what she calls 'her hybrid reading cabinet'. Her reading cabinet combines understanding of Miranda Frickers' epistemic injustice with Judith Butler's understanding of performativity and precarity and Donna Haraway's situated knowledge as tools for analysing and escaping *epistemonormativity*. In this chapter, engagement with feminist theory works as a lens able to shed light on the epistemic structures of power and how academics are situated within them, not only by choice, but sometimes also by need. What theory in this case also offers is an alternative to the epistemic stance that many times even the subaltern ends up adopting. What Winter Pereira proposes, then, is the cultivation of an alternative model of knowledge production and of one's location within the higher education system; a model that fosters self and collective care as a solidarious act able to counteract the effects neoliberalism has on both the university and the individual. In times when citizenship has been re-appropriated, and to a certain extent, commodified in academia, a proposal of caringzenship does not only sound appealing, but necessary.

The final chapter of this section is focused on the casualisation of academic work and its impact on academics' identities. Alexandra Jones, Jess Harris, Nerida Spina and Jen Azordegan discuss the problem of casualisation from a perspective of precarity at the hands of the neoliberal university and the impact it has on casual academics' identities. The chapter incorporates the work of Foucault to examine how relations of privilege are operationalised in universities and how 'dividing practices' have ensued through casual work and insecure contracts. Their inquiry is shaped by the blend of Foucault's concepts of 'governmentality' and 'discourse' and Dorothy Smith's guidance on the development of empirical work and notions of 'bifurcated consciousness' to develop their research instruments and process of analysis. This approach proves an effective combination in teasing out the positionality of academics on casual contracts and thus reaching understandings of participants' identities, while bringing out a thorough understanding of how perspectives of 'othering' are created in academia through the enabling of casual and precarious practices. This chapter helpfully unpacks the research process in crystal clear ways. What is more, the authors provide a much needed account of 'how the dominant discourse establishes and reinforces relations of privilege in university workplaces' while giving voice to the experiences of academics that have often been silenced. This is a critical step in undoing the 'othering' that is increasingly persistent in academia.

Section 3: Social theory and the politics of student experience

Rille Raaper and Ciaran Burke open Section 3 with a chapter that explores the contested nature of student politics in contemporary higher education settings. They start by framing the issue in the context of neoliberal regimes and move on to exploring student politics as a multi-faceted phenomenon. In order to support their conceptualisation, they draw on a wide range of relevant social theorists, including the works of Hannah Arendt (on the formation of political action), Pierre Bourdieu (acts of resistance and the challenge of social reproduction in the face of resistance), Jürgen Habermas (opportunities for the public sphere and the increasing danger to the viability of these spaces) and Michel Foucault (on the subtle construction of political subjectivity within dominant discursive power relations).

In Chapter 13, Cedomir Vuckovic focuses on English higher education and discusses how higher education research literature has tended to focus on organised student protests when considering the consequences of tuition fees and tuition fee rises. Placing the works of Habermas and Foucault in dialogue, Vuckovic argues for the need to consider alternative strategies of resistance and non-conformity. The research presented in this chapter applies critical concepts of communicative action, power and resistance, exemplifying the development of participatory design methods. This approach does not come without challenges regarding the operationalisation of Habermasian concepts, such as communicative action and mutual consensus, when participants respond in unpredictable ways to the tasks at hand. This chapter illustrates how overlooked forms of resistance within higher education may effectively be explored in theoretical dialogue between Habermas and Foucault even if not a straightforward process to either researchers or participants. Considering alternatives and undoing unequal realities is not an easy task, but is one that social theory has as one of its core missions.

Diego Salazar-Morales employs Foucauldian concepts of governmentality and counter-conduct in Chapter 14 to cast light on the government and media representations of public universities in Peru and the process on how students' unions have resisted, and in some cases, challenged these representations. Salazar-Morales suggests that, applied to the Peruvian context, Foucault's analysis of neoliberal governmentality can help to examine the workings of a post-colonial society and its indigenous people, indicating that when carefully applied Foucault's work can travel across continents and contexts. This is not to create uniformed explanations of different phenomena, but rather to develop a genealogical reading of the problematic under investigation. This is where Salazar-Morales finds Foucault's work pertinent. The genealogical approach is enacted in this chapter in a first instance through the identification of the 'discursive formation' sustaining higher education conflict in Peru. In a second phase, the genealogical approach encounters 'history' illustrative of practices evidencing the dynamics of 'power-knowledge'. Lastly, in a final phase, the genealogical approach of this study situates theoretical work as an essential aspect of writing the research narrative. The result of this methodological apparatus is an account of a Peruvian neoliberal governmentality that is intrinsically connected to its historical context and to which a proper theoretical iteration is essential. Salazar-Morales delivers an excellent example of how Foucault can be put to work under such conditions.

The final chapter is written by Fiona Christie, James Rattenbury and Fiona Creaby. It exemplifies the application of Figured Worlds theory to the exploration of student and graduate identities. The authors argue that Holland's Figured Worlds offers a novel lens with which to explore contemporary identity in the context of a competitive graduate labour market that puts added pressure on individuals' sense of who they are and want to become. In considering the challenges faced in bridging the theory–method relationship together, the authors offer reflections pertaining to the complexity of the Figured Worlds framework regarding researchers' own positionality, bias and assumptions as well as degrees of power and privilege of the different actors involved in the research: concerns that should always be at the forefront of ethical research. The authors find that Figured Worlds constitutes a useful tool for the study of identities, also in its relation to possible and agentic selves. They conclude that this theoretical lens helps researchers and readers to go 'beyond the dominant ways in which "Student Voice" and "Graduate Outcomes" are constructed' to produce thoughtful and critical insights of student and graduate journeys.

References

Murphy, M. (2011), 'Troubled by the past: History, identity and the university', *Journal of Higher Education Policy and Management*, 33 (5): 509–517.

Zumeta, W. (2011), 'What does it mean to be accountable? Dimensions and implications of higher education's public accountability', *The Review of Higher Education*, 35 (1): 131–148.

Part One

Social Theory and University Governance

2

Governing Universities: Power, Prestige and Performance

Mark Murphy

Introduction

This opening chapter to the section provides an introduction to the governance of universities. University governance, it is fair to say, has been dramatically transformed in only a matter of decades, moving swiftly in the twenty-first century to a more intense and concentrated version of the business-oriented and marketised model that took hold in the latter part of the twentieth century. The 'traditional' collegial model of institutional governance, while a somewhat romanticised conception of academic history, could not compete with the mounting pressures that came with managerialist demands for efficiency and surveillance, alongside the financial imperatives that resulted from immersion in an uber-competitive environment.

The chapter will briefly detail the rise of new public management, the key ideology that has swept across the sector, identify its impact and the responses to this impact. Also covered is the style shift to 'new governance' that has paved the way for a heightened accountability regime to take hold of the sector. Much has been written about how universities have responded to new forms of governance that have applied an 'arm's length' model of management to university administration. This altered form of control has significant implications when it comes to issues of regulation, accountability, surveillance and managerial oversight. Also included in the chapter is a brief account of how social theory has grappled with the kinds of problematic issues that have emerged in the aftermath of such a seismic change.

Higher education and the onward march of marketisation

New public management, or NPM for short (and often referred to simply as 'managerialism'), became a popular, even dominant, way to assess the changes that were imposed on the public sector in many countries in the late twentieth century (Hood and Dixon 2016; Lyons 1998; Pollitt and Bouckaert 2017). As a governance approach, NPM was new precisely because it viewed public services as a poor relation to the private marketised sphere, a sphere where notions of efficiency and economy were paramount. It borrowed a great deal of its managerial philosophy from the operations of the market, especially the relation at the heart of modern economies, that between producer and consumer. Traditional values of public sector planning were substituted with a supposedly more efficient 'business-like' approach to management – an approach that set great store by performance management, target-setting and output measurement, competition and consumer choice, marketisation, contractualism and privatisation.

In recent decades, NPM has seeped into the governance of higher education institutions (HEIs), emboldened by a broader spirit of neoliberalisaton of public institutions taking place across the globe (Deem et al. 2007; Murphy 2016; Slaughter and Rhoades 2004; Stevenson and Bell 2009; Sultana 2012). This is an important shift in academic governance for a number of reasons, chief among them a radically transformed conception of academic quality. The underlying assumption of NPM was that competition, enabled via a marketised higher education context, would help to drive up standards in universities, and deliver a more responsive and consumer-oriented institution.

Enhanced quality in this marketised space would be a consequence of a new competitive landscape, bringing with it a pedagogical and research infrastructure better suited to the political and economic demands of the modern world. This was implemented in academic institutions (and before it, further education colleges; see Longhurst 1996; McTavish 2003; Newman and Jahdi 2009), delivered as an unshakeable set of beliefs about how institutions should be governed. This ideological package, bundled up into the signifiers of efficiency, productivity and performativity, has now become commonplace, altering in numerous ways institutional practices and the life worlds of legions of academics and students alike.

This drastic transformation of academic governance was always going to encounter some level of resistance and criticism from the profession and elsewhere. This critique came in two forms – first, as a response to its implementation, and second, as a response to its underpinning rationale. The first set of criticisms relate to how NPM has been implemented at the institutional level. This critique centres on the barrage of unwanted consequences that have been generated as a result of these reforms, such as the questionable impact on quality and standards (Huisman and Currie 2004), the overemphasis on students as consumers (Todd et al. 2017), funding changes and the resulting institutional disempowerment (Shattock and Horvath 2020: 43), as well as the malign effects on academic working conditions and professional life (Cribb and Gewirtz 2013; Dowling-Hetherington 2014) (see Section 2 for more on this).

The second set of criticisms relate to the reasons behind the imposition of NPM in higher education. Suspicion has endured among academic commentators that NPM was a policy trojan horse for a land grab of institutional autonomy (Christensen 2011; Welsh 2017). This suspicion is warranted, as the advent of the knowledge economy has placed the university at the centre of political power, becoming a prized conduit of competitive advantage in a globalised economy. In turn, the pressures driving the field of higher education governance stemming from this imposition of market forces, turns the heads of senior management towards higher income generation, risk reduction and market survival (Shattock and Horvath 2020). Control of academic affairs in such a hothouse environment inevitably takes precedence over age-old concerns with institutional differentiation and academic freedom.

NPM is not the only ideology exerting pressure on higher education governance. It has significant if underplayed competition in the shape of a social justice agenda that positions access to higher education as a crucial tool of equal opportunity and social mobility. These outcomes are a powerful measure of institutional and sectoral legitimacy, to the extent that policies have been introduced in some cases to penalise universities for missing widening participation targets. In the current hyper-aware political climate, universities and other HEIs can literally not afford to avoid their obligation to a society that still sees higher education as a route to a better life, greater social standing and even enhanced well-being.

While this is true, the marketised university has become remarkably adept at incorporating social justice concerns into its mode of operation. This is evident when it comes to the widening participation agenda itself. Evident in the UK, for example, is a conflation of widening participation with a strategic recruitment agenda, a situation that reflects a highly competitive marketplace. This 'hijacking' of the access agenda is compounded by the highly institutionalised response to this agenda, one in which some institutions, due to their relative positioning in the higher education prestige economy, 'are driven to increase recruitment and identify new markets as part of a strategy for institutional survival' (Murphy 2002: 287).

Ideologies such as marketisation, once they embed themselves in forms of institutional and professional practice, have an unwelcome habit of 'bulldozing' other ideologies into submission. While access is one, consider the example of 'impact', and how this has played out at an institutional governance level. The demand for societal impact on the part of HEIs is a laudable aim, one that speaks to a desire to contribute to the process of societal change. In the marketised university, however, this demand has a tendency to become a marketing and promotional tool, a form of impression management that lends a gloss to institutional governance (Murphy and Costa 2019; Watermeyer 2016). Can HEIs be trusted to park their institutional imperatives to serve the greater good of democratic deliberation, even if it impacts their own institutional reputation and income-generating activities?

This appropriation of the public engagement agenda has unfortunately come at the expense of a more expansive vision of societal impact. Institutional governance currently operates in a challenging political hinterland that combines significant fiscal constraint with heightened responsibility for human capital and knowledge production. The scope for establishing a more progressive university sector has arguably never been more narrow and instead one has a diminished university sector with its value and potential curtailed by an over-excited prestige economy.

Governance and accountability

New public management brought with it a transformation in the style of governance that took hold in the public sector as well as in higher education. Often termed the new governance (Murphy 2018), the style shift to 'governing without government' (Rhodes 1996) became an increasingly prominent way to manage public services in more decentralised regimes, employing techniques of arm's length 'steering at a distance' (Kickert 1995) to achieve public sector reforms. As with NPM, these techniques gradually spread to the higher education sector (King 2007), techniques spearheaded by the imposition of accountability measures in academic governance structures. The twenty-first century has witnessed a dramatic transformation in how both institutions and academics are made answerable to the state and the public, a trend evident at the global level

(Cheng 2012; Gouvias 2012; Kai 2009; McLendon et al. 2006; Murphy 2009; Vidovich et al. 2007). This transformation has seen a wholesale 'reinvention' of accountability across the sector (Burke 2005), one that has sought to replace traditional bureaucratic rules with performance results.

These techniques of surveillance, discipline and compliance, including performance indicators, league tables, student satisfaction surveys, institutional audits and professional development reviews, are now commonplace and cover the work of departments and research groups as well as individual academics (Fejes 2016: 296). But this high level of answerability has come at a substantial cost, as the emphasis on accountability mechanisms to ensure compliance and surveillance has to some extent reduced governance to a form of regulatory oversight. As well as this, the immense efforts to assure and improve quality have been accused of facilitating the introduction of damaging practices into the higher education sector (Schwier 2012), such as institutional gaming and impression management (Gouvias 2012) and, far from increasing quality, have been blamed for reducing the overall quality of teaching and learning (Murphy 2019). On top of that, the evidence that they work (i.e. that they deliver the intended results, such as improved student outcomes) is highly debatable (Senechal 2013; Zepke and Leach 2007).

Arguably more concerning is the way in which accountability regimes help reframe common understandings of the public university, shifting the moral centre towards a focus on competition, mobility and the knowledge economy (Jayasuriya 2010: 13). In the long run, the cumulative nature of accountability mechanisms, alongside their numerous unforeseen consequences, may result in a level of damage to publicness that cannot simply be reversed. If this is correct, then the concept of the hollowed-out university may yet become the defining feature of academic institutions (Cribb and Gewirtz 2013).

At this stage, it is useful to mention a number of caveats to the above discussion. First, it should at this point be appreciated that academic governance, not dissimilar to the forces at work in the public sector, has to balance a number of distinct accountability demands – those from the state, the market as well as civil society more generally. It is a mistake to view accountability in one-dimensional terms. As a result, universities struggle to balance demand for academic autonomy with the loud calls for greater responsibility, a struggle that places them in an awkward position, to put it mildly. One might even refer to academic governance as a thankless task. Second, the impact of accountability regimes, as well as broader marketisation strategies, can differ from one institution to another, a situation which also applies to the ways in which institutions respond and adapt to these contemporary pressures (Ek et al. 2013). The higher education sector is far from a monolithic or homogeneous entity as sometimes portrayed in the literature. Granted, it is often the case that there is a need to write in shorthand to present what amounts to quite complex governance issues, but this should not detract from the need to better understand the extent to which variables such as institutional type and discipline mediate the impact of NPM, marketisation and neoliberalism. This also applies to our understanding of the ways in which globalising processes of academic governance produce highly localised effects at the national and regional level (Brankovic 2018; Paradeise and Thoenig 2013).

Theorising academic governance

As a result of these changing dynamics, university governance provides fertile ground for socio-theoretical exploration. We are living through a period of academic reformation arguably unparalleled in the modern era, the politics surrounding higher education a constant presence in political debates and public discourse. That said, the history of social theory is no stranger to the problems of university governance – Max Weber (1974) in particular was a vocal critic of attempts to curtail academic freedom and institutional autonomy on behalf of the state and the market (Josephson 2004; Murphy 2009). The concern over institutional autonomy and control runs deep in social theory, and is a particular focus for Foucault-inspired analyses of university politics. Authors such as Amit (2000), Fejes (2016) and Suspitsyna (2010) view NPM techniques and accountability regimes as panopticon-like, ushering in an era of governmentality that produces a set of disciplining practices for both institutions and academics.

The thematic nature of Foucault's work lends itself well to such forms of interrogation. Conceptual tools provided by Habermas have also been deployed in critical analyses of academic governance. One way his work has proved fruitful is in relation to the concept of steering mechanisms as a form of regulatory control system imposed on higher education. In the work of Broadbent et al. (2010), this steering refers to finance, while for Murphy (2009), accountability mechanisms are the focus. But in both cases, conclusions are drawn regarding the restrictive nature of these mechanisms and their damaging consequences for higher education governance.

Another socio-theoretical concept that has been put to work in governance studies is attributable to Bourdieu, that of field. The concept of field has been successfully utilised to examine forms of institutional strategy and institutional change – see the work of Kloot (2013) and Naidoo (2004) on academic governance in the case of South Africa. Bourdieu's conceptual toolkit has proven especially useful when exploring the impact of globalisation on institutional policy and strategy (Marginson 2008). This application of Bourdieu's ideas makes sense, as Bourdieu himself invested considerable energy in understanding the field of higher education, as evidenced in his classic text, *Homo Academicus* (1988).

Given the commodifying and marketised nature of this change, Marxist critiques are surprisingly thin on the ground. It could be argued that the work of Foucault has occupied some of the intellectual space that previously would have been dominated by Marxist analyses of labour power, competition and exploitation. They do exist however, a good example being that of Szadkowski and Krzeski (2019). They apply a Marxist analysis to contemporary higher education in order to identify the manner in which the operations of what they call 'prestige distribution' not only 'relate to the mechanisms of extraction of surplus value from academic labour but also condition them' (2019: 8). This type of analysis is an important counter-foil to other critiques inspired by Foucault, Bourdieu and Habermas (to name but three of the most utilised theorists), as it quite explicitly and unashamedly places higher education within a world capitalist order. It is important to remember this context, a context that, after all, has had a major role to play in the drive towards privatisation, marketisation and competition in the higher education sector.

References

Amit, V. (2000), 'The university as panopticon: Moral claims and attacks on academic freedom', in M. Strathearn (ed.), *Audit Cultures: Anthropological Studies in Accountability, Ethics and the Academy*, 215–235, Abingdon: Routledge.

Bourdieu, P. (1988), *Homo Academicus*, trans. P. Collier, Cambridge: Polity Press.

Brankovic, J. (2018), 'Between world culture and local context: The university as an empowered actor in national higher education governance', *Acta Sociologica*, 61 (4): 374–388.

Broadbent, J., Gallop, C. and Laughlin, R. (2010), 'Analysing societal regulatory control systems with specific reference to higher education in England', *Accounting, Auditing and Accountability Journal*, 23 (4): 506–531.

Burke, J. (2005), 'Reinventing accountability: From bureaucratic rules to performance results', in J. Burke (ed.), *Achieving Accountability in Higher Education: Balancing Public, Academic and Market Demands*, 216–245, San Francisco, CA: Jossey-Bass.

Cheng, M. (2012), 'Accountability and professionalism: A contradiction in terms?', *Higher Education Research and Development*, 31 (6): 785–795.

Christensen, T. (2011), 'University governance reforms: Potential problems of more autonomy?', *Higher Education*, 62 (4): 503–517.

Cribb, C. and Gewirtz, S. (2013), 'The hollowed-out university? A critical analysis of changing institutional and academic norms in UK higher education', *Discourse: Studies in the Cultural Politics of Education*, 34 (3): 338–350.

Deem, R., Hillyard, S. and Reed, M. (2007), *Knowledge, Higher Education, and the New Managerialism: The Changing Management of UK Universities*, Oxford: Oxford University Press.

Dowling-Hetherington, L. (2014), 'The changing demands of academic life in Ireland', *International Journal of Educational Management*, 28 (2): 141–151.

Ek, A.-C., Ideland, M., Jönsson, S. and Malmberg, C. (2013), 'The tension between marketisation and academisation in higher education', *Studies in Higher Education*, 38 (9): 1305–1318.

Fejes, A. (2016), 'The confessing academic and living the present otherwise: Appraisal interviews and logbooks in academia', *European Educational Research Journal*, 15 (4): 395–409.

Gouvias, D. (2012), 'Accountability in the Greek higher education system as a high-stakes policymaking instrument', *Higher Education Policy*, 25 (1): 65–86.

Hood, C. and Dixon, R. (2016), 'Not what it said on the tin? Reflections on three decades of UK public management reform', *Financial Accountability and Management*, 32 (4): 409–428.

Huisman, J. and Currie, J. (2004), 'Accountability in higher education: Bridge over troubled water?', *Higher Education*, 48 (4): 529–551.

Jayasuriya, K. (2010), 'Learning by the market: Regulatory regionalism, Bologna, and accountability communities', *Globalisation, Societies and Education*, 8 (1): 7–22.

Josephson, P. (2004), 'Lehrfreiheit, Lernfreiheit, Wertfreiheit: Max Weber and the university teachers. Congress in Jena 1908', *Max Weber Studies*, 4 (2): 201–219.

Kai, J. (2009), 'A critical analysis of accountability in higher education', *Chinese Education and Society*, 42 (2): 39–51.

Kickert, W. (1995), 'Steering at a distance: A new paradigm of public governance in Dutch higher education', *Governance: An International Journal of Policy and Administration*, 8 (1): 135–157.

King, R. (2007), 'Governance and accountability in the higher education regulatory state', *Higher Education*, 53 (4): 411–430.

Kloot, B. (2013), 'Exploring the value of Bourdieu's framework in the context of institutional change', in M. Murphy (ed.), *Social Theory and Education Research*, vol. 4: *Governance and Management*, 129–144, London: Sage.

Longhurst, R. (1996), 'Education as a commodity: The political economy of the new further education', *Journal of Further and Higher Education*, 20 (2): 49–66.

Lyons, M. (1998), 'The impact of managerialism on social policy: The case of social services', *Public Productivity and Management Review*, 21 (4): 419–432.

Marginson, S. (2008), 'Global field and global imagining: Bourdieu and worldwide higher education', *British Journal of Sociology of Education*, 29 (3): 303–315.

McLendon, M., Hearn, J. and Deaton, R. (2006), 'Called to account: Analyzing the origins and spread of state performance-accountability policies for higher education', *Educational Evaluation and Policy Analysis*, 28 (1): 1–24.

McTavish, D. (2003), 'Aspects of public sector management: A case study of further education, ten years from the passage of the Further and Higher Education Act', *Educational Management and Administration*, 31 (2): 175–187.

Murphy, M. (2002), 'Creating new demand? The development of out-reach access initiatives in higher education research in post-compulsory education', *Research in Post-Compulsory Education*, 7 (3): 273–92.

Murphy, M. (2009), 'Bureaucracy and its limits: Accountability and rationality in higher education', *British Journal of Sociology of Education*, 30 (6): 683–695.

Murphy, M. (2016), 'Universities and the politics of autonomy', in M. Peters (ed.), *Encyclopedia of Educational Philosophy and Theory*, 1–5, Dordrecht: Springe

Murphy, M. (2018), 'Ever greater scrutiny: Researching the bureaucracy of educational accountability', in A. Wilkins and A. Olmedo (eds.), *Education Governance and Social Theory: Interdisciplinary Approaches to Research*, 193–207, London: Bloomsbury.

Murphy, M. (2019), 'Public sector accountability and the contradictions of the regulatory state', *Administrative Theory and Praxis* 193–207 (DOI: 10.1080/10841806.2019. 1700455).

Murphy, M. and Costa, C. (2019), 'Digital scholarship, higher education and the future of the public intellectual', *Futures*, 111: 205–212.

Naidoo, R. (2004), 'Fields and institutional strategy: Bourdieu on the relationship between higher education, inequality and society', *British Journal of Sociology of Education*, 25 (4): 457–471.

Newman, S. and Jahdi, K. (2009), 'Marketisation of education: Marketing, rhetoric and reality', *Journal of Further and Higher Education*, 33 (1): 1–11.

Paradeise, C. and Thoenig, J.-C. (2013), 'Academic institutions in search of quality: Local orders and global standards', *Organization Studies,* 34 (2): 189–218.

Pollitt, C. and Bouckaert, G. (2017), *Public Management Reform: A Comparative Analysis – into the Age of Austerity*, 4th edition, Oxford: Oxford University Press.

Rhodes, R. (1996), 'The new governance: Governing without government', *Political Studies*, 44 (4): 652–667.

Schwier, R. (2012), 'The corrosive influence of competition, growth, and accountability on institutions of higher education', *Journal of Computing in Higher Education*, 24 (2): 96–103.

Senechal, D. (2013), 'Measure against measure: Responsibility versus accountability in education', *Arts Education Policy Review*, 114 (2): 47–53.

Shattock. M. and Horvath, A. (2020), *The Governance of British Higher Education: The Impact of Governmental, Financial and Market Pressures*, London: Bloomsbury.

Slaughter, S. and Rhoades, G. (2004), *Academic Capitalism and the New Economy: Markets, State and Higher Education*, Baltimore, MD: Johns Hopkins University Press.

Stevenson, H. and Bell, L. (2009), 'Universities in transition: Themes in higher education policy', in L. Bell, H. Stevenson and M. Neary (eds.), *The Future of Higher Education: Policy, Pedagogy and the Student Experience*, 1–14, London: Continuum.

Sultana, R. (2012), 'Higher education governance: A critical mapping of key themes and issues', *European Journal of Higher Education*, 2 (4): 345–369.

Suspitsyna, T. (2010), 'Accountability in American education as a rhetoric and a technology of governmentality', *Journal of Education Policy*, 25 (5): 567–586.

Szadkowski, K. and Krzeski, J. (2019), 'In, against, and beyond: A Marxist critique for higher education in crisis, *Social Epistemology*, 33 (6): 463–476.

Todd, S., Barnoff, L., Moffatt, K., Panitch, M., Parada, H. and Strumm, B. (2017), 'A social work re-reading of students as consumers', *Social Work Education*, 36 (5): 542–556.

Vidovich, L., Yang, R. and Currie, J. (2007), 'Changing accountabilities in higher education as China "opens up" to globalisation', *Globalisation, Societies and Education*, 5 (1): 89–107.

Watermeyer, R. (2016), 'Public intellectuals vs. new public management: The defeat of public engagement in higher education', *Studies in Higher Education*, 41 (12): 2271–2285.

Weber, M. (1974), *Max Weber on Universities: The Power of the State and the Dignity of the Academic Calling in Imperial Germany*, Chicago, IL: University of Chicago Press.

Welsh, J. (2017), 'Governing academics: The historical transformation from discipline to control', *International Journal of Politics, Culture and Society*, 30 (1): 83–106.

Zepke, N. and Leach, L. (2007), 'Educational quality, institutional accountability and the retention discourse', *Quality in Higher Education*, 13 (3): 237–248.

3

University Management as Court Society: A Processual Analysis of the Rise of University Management

Eric Lybeck

Vive l'Université!

In 1789, the king of France, Louis XVI, had a financial crisis on his hands. To resolve this via new taxation, he convened the Estates-General for the first time in 175 years, a decision that quickly devolved out of his hands and into those of the people of France. After the Estates' first meeting, a question of representation emerged regarding whether votes should be tallied according to head or order, with the former proposal suggesting one house consisting of the first (clergy), second (nobility) and third (middle and popular classes) estates, and the latter proposal recommending an upper chamber for the first and second and a lower for the third. Decamping to a nearby tennis court, the third estate declared an oath that they would remain assembled until a constitution was established. Soon thereafter, the representatives declared themselves a National Assembly. In the following month, the king sacked his finance minister, Jacques Necker, for publishing documents revealing the fully debased state of the kingdom's financial health, which the population perceived as an act directed against the National Assembly. Riots ensued, culminating in the storming of the Bastille prison, a potent symbol of royal power. The French Revolution had begun. It was not long before all special privileges of the first and second estates were abolished, and the Rights of Man were declared.

Without the same level of international political significance, a more recent event can be recounted here for comparison. In 2018, the University and College Union (UCU), representing over 100,000 university staff in the UK, balloted to begin strike action to prevent changes to their Universities Superannuation Scheme (USS) pension after negotiations with university 'employers' represented by Universities UK (UUK) stalled. This led to the largest and longest industrial action in British university history, with more than a million students affected by the withdrawal of over 575,000 teaching hours during the month of sustained strike action. While changes to pensions were the proximate cause, the strikes soon took on a broader, critical dimension against sector-wide trends within UK universities towards more marketisation, performance management and unaccountable decision-making.[1]

In the run up to strikes, reports emerged of a disproportionate influence played by constituent colleges at the universities of Cambridge and Oxford. Focused attention was accordingly directed at Oxford ahead of a 6 March meeting of congregation – the 'supreme governing body' of the university, consisting of all academic staff – which sought a vote on changing the university's position *vis-à-vis* the pension dispute. Hitherto, the university's vice chancellor, Louise Richardson, towed the USS line, and, though she was abroad at the time of congregation, her office arranged for suspension of debate using a legislative technicality. This resulted in outraged members of the governing body staging an ad hoc meeting outside, where a vote was taken of 442-2 against senior management. Two days later, the vice chancellor adjusted the universities' formal position in light of the 'depth of feeling'. Thus, just as the tennis court oath taken by members of the third estate asserted their representation of the people *vis-à-vis* the monarchy in the French Revolution, at least for this moment – and within a much more limited institutional sphere of university, rather than national governance – academics at Oxford performatively re-asserted their control of the university *vis-à-vis* university management.

Since their foundation in the Middle Ages, universities have been autonomous, self-governing institutions of higher learning. How was it the case that, in 2018, the gulf between management/employers and academics/employees had grown so wide as to necessitate such a dramatic and contentious event? In this chapter, we can learn even more about the dynamics driving present higher education policy and practice, if we retain parallel analysis of the French Revolution. Drawing particularly on the social theory of Norbert Elias, but extending this within a broader processual sociology of higher education, we can see that changes within the governance and management of universities have structural homologies with the court society that developed in the decades prior to the storming of the Bastille in 1789.

Processual sociology of higher education

The following analysis of university management as court society applies theoretical concepts and frameworks developed in my recent book, *Norbert*

Elias and the Sociology of Education (Lybeck 2019). Despite being a well-known, if initially neglected, sociologist of the twentieth century, Elias's social theory is not widely applied within education studies. This is due to his own neglect of the topic area within his otherwise comprehensive analyses of modern society, certainly compared to more familiar social theorists, such as Pierre Bourdieu and Michel Foucault. The book introduces readers to Eliasian – or, figurational – sociology, as it is called, including several concepts and analyses introduced in less detail here, namely 'court society', 'game models' and figurations/processes, in general. Indeed, the most important contribution Elias adds to our understanding of social phenomena is recognition that these are all processes. In other words, historical interpretations are essential to capture the unplanned, temporal dimensions of social configurations, structures and identities, particularly those that occur over long timescales.

The period under consideration – the decades prior to 2018 – certainly involve tremendous changes to the linkages between and across universities, the government, professions and markets, which have had internal and external effects within the ways universities operate and are governed. The dramatic growth of functions, including new demands to accommodate expanding numbers of students enrolled in higher education (Marginson 2016), to produce economic growth through technology transfer and professional skills development (Block and Keller 2009), as a leading cultural institution projecting soft power overseas (Lomer 2017), as a presumed contributor to the ecological transformation of a warming planet (McCowan 2019) and more, means higher education institutions have become more and more complex. Smelser (2013) noted the way in which universities develop via a form of 'structural accretion' in which new functions are added without functions being removed, becoming bulging, unwieldy structures with dramatically increased complexity.

Drawing on Elias, this can all be interpreted using his theory of 'game models', as explained in greater detail both in Lybeck (2019) and Elias' original essay itself (1978: 71–103). The model begins using a simple example of a 'primal contest' in which two groups are competing over food, one (A) being stronger than the other (B). Though A can dominate in certain regards, B does have room to manoeuvre, thus highlighting that no power imbalance is absolute and the figuration consists of the relations between the groups as much as the qualities of any group independently. Elias adds more and more complex examples to highlight ways in which multiple groups can become involved in coalitions for and against a more dominant actor, who may lose control of both their own room for manoeuvre, and their control of the overall rules of the game. Thus, paradoxically, as the distance between power actors diminishes, more chaos and uncertainty can emerge. This might necessitate articulation of a second tier – something akin to a parliamentary government – which establishes representatives of the population and groups competing on the first level, but now engaged in competition, coalitions and power struggles on the second tier. In oligopolistic configurations, the second tier might distance itself entirely from the people, as in aristocracies or out-of-touch political establishments whose genuine relation to the people becomes increasingly nominal. This can result in a power contest across the tiers, resulting in a revolution or democratic reform. The tennis court oath, for example, amounted to a reclamation of the rights of the 'people' to be represented fairly relative to the out-of-touch, unelected and privileged estates in the French clergy, aristocracy and monarchy.

Prior to the revolution, the monarchy in France had played aristocracy and bourgeois classes against one another via what Elias called the 'royal mechanism'.

> When the situation of the bulk of the various functional classes, or at least their active leading groups, is not yet so bad that they are willing to put their social existence at risk, and yet when they feel themselves so threatened by each other, and power is so evenly distributed between them, that each fears the slightest advantage of the other side, they tie each other's hands: this gives the central authority better chances than any other constellation within society.
>
> Elias 2000: 320

With dominated groups competing amongst themselves, rather than directing their power collectively against the king, the central authority has greater control over the rules of the game. From this vantage, they can better observe the overall field of power and make strategic moves and interventions more predictably and effectively. During the long-term 'civilizing process' across the early modern era Elias (2000) described, monarchs managed to secure the monopoly of violence through the elimination of territorial rivals, generally by fielding large standing armies. To pay for these armies, the monarch introduced currency into the economy, thereby contributing to the ascent of the bourgeois classes of merchants and financiers in towns and cities. However, as military and naval campaigns became more extensive and unpredictable, this led to fiscal crises and arbitrary taxation patterns that proved unacceptable to the bourgeoisie. In many ways, their demand for greater rights in parliament on behalf of the 'people' meant control over public finance: in other words, seizure of the monopoly of taxation from the unaccountable monarchy.

Meanwhile, during the civilizing process, the monarchs not only had to eliminate foreign rivals through territorial expansion, they needed to remove the existing military power of local aristocracies, who historically emerged from warrior classes. Securing the monopoly of violence meant defanging the existing aristocracies so these could not function as viable counterpowers. In *The Civilizing Process* (2000), Elias traced the long-term change in manners and ideas of 'civility' that occurred as the upper classes learned new standards of acceptable behaviour, reflecting the sublimation of their more violent instincts in the form of etiquette. Drawing on his earlier study of court society under Louis XIV, Elias demonstrated the way in which the sun king managed to remove aristocrats from their territorial homes by making them participate in increasingly elaborate rituals of etiquette and style within the court of Versailles (Elias 1983).

Elias captured the fundamental lack of freedom – that is, constraint – within this particular figuration.

> Etiquette and ceremony increasingly became ... a ghostly *perpetuum mobile* that continued to operate regardless of any direct use-value, being impelled, as by an inexhaustible motor, by the competition for status and power of the people enmeshed in it – a competition both between themselves and with the mass of those excluded – and by their need for a clearly graded scale of prestige ... No single person within the figuration was able to initiate a reform of the tradition. Every slightest attempt to reform, to change the precarious structure of tensions, inevitably entailed an upheaval, a reduction or even abolition of the rights of certain individuals and families. To jeopardise such privileges was, to the ruling class of this society a kind of taboo. The attempt would be opposed by broad sections of the privileged who feared, perhaps not without justification, that the whole system of rule that gave them privilege would be threatened or would collapse if the slightest detail of the traditional order were altered. So everything remained as it was.
>
> Elias 1983: 93

Thus, we can see the manner in which social constraint became embodied as self-constraint. Even if a particular individual wanted to change their manners and habits, they would risk so much – effectively, excommunication from the central court society – so, they did not even consider this as an option. Further, to reject these patterns of behaviour would be to, in effect, criticise the very status one held; in a sense, this would amount to rejecting one's self and one's identity. The result was an ultimately highly conservative structure that was nonetheless constantly changing in terms of new participants, new events, even new manners – as the textbooks of manners reveal changes occurring over the long term.

The aristocracy bought into and assimilated into this system through a range of incentives, including retention of historic rights to be exempt from taxation. However, the high expense of retaining position in court, including extensive gambling, socialising, formal dancing and currying favour with the monarch and his inner circle, often debased the wealth of aristocracies. All the while, the disgruntled bourgeois classes demanded representation and positioned themselves and their values (of utility, prudence, industry) against those of what the decadent aristocracy had become.

In terms of game models, we can see the initial (all unplanned and long-term) moves made by the monarch to gain control over a complex field of territorial power by spatially constructing and concentrating rivals within court – effectively a second tier made manifest within the royal palace. From there, he could view the entire field of power ostensibly represented by the territorial rulers competing for his favour. Enlisting a burgeoning class of advisors, often from educated members of the clergy, bourgeois and aristocratic classes, he and his cabinet could gain an overview of the second tier. One could interpret this as a limited third tier observing the second – but, one ultimately dependent on the reduction of complexity provided by the physical space of court, the willing participation of members of court society in rituals of deference, and the wider relations that linked those representatives to the growing nation's far-flung territories. Once these relations and conditions had broken down, the opportunity for revolution emerged, resulting in a new configuration of games, tiers and processual openings, including, I argue elsewhere, the rise of the modern higher education system (Lybeck 2020).

Combining the various theoretical insights introduced here before turning to the recent rise of university management, we can see the value of adopting a processual perspective in order to see the unplanned and initially partly disconnected developments that produce a particular configuration. The figurational game models demonstrate the way in which changing power relations can produce multiple tiers, which provide different power actors with better or worse knowledge of the overall game, which may be leveraged into greater power chances. In the early modern era, this resulted in the consolidation of absolutist courts as monarchs managed to pacify the aristocracy through separation of this class from its territorial constituents on the first tier, as well as the ascending bourgeois classes, by encouraging their competition over style and favour on an increasingly detached second tier. This established new patterns of behaviour, selection mechanisms and socialisation, which not only influenced the courtiers, but their enemies who defined themselves in opposition. This highlights the relational character of such power figurations. Finally, we have seen the way complexity itself begins to increase due to functional differentiation – and, indeed, through power equalisation and fragmentation itself – which may compel articulation of further tiers in order to get a (potentially illusory) reflexive grasp on the situation on a lower tier. All of these insights will inform our analysis of the recent consolidation of university management as a kind of court society.

The rise of management as a third tier

Drawing on the game model theory provided by Elias, we can arrange our study in order to observe and interpret certain aspects of recent history. Within the topic area of university management, we are interested in the ways in which management begins to distance itself across a differentiated tier: on the one hand, claiming to represent the masses of academic staff upon whose authority they govern; on the other hand, becoming involved in their own patterns of behaviour just as Louis XIV organised in his absolutist court. Methodologically, our challenge is how to capture this history and the manner in which these unplanned processes developed over time. My aim in this initial scoping study was not to 'prove' the theory, but rather to demonstrate proof of concept: to demonstrate that adopting an Eliasian perspective can facilitate our search for new materials in a way that helps explain the outcome of interest, i.e. the USS strike of 2018. Accordingly, the methods here are rather tentative and historical. Still, in this initial study, I opted to study documents in sequence, akin to Elias' study of books on manners (Elias 2000). These included Senate and Council documents in the archives, and policy and regulation documents available online. I compared these to similar documents at other universities to gain a sense of broader trends. However, this comparison was not systemic and, as noted in conclusion, a more robust comparative historical study can be envisaged to further refine and confirm the findings tentatively presented here.

The following narrative provides an account of a pseudonymised university's history based on a number of qualitative sources – largely interviews and archival material – as well as experiences gained through personal efforts at university reform within and beyond particular institutions. It would be difficult to provide reference to much of this material without revealing the identity of the institution and actors therein. Effort has also been made to integrate similar events, policies and experiences from other institutions to further disguise the case, which should be understood as an ideal type in any event. The narrative should accordingly be understood as a story, rather than as a specific historical instance, although the story is rooted in real historical events and should illuminate more generalisable processes. By narrating a story of one institution, we can better see the many contingent and unplanned ways in which the process developed locally and in relation to broader contexts.

As Elias noted, no social process ever really has a beginning, since one could always point to the significance of prehistory. However, for present purposes, we can begin in the mid to late 1970s at a time just after the broad expansion of higher education in Britain following the Robbins Report (1963), the establishment of new plate glass universities, and the coming-of-age of student radicals from the late 1960s and early 1970s. Our university, called here the University of Wessex, was founded as a plate glass university in order to provide higher education within an underserved region. Initially drawing on Oxbridge and University of London professors and graduates as its first generation of lecturers, the original dons wore robes and segregated themselves by gender in a club-like atmosphere. In this condition, self-governance was presupposed and relatively smooth due to the similarities of social backgrounds, values and assumptions of the professoriate. Organised and chartered as a Council and academic Senate, which managed the curriculum and research, the faculty also elected department chairs, deans and the vice chancellor, who was drawn from their ranks and managed a small executive committee accountable to the governing board (Council).

The first signs of strain emerged internally as a younger generation of lecturers from different social and institutional backgrounds, often more politically left wing, having come of age within the era of student activism, rejected the culture and governance arrangements wherein the professoriate dominated decision-making, often at the expense of more junior lecturers and students. Indeed, demands for devolution of more representation below the professorial level were concurrent with student demands to establish a robust students' union and to obtain representation on university committees, including Council. By the end of the 1970s, these efforts to formally and culturally democratise the university were successful, and for a decade or so, the same activists who led initial reforms encouraged wide participation in governance, including a larger academic Senate akin to Oxford's congregation mentioned above. By the 1980s, however, participation rates began to wane, not least due to the continued expansion of academic staff numbers, resulting in unwieldy staff meetings dominated by unrepresentative, oppositional academics and lingering, conservative dons, who retained interest in Senate proceedings.

Concurrent to this internal decline, the broader political context of Thatcherism put pressure on the governing Council as well and public pressure on the academic profession, demanding both wider student participation and more economic utility to be delivered with fewer resources, new accountability exercises including the Research Assessment Exercise, and diminishing long-term security. This began to tie university vice chancellors together across the sector, in order to consider means of defending themselves, collectively, in a context of increasing uncertainty. The significance of Universities UK as the committee of university vice chancellors grew, eventually culminating in the Jarratt Report published in 1985 as an attempt to thwart further Thatcherite interference in the sector, by voluntarily submitting to self-organised accountability mechanisms and moves towards what would later be called 'neoliberal' university management organised around targets and performance management (Deem 2004; Parry 1999). Consolidation of the position of the older universities, including ancient, red brick and plate glass institutions was deepened with the formation of the Russell Group in 1994 after a large number of former polytechnic institutes were granted university status in 1992.

Increasingly, university senior managers saw themselves as a distinct tier representing their institutions in policy and business sectors. At Wessex, this was evident in the distinctions between roles – with the workload of the vice chancellor involving 'external' partnerships, and a provost managing internal institutional issues. As Jarratt articulated, academics were to be thought of less as self-governing members of autonomous corporations pursuing higher learning, but as shop-floor producers delivering educational and research services to customers, be they students or external partners. Throughout the period, resistance could be observed here and there, but as the scale of activities increased, it became more difficult for academics to gain an upper hand on management within their institutions or on a national bargaining platform beyond trade union issues of pay as the newly formed UCU obtained in 2006.

Locally, at the University of Wessex, we see a gradual and largely unplanned chipping away at the authority and rights of Senates and academics, often under the guise of plausible practicalities, such as the unwieldy size of a Senate consisting of the entire faculty. Instead, departments were allowed to elect representatives to Senate, where *ex officio* members of the executive group, including deans, who were also elected, joined them. As further rapid changes developed externally, council and executives became wary of the delays inherent in waiting for approval and deliberation amongst Senates that might meet only three or four times a year. Increasingly, committees began to proliferate to progress certain agendas, for example, research, education, engagement, finance and so on. Each of these committees was linked to members of the executive team, each of which might involve a new role – Director or Deputy Vice Chancellor of Research, etc. These members, too, would be represented as *ex officio* members of Senate and often Council.

Following a poor performance in the Research Assessment Exercise (RAE), resulting in a dramatic withdrawal of government direct grant funding, concurrent with a scandal that saw the elected vice chancellor involved in minor, but embarrassing corruption surrounding use of staff and resources, the governing board opted to invest in obtaining a visionary leader for the executive. The new chief executive officer (CEO), as he would come to be called, modelled himself on an idea of business leaders dominating the corporate economy, despite having no non-academic, business experience himself. The vice chancellor/CEO's first priority was to 'see' the institution and hired the most innovative technicians in data analytics who developed statistical models enabling forecasting. Together with the Chair of Council, a former executive at one of the leading logistics companies, he created a set of twenty key performance indicators (KPIs) by which he would be judged year by year, including global ranking position, number of students, staff satisfaction, grant income and so forth.

Of course, such indicators largely measured the performance of others – academic and non-academic staff, and so to increase performance, meant 'change' amongst departments, finance offices, human resources and so on. Activities that did not contribute to the 'bottom line' were cut, including departments, local history associations and staff meeting rooms. Meanwhile, growth areas were identified by deploying a 'SWOT' analysis to identify strengths, weaknesses, opportunities and threats. These included mergers with nearby institutions, including art schools, polytechnics and teachers' colleges, to incorporate their successful programmes, while eliminating deadweight and obtaining new estate. At the same time, ambitious plans to develop new buildings, many show-stopping student-facing venues to attract new applicants, resulted in complex financial arrangements involving large loans obtained by international investment banks at not particularly attractive interest rates.

Still, the university was growing. The executive team hit their KPIs, and initial resistance by academic staff diminished with the appearance of both financial security and success as more and more students enrolled. Still, not every policy travelled smoothly through Senate, and department heads continued to irritate the executive committees with parochial demands that failed to see the bigger picture revealed by the data. In 2009, the university Council and executive group conducted a wholesale revision of the governance of the statutes, ordinances and charters. They re-applied to the Privy Council to move many provisions from statutes to ordinances, where changes could be made without further re-chartering – that is, internally, amongst Council, Senate and executive committees.

While nominally retaining departments, these were merged in more-or-less arbitrary configurations to fudge KPIs and to diminish the authority of department heads. The departments were reorganised into five different schools consisting of anywhere from two to eight departments. The deans of these schools were renamed pro-vice chancellors (PVCs). Each PVC was provided with an executive committee that mirrored the top. A few years later, without notice, ordinances were changed so PVCs were no longer elected, but hired via executive search. Another ordinance change dramatically reduced the number of academic senators in Senate, allowing for only four per school for a total of twenty. Meanwhile, *ex officio* positions had grown to such an extent that academic senators amounted to less than half of the voting members, most of whom were directly accountable to the vice chancellor/CEO.

Concurrently, since the vice chancellor had been in office for so long, the appointment of external governors had been conducted to ensure that, although governors were ostensibly responsible for holding the executive to account, none would dramatically challenge the strategy, reports or activities of the senior management. By this stage, little visible resistance to the chief executive remained – all reports demonstrated progress, especially after the metric measuring staff satisfaction (hovering between 20 and 30 per cent) was removed as a KPI. Everyone surrounding the vice chancellor agreed with the direction of travel. The restructuring of governance via committees and a defanged Senate meant decisions and policies could be prefigured entirely by deputy vice chancellors; Senate meetings took the form of information delivery, wherein PowerPoints explained what was going to happen, without asking questions about 'what should happen?'

At every level, all involved used metrics they knew were incredibly flawed, including surveys with completion rates in the single digits. But, none would dare draw attention. As in the absolutist court of Louis XIV, organised around etiquette, in this instance, measurement became the ritual around which internal compliance was ensured. If one challenged these, they exposed themselves as an individual at odds with the entire configuration. Many preferred the option of resigning and returning to academic work rather than push against the machine that ran according to its own logic. The roles demanded that the actor submit to the emergent hierarchy in order to survive within it – if one stepped out of line, she or he was selected out and replaced by a firm believer in both the validity of the metrics, and the suzerainty of the vice chancellor/CEO as the captain of the great ship Wessex.

Breaking the social contract

The crisis that enveloped the universities in the wake of the 2018 USS strike should be understood within the context described above – which, although based largely on one institutional history, was common across the sector. Homology was partly due to institutional isomorphism (DiMaggio and Powell 1983), in which universities copied one another's 'best practices' in order to deal with common challenges on the market and with respect to increasing governmental regulation. As complexity increased, many relied on consultants, including lawyers, accountants and human resource gurus, to provide advice about how, for example, to remove statutes and reposition these in ordinances; how to establish 'interdisciplinary institutes' in order to avoid the insularity of 'academic tribes'. As these consultancies linked themselves together within the burgeoning networks created within *Times Higher Education* summits, or higher education expos, and as the consultants themselves developed collective consciousness amongst themselves as 'wonks', as defined within the blog WonkHE established in 2012, a new layer of technicians and 'professional service' administrators was introduced into universities' operations. On the frontlines, these workers might identify with, interact with and sympathise with academics, but many would enter the senior management courts, promising to deliver 'change' regardless of whether such change was good or bad for the institution or sector.

Through UUK, university executives coordinated their actions *vis-à-vis* the government and international markets – although many would remain competitive as each institution struggled for advantage in rankings and governmental metrics. Thus, just as the court society established in Versailles was emulated across European courts, down to the level of minor princes in German- or Slavic-speaking states, so have university courts become a national – indeed, an international – society operating on its own tier.

However, this tier was becoming more and more detached from everyday experiences of the academic staff and stakeholders who the vice chancellors ostensibly represented. It became ever-more difficult, even for professional associations and government ministers to determine whether vice chancellors spoke for their own interests or for their institutions. The most evident public expression emerged during the 2017 scandals over vice chancellor pay, leading to the resignation of Dame Glynis Breakwell as leader of the University of Bath. It appeared not even the titles and honours vice chancellors helped confer upon one another could protect an individual 'bad apple' who made their cohort look bad. Meanwhile, nearly all had participated in the scandalous activity in question: namely, sitting on the pay committees that determined their own extravagant pay – all of which consisted of members of court.

Operating on an increasingly autonomous tier meant university leaders had become less aware of conditions on the ground, particularly amongst academic staff, who had been disenfranchised and were losing control of their conditions of professional work. Academics had been, by and large, unaware of these changes themselves, and experienced only a general dissatisfaction with the direction of travel and local frustrations. Finding no suitable outlets for expression of grievances, the profession knew that something was wrong, but felt powerless to do anything. The cut in pension benefits was the final straw that broke the camel's back.

Obliviously, the chief executives of universities and UUK thought the matter would be quickly resolved; none expected the scale of industrial action taken. Once academics came out on the picket lines, they established themselves as truly interdisciplinary cohorts; they established collective consciousness and shared local grievances, which became recognisable as general patterns. All became increasingly aware that the pensions crisis was merely a symptom of the deeper problem: namely, that the social contract that linked the tiers together had been broken. The vice chancellors claimed to speak on behalf of universities, but as the dramatic vote at Oxford demonstrated, the universities themselves begged to differ.

Still, this was only possible at Oxford in so far as the governance structures had not changed as radically as those at the University of Wessex, in part due to their antiquity, in part due to tradition, and in part due to the sustained defence of academic decision-making Oxford academics made during the entire period in question, even when they faced similar problems of participation and large congregations. Now, in the wake of the 2018 strikes, with the pension dispute still unresolved; when academics have returned to their offices, back to similar conditions of work as before, the question remains whether we can point to any similarities between the revolutions of 1789 and the present. More than likely, beyond some minor reforms – and some greater attention paid by courts to their nominal constituencies – the court society structure that had developed before remains in place today.

Academics on the lower tier – historically tasked with the self-governance of our institutions – need to determine a path forward. Do we continue to demonstrate deference to our university courts and their monarchs? Do we look to establish alliances or clashes with the growing body of professional service administrators and consultants coming between us and the management tiers? Do we revitalise and reform the remaining institutions for academic decision-making and resistance that have been defanged? Senates. Departments. Unions. These are choices yet to be made. But, only by first understanding and, indeed, observing that, due to a range of unplanned processes, such a structure now exists can we hope to regain some agency in the ways our universities and our work are run.

Critical reflections on social theory and methodology

The analysis above demonstrates the value of remaining attentive to situations one finds oneself in, particularly when researching universities (in which many of us work). In this instance, in early 2018, I was writing my book on Norbert Elias and the sociology of education, doing a lot of re-reading, including his analysis of court society. Meanwhile, as a member of my university's UCU branch, I became involved in the industrial action over pensions, and was asked to prepare a public talk as part of the teach-out programme. I decided to apply the theory I was developing to the situation, and immediately found the quotation above in which Elias described how no individual courtier could opt out of the figuration and came to believe in the irrationality of the system. My tentative explanation to striking staff proved effective, as many academics said this conformed with their own experience.

In the months that followed, I began further data collection, including especially interviews with key members of staff who had been involved in governance for decades. I began review of the university archives, looking at Council and Senate papers beginning in the 1980s. When, in summer, a graduate student visited me on a research placement, we both went through the archives to gather a chronological picture of how power arrangements changed. Lastly, I took advantage of the fact that the university's statutes, ordinances and other policies are posted publicly online and have been for some time. Annual reports were interesting in so far as the page length of these documents was reduced across the period from an average of forty-five pages in 2005 to eight in 2015, demonstrating the relative disinterest in justifying activities beyond court. Using the 'internet wayback' machine (https://archive.org/web/), I accessed changes in these statutes and ordinances, both locally, and across the sector – revealing the scale of the problem, which was not specific to the institution I focused my research on.

These methods proved adequate for the task I set myself, which was not comprehensive and definitive evidence of the entire process or historical reality as such. Rather, my goal was to demonstrate the utility of a concept – management as court society – which I deductively derived from theoretical work. Within my general framework of processual sociology, the theory was coherent, but I was interested in applying the theory to a new field of study to see which new aspects of reality would be revealed. In this instance, the confusion surrounding the strike began to make sense to me and to my colleagues, suggesting the concept was worthy of further application. Since I did not have a large grant or much time beyond my primary research on nineteenth-century university history, I could only explore the concept locally, drawing on resources ready to hand. The analysis should accordingly be understood as a test, or proof of concept. The theoretical lens provided by Elias applied within the local situation and initial exploration of further evidence demonstrated this held further purchase across the sector. The figurational perspective on court society provides a perspective on higher education policy that has not yet been represented in the literature – highlighting the distance between managers and academics. Identifying homologies between absolutist court societies and senior management surrounding contemporary vice chancellors could provide further insight into how these configurations work, particularly in terms of the way in which measurement and etiquette serve different forms of constraints. It should, however, be said that the stakes in politics and higher education are different, and there are undoubtedly many areas wherein the analogy does not hold sway. The theory should not be forced. Rather, this tentative study should demonstrate the potential utility in adopting an Eliasian approach.

More research would need to be conducted to fully document the phenomena and processes in question. Undoubtedly variations and particularities could be identified across different types of institutions and national higher education systems. However, in demonstrating the utility of the concept, trial research into the emergence of court society in contemporary universities recommends both the processual theory and concept in particular, and, more broadly, the value of educational research that engages and moves back and forth between theory, evidence and method throughout all stages of discovery.

Note

1 The USS pension crisis was complicated due to the lack of transparency surrounding the way the USS firm prepared its valuation, projecting a contested deficit of £17.5 billion. This led employers (UUK) to replace the defined benefits scheme with a defined contribution scheme. During the course of the strike, members of UCU calculated alternative valuations which not only projected no deficit, but even interpreted the scheme as being in surplus. The eventual resolution to the industrial action involved the creation of a Joint Expert Panel to assess these contradictory valuations.

References

Block, F. and Keller, M.R. (2009), 'Where Do Innovations Come from? Transformations in the US Economy, 1970–2006', *Socioeconomic Review*, 7 (3): 459–483.

Deem, R. (2004), 'The Knowledge Worker, the Manager-academic and the Contemporary UK University: New and Old Forms of Public Management?', *Financial Accountability and Management*, 20 (2): 107–128.

DiMaggio, P.J. and Powell, W.W. (1983), 'The Iron Cage Revisited: Institutional Isomorphism and Collective Rationality in Organizational Fields', *American Sociological Review*, 48 (2): 147–160.

Elias, N. (1978), *What is Sociology?*, New York: Columbia University Press.

Elias, N. (1983), *The Court Society*, New York: Pantheon Books.

Elias, N. (2000), *The Civilizing Process: Sociogenetic and Psychogenetic Investigations*, Oxford: Blackwell.

Jarratt, A. (1985), *Report of the Steering Committee for Efficiency Studies in Universities* (The Jarratt Report), London: CVCP.

Lomer, S. (2017), 'Soft Power as a Policy Rationale for International Education in the UK: A Critical Analysis', *Higher Education*, 74 (4): 581–598.

Lybeck, E. (2019), *Nobert Elias and the Sociology of Education*, London: Bloomsbury Academic.

Lybeck, E. (2020), *The University Revolution: The Academization Process and the Emergence of Modern Higher Education since 1800*, Abingdon: Routledge.

Marginson, S. (2016), 'The Worldwide Trend to High Participation Higher Education: Dynamics of Social Stratification in Inclusive Systems', *Higher Education*, 72 (4): 413–434.

McCowan, T. (2019), *Higher Education For and Beyond the Sustainable Development Goals*, Dordrecht: Springer.

Parry, G. (1999), 'Education Research and Policy Making in Higher Education: The Case of Dearing', *Journal of Education Policy*, 14 (3): 225–241.

Robbins, Lord (1963), *Higher Education* (The Robbins Report), Cmnd. 2154, London: HMSO.

Smelser, N.J. (2013), *Dynamics of the Contemporary University: Growth, Accretion, and Conflict*, Berkeley, CA: University of California Press.

4

Tales from the Matrix: Student Satisfaction as a Form of Governmentality

Stephen Day and Anne Pirrie

The title of this chapter is derived from the sci-fi film The Matrix (1999). The story goes roughly like this. Morpheus and Trinity head up a group of cyber-rebels who have discovered that the world as their fellow mortals know it doesn't exist. They hire Neo, a young computer nerd who seems to have great potential. So much so that Morpheus and Trinity see him as a potential saviour. They persuade him to lead a rebellion against the powers of oppression, to break out of the prison of humdrum existence. The Matrix is a virtual reality designed to enslave humanity. All it takes to be free of it is to swallow a little red pill. But the red pill doesn't come with a Patient Information Leaflet. We have attempted to supply one below.

Introduction

This chapter explores how three related Foucauldian concepts – *governmentality, subjectification* and *technologies of self* – might support an analysis of how measures of student satisfaction alter the nature of the relationship between academics and students and working practices in the university. By focusing on how these measures mould and shape academic practices, we aim to render visible the pervasive and coercive nature of such measures within contemporary higher education, with particular reference to the UK context. In so doing, we shall problematise the seemingly mundane and quotidian policy narratives that govern contemporary academic practices.

By way of context, we acknowledge that higher education systems across Europe are in the throes of governance reforms that encourage senior managers to adopt and apply a 'new public management' approach to leadership. As a result, 'governing by number' (Ozga 2009) has become commonplace. Although it is interesting to understand how management systems have changed, both in individual institutions and in the management of the higher education system as a whole, such a discussion is beyond the scope of this chapter. For those interested in such a critique, we might suggest reading Radice (2013) and Collini (2017) for a detailed analysis of the impact of the neoliberal agenda on education, particularly in respect of the wholesale marketisation of the sector in the UK.

For our current purposes, it will suffice to note that over the past two decades neoliberal reforms within higher education have resulted in a shift in the meaning, purpose and mission of the public university, particularly in the UK. This shift has transformed the university from an institution primarily concerned with the promotion of higher learning, the disinterested pursuit of knowledge and research for the public good and nation-building, into one that has been remodelled to resemble a transnational business corporation operating in a competitive global knowledge economy (Shore and Davidson 2014). In an increasingly competitive environment, these developments often manifest themselves in the drive towards becoming an 'international' university, as university managers strive to attract ever-growing numbers of international students to their institutions. In the UK over the last decade, universities have increasingly engaged in a game of one-upmanship regarding their respective standings in league tables such as the *Complete University Guide*, *The Guardian*'s University Rankings or those compiled by the *Times/Sunday Times*. This highly competitive, marketised higher education environment forms the backdrop to our inquiry.

This chapter comprises four sections. These are a testament to the role of theory, coupled with dialogic and collegial relations, as a means of generating powerful counter-narratives and exercising resistance to particular trends within higher education. The inexorable rise of the 'student satisfaction' agenda is a case in point. The first section critically discusses how the application of social theory supports the notion that academics need to 'think differently' about contemporary higher education in order better to understand the working environment within which they find themselves. By so doing, we seek to undermine what is regarded as self-evident and to open up spaces for acting and thinking differently about our relationships to ourselves and to others. We also explore the impact of the prevailing climate on constructions of personal and professional identity in the academy. The second section outlines our understanding of the Foucauldian conceptual tools that frame our analysis of how student satisfaction shapes academic practice. The third section describes the contemporary higher education environment by characterising the 'matrix', which is how we conceptualise the simulated reality that has inflected the socio-political culture of higher education. The reference to The Matrix (1999) at the beginning of this chapter suggests that we are enslaved by a totalising virtual reality that demands absolute compliance. In short, this is a social system that is premised on the exercise of total control and manipulation. In a higher education system in which 'vestiges of academic self-government have largely been removed and replaced by the top-down control of a "senior management team" implementing the latest government directions' (Collini 2017: 1), the analogy with an iconic sci-fi movie will not stretch the imagination of most readers. In the context of higher education, the expression *to measure up* has lost its metaphorical value in the face of sustained attempts to render a complex system manageable, accountable and thereby controllable by the manipulation of data and the enshrinement of metrics as the key driver of change. The fourth section explores how our understanding of the Foucauldian concepts of governmentality, subjectification and technologies of the self provides a lens through which to critique both the higher educational environment and the manner in which it constructs professional identity.

Critical reflections on social theory

Since social theories are broadly understood to be analytical frameworks (or paradigms) used to examine social phenomena (Harrington 2005), we chose to focus our analysis on an existing area of mutual research interest, namely student satisfaction (see Pirrie 2018; Pirrie and Day 2019). This chapter marks our attempt to reconceptualise our thinking in this area through the prism of social theory (in this case, a Foucauldian perspective).

Why Foucault? As Ball (2019) suggests, Foucault's curiosity towards the art of governing and by extension being governed, provides a suitable canvas upon which to develop our thinking regarding the use of student satisfaction as a proxy measure of academic quality. We would like to trouble the notion that the logic of competition that underpins the widespread use of metrics is benign. In order to do this, we have problematised student satisfaction as an agenda that has been galvanised by the pivotal role that it plays in the compilation of institutional rankings, which only serve to reinforce the logic of competition that pervades contemporary higher education.

Prior to a discussion of the application of governmentality, subjectification and technologies of the self as an analytical lens, we outline our understanding of these concepts. We then proceed to matters of methodology by describing how we operationalised our analysis through a directed content analysis. The aim of this approach was to describe the characteristics of documentary artefacts relating to student satisfaction using an inductive/deductive approach to our use of the three Foucauldian concepts.

Governmentality

We subscribe to the view that governmentality can be applied as an analytical tool for the study of networked governance beyond the state. The aim here is critically to explore government as a form of power by understanding the micro-practices used to govern, and the mentality that underpins those practices (Merlingen 2011). Foucault's notion of 'governmentality' is semantically linked to the following terms: government (or governing), and rationality or modes of thought (*mentalité*). Foucault coined the concept of governmentality as a guideline for analysis during his 1978 and 1979 lectures at the Collège de France, focusing on the 'genealogy of the modern state' (Foucault 1982a). However, Foucault's notion of government harks back to an older meaning of the term and adumbrates the close link between forms of power and processes of subjectification (Lemke 2002). Here government is seen not only in political terms, but also in philosophical, religious, medical and pedagogical terms. As well as management (or administration) by the state, 'government' signifies issues of self-control or discipline. It was for this reason that Foucault defined government as 'the conduct of conduct', as the term encompasses both governing the self and governing others. Thus, governmentality offers a view on power beyond political or (micro-political) consensus by linking it to technologies of the self through mechanisms of subjectification, i.e. the processes that constitute the subject. In short, governmentality encapsulates the relations between power and the subject. Governmentality represents what Foucault called an unstable 'contact point' between techniques of domination (or subjection) and the actual practices of subjectification by which neoliberal subjects govern themselves (Lemke 2002). Therefore, we suggest that governmentality is a valuable tool for the study of the processes of governance in the contemporary university. In the case under consideration below, it provides the theoretical lens through which to explore the various 'performative technologies' that have disfigured higher education in recent decades (Englund and Gerdin 2019).

That said, we acknowledge that governmentality is conceptually more complex than our brief characterisation suggests. There are various ways in which the concept of governmentality can be applied, depending on one's positionality regarding higher education practice. The literature on governmentality exposes the complex array of different forms or regimes, for example, disciplinary, liberal, neoliberal and affective governmentality (Kantola et al. 2019; Thiel 2019). Despite this complexity, Merlingen (2011) argues that governmentality is a thin theory with a light conceptual apparatus that does not offer causal models that can be used to formulate testable hypotheses. Rather, it enables us to study the processes of co-option and administration in terms of the 'heterogeneous intellectual and technical conditions … that link aspirations of rulers with the conduct of the ruled' (Miller and Rose 1995: 594).

Through the use of governmentality as an analytical tool, we will focus our analysis on how certain identities and action-orientations (i.e. the disposition of the subject to act in certain ways given a level of autonomy and feelings of personal agency) are defined as appropriate and normal, and how relations of power are implicated in those processes. In so doing, we seek to analyse the relation between individuals and the 'micro-political' order from the perspective of the different processes, whereby the former are objectified as certain kinds of subject through the ways in which their conduct is governed.

Subjectification as a form of domination

Subjectification is conceptually linked to governmentality by the way in which the rationality of the disciplinary discourse positions the individual relative to their professional identity, ethics and code of conduct within institutional governance structures. Foucault (1982b: 331) suggests that

> … the subject is constituted through practices of subjection, or … through practices of liberation, of freedom … starting of course from a certain number of rules, styles and conventions that are found in the culture.

Subjectification takes many forms, but these coalesce on rational grounds both directly, through formal management and accountability systems (regimes of performance), and indirectly, through techniques for leading and controlling individuals, such as gentle persuasion or words to the wise from those in positions of influence. The strategy of rendering individual subjects (academics) 'responsible' entails the shifting of responsibility from the institution to the individual by transforming it into a problem of self-care (Lemke 2002). A key feature of neoliberal rationality is that 'it aspires to construct responsible subjects whose moral quality is based on the fact that they rationally assess the costs and benefits of a certain act as opposed to alternative acts' (Lemke 2002: 59). This line of thinking extends to the choice of action taken by individuals, in so far as such choices are expressions of free will on the basis of self-determined decisions. In this case, the consequences of the action are borne by the subject alone, as they have sole responsibility for their actions. The dominant discourse renders the individual (subject) through processes of subjectification within the confines of 'reasonable expectation' in terms of their conduct and active decision-making. These must align with and at times mirror the institutional rationality and corporate (self-) image.

Technologies of the self

Technologies of the self relate to subjectification through modes of subjectivity, which in turn are associated with the practice of governing and its underlying rationality. This shift in responsibility for action from the institution to the individual is achieved by playing on and appealing to notions of professional identity, ethics and codes of conduct. For Foucault (1997), the concept of technologies of the self was seen as 'games of truth', not as a coercive practice but as an ascetic practice of self-formation. 'Ascetic' here means an 'exercise of self upon the self by which one attempts to develop and transform oneself, and to attain a certain mode of being' (Foucault 1997: 282).

This suggests that the borders between the individual (personal) and the institution (corporate) are redrawn within the neoliberal model of rationality. Barbara Cruikshank's work on the self-esteem movement in the US provides some insight into how such processes of subjectification subtly alter individuals' practices through an appeal to professional (self-) esteem. According to Cruikshank (1999), self-esteem has more to do with self-assessment than with self-respect, as the self is continuously measured, judged and disciplined in order to gear personal 'empowerment' towards collective yardsticks (a process of normalising judgement). Through this process, the individual governs her own behaviours and practices in order to align them with institutional expectations. The result is a precarious harmony between the institutional goals and the subject's personal 'state of esteem' (Cruikshank 1999). This suggests that one is only as good as one's most recent performance development review.

Foucault's notion of technologies of the self suggests that the regimes of governmentality are not restricted to rationalities but also pertain to the subject's affective life. This affective element is clear in *confessions*, a topic that Foucault was interested in early on in his thinking (Foucault 1988). In confessions, the self-mortifying emotions of guilt, shame and remorse play a key role in constituting a new self (Foucault 1988). Reflecting upon the notion of technologies of the self permits individuals

> ... to effect by their own means or with the help of others a certain number of operations on their own bodies and souls, thought, conduct, and way of being. The aim is to help the individual transform themselves, and this takes place not only rationally, but also in a more fundamental way to attain a certain state of happiness, purity, wisdom, perfection, or immortality.
>
> Foucault 1988: 18

Methodology

Reflecting upon the possible methodological approaches that we might take for this research, we discussed how we might apply the Foucauldian concepts as analytical tools for the documentary analysis that formed the basis of the research approach. The documentation reviewed comprised university league tables and their associated methodologies, university websites and those of Schools of Education, and publicly available documents relating to regulations and 'student experience'. This led to discussions around the ontological and epistemological assumptions that underpinned possible methodologies. Since the research follows an interpretivist ontology and is epistemologically underpinned by post-structuralism aligned with a Foucauldian perspective, the method of analysis adopted within this research was conducted in two discrete phases, each comprising several different stages of analysis.

The *first phase of analysis* comprised a directed content analysis (DCA) of key documentary artefacts relating to the assessment of student satisfaction within the UK. The purpose of a DCA is to describe the characteristics of the content of documents by examining who says what, to whom and with what effect (Bloor and Wood 2006). This entails using a descriptive approach to the coding of data, and its interpretation through an inductive/deductive approach to the analysis. This methodology was applied in several stages. During the first stage, the DCA was to characterise the 'matrix'. This was performed by first identifying the main matrices used by external actors (government agencies, the media and third sector organisations) in order to assess student satisfaction within the UK. Documentary artefacts (e.g. explanatory notes, opinion pieces, assessment and feedback policies, regulatory frameworks and research articles) relating to each matrix were also accessed. The second stage was to upload and read the documents using NVIVO 12. The third stage of analysis was the development of a range of codes, in the form of 'nodes', for example SubNJ (subjectification normalising judgement), to be used to mark relevant concepts (governmentality, subjectification and technologies of the self) and topics within the documents reviewed. The fourth stage was to make memos in order to record observations about emerging themes or thoughts about issues that drew our attention, questions these raised in our minds, or issues pertaining to the data that required further investigation. For example, under the node of SubNJ, the associated memo was as follows: *most universities in the sample have processes that relate to normalising judgement such as module reviews and programme reviews. These processes are open to scrutiny from management and subject to apparently arbitrary measures of satisfaction.* The fifth stage involved drawing together the nodes and memos in order to synthesise a critical perspective on the object of analysis (i.e. student satisfaction).

The *second phase of analysis*, drawing on the first, was a critical reflection on the extent to which market forces act upon universities; how they position academics working in higher education (focusing specifically on those working in initial teacher education (ITE) within one institution); and how they subtly and coercively subject them and alter their practices in the interests of improving 'student satisfaction'.

From the Foucauldian perspective inherent in the methodology, it was relatively simple to access the documentary artefacts required to characterise the 'matrix'. Subjecting documentary artefacts to careful scrutiny (with no help from a cyber-nerd like Neo) enabled us to assess the governmentality of the university sector without engaging in the virtual tussles embraced with such alacrity by our avatars Morpheus and Trinity. Ours was a much simpler (and cost-effective) mode of working: setting forth together on a path of inquiry and bringing to bear on the object of inquiry the resources from our different disciplinary backgrounds (the natural sciences and the humanities, respectively). Most documents were publicly available, especially those used by universities to govern academic practices that relate the 'student experience' within each institution. Adherence to the principle of 'transparency' is another key feature of the discourse of contemporary higher education. What we could not access using this methodology were the subtle technologies of the self through which individual academics govern themselves. This would have necessitated a different type of empirical research design. We acknowledge the limitations of our chosen methodology in respect of our capacity to scrutinise one of the three concepts. One way to bridge this gap between our methodological reach and our application of Foucauldian theory was for us critically to reflect (individually and dialogically) upon our own working practices when dealing with issues of 'student satisfaction', in the light of our combined experience within higher education practice (Pirrie 2018; Pirrie and Day 2019; Pirrie and Fang 2021). This limitation of our methodology has, however, opened up a rich seam of thought that can be further explored in future research. We intend to develop our work in the area of technologies of the self by conducting empirical research into the lived experience and working practices of academics. In the sections that follow, we outline our analysis, interpretations and reflections on our current study.

Characterising the 'matrix'

In order to develop a richer understanding of the many matrices that universities use to position themselves relative to one another, we begin by characterising the 'matrix' relating to student satisfaction. The matrix comprises five matrices or 'league tables' used by many UK Universities: *The Complete University Guide*; *The Guardian*'s University Rankings; *The Times/Sunday Times* League Tables; the *Times Higher Education* World University Rankings; and the *Teaching Excellence Framework* (TEF).

All of the above use metrics that form a holistic input/output model, with an emphasis on the output side of the model. Each metric uses measures of student satisfaction. It is interesting to note that *The Guardian*'s University Rankings and TEF[1] rely more heavily than the others on measures of 'student satisfaction'. These league tables characterise the contemporary higher education landscape. They also set up the environmental conditions that have favoured the emergence and evolution of neoliberal forms of governmentality.

Governmentality

When searching the main university webpages of the nineteen Scottish higher education institutions (HEIs), we found that eleven make no reference to their relative league table position in relation to the 'matrix' or to student satisfaction. However, five institutions draw attention to their standing in terms of research excellence and research quality indicators.

Close inspection of the webpages of university Schools of Education revealed that only four of the ten ITE provider institutions in Scotland refer to their

Table 4.1 The 'matrix' of measures used by universities to position themselves within the UK higher education arena

Matric data	Source	The Complete University Guide	The Guardian University Rankings	Times/Sunday Times League Tables	Teaching Excellence Framework (TEF)
Overall student satisfaction	NSS[1]	•	•	•	•
Course satisfaction	NSS	○	•	○	•
Teaching quality	NSS	○	•	○	•
Feedback	NSS	○	•	○	•
Entry standards/average entry tariff	HESA[2]	•	•	•	○
Graduate prospects / employability	HESA	•	•	•	•
Staff / student ratio	HESA	•	•	•	○
Degree completion	HESA	•	•	•	•
Good honours	HESA	•	○	•	○
Academic services spend	HESA	•	•	•	○
Facilities Spend	HESA	•	○	•	○
Value-added score	HESA	○	•	○	○
Continuation rate	HESA	○	•	•	•
Teaching excellence	SHEFC[3]	○	○	•	•
Heads assessment	Sunday Times Heads Survey	○	○	•	○
Research quality	REF[4]	•	○	•	○
Research intensity	REF/HESA	•	○	○	○

Note: Bullet point represents matric data present and open circles represent metric data absent.

[1]National Student Survey; [2]Higher Education Statistics Agency; [3]Scottish Higher Education Funding Council; [4]Research Excellence Framework.

league table position. This may suggest that Scottish ITE providers do not explicitly focus on league table positions to market themselves via their respective websites. However, this interpretation fails to take account of the potential pressure placed on academics within each institution to meet institutional key performance indicators relating to improving student satisfaction, as this pressure is not visible within the public domain. These findings lead us to reflect on where we might find indicators of institutional governmentality that are visible in public discourse as opposed to the internal discourse of the institution. This led us to explore each of the Scottish university websites for academic quality/regulatory frameworks and assessment and feedback policy handbooks in order to assess the extent to which their governance structures emphasise practices that maximise student satisfaction.

Subjectification

Our analysis of publicly available academic quality documentation, regulatory frameworks, and assessment and feedback policies indicates that all nineteen Scottish universities have internal procedures for annual, periodic and external reviews of student experience. Our analysis also indicates that the documents relating to these procedures clearly outline the lines of accountability and responsibilities of academic staff. We read these as technologies of subjectification. In addition, the majority of the documents scrutinised make statements regarding students' responsibilities in respect of engagement, assessment and the use of feedback mechanisms, thereby also positioning the student within the process of subjectification.

The following extracts from documentation from two universities exemplify this point.

> Staff are expected to *explain* the purpose of collecting feedback, the methods that will be utilised, how the feedback will be analysed, how and when the findings will be considered and how actions taken as a result of the findings will be communicated back; *encourage* students to reflect on their learning experience; *communicate* responses to students and staff; *communicate matters of interest and import arising from feedback from students onwards to School, College and the University*
>
> University of Glasgow 2018: 9, emphasis added

> Staff involved in assessing students' work are responsible for *designing* assessments that effectively facilitate and measure students' achievement of

intended learning outcomes; *assessing* students' work according to published assessment criteria which are aligned to intended learning outcomes and the University's Guidance on Marking Assessments in Undergraduate and Postgraduate Taught programmes; *providing timely, informative and helpful feedback* which enables students to further improve their learning and performance wherever possible; *informing students when, where and how feedback will be provided*; *engaging in dialogue* with students about assessment and feedback; and *continuously reviewing* their approaches to assessment and feedback to reflect effective practice.

University of Strathclyde 2019: 6, emphasis added

As we reflect upon these two examples, a few points emerge. First, there is an emphasis on feedback to students (a theme identified in all the documents). This is often a contentious component of the National Student Survey, due in part to the fact that students tend to have rather limited conceptions of feedback and regard it as something that is presented in written form, mostly within the context of formal assessment. There is a tendency to overlook feedback that is provided orally in teaching situations or written feedback in the form of moderation in a virtual learning environment. Second, responsibility is placed on staff to explain, encourage and communicate with students in an informative and timely manner. Academics are free to exercise a degree of discretion in respect of how this is to be achieved. However, discretion can also be exercised in how this is interpreted. Does it constitute academic freedom or is it more accurately conceived as room to manoeuvre? Third, the tone of both examples is interesting, in so far as the emphasis is on *expectation* in the case of the first example, and the positioning of staff within the corporate body as *responsible,* as in the second example. Fourth, both examples stipulate referring to issues arising from assessment, and regard the use of assessment feedback as 'evidence' of the process of reflection. In respect of the latter, staff are expected to evaluate their teaching, learning and assessment practice within the annual review processes. While all this may seem reasonable given the interactional nature of the teaching and learning process, we suggest that it may also point towards the governance structures used to position academics as subjects (mechanisms of subjectification) and to emphasise the means of *self-governance* as a technology of the self. This has led us to reflect upon the mechanisms for regular, annual, periodic and external reviews of teaching and learning as technologies of subjectification within the governmentality of student satisfaction.

Technologies of subjectification: Internal review/evaluations of students' experience

When we looked more closely at the nineteen Scottish universities' regulatory frameworks and quality assurance handbooks, we found that all Scottish HEIs utilise module/course evaluation surveys, module and programme evaluation forms or questionnaires designed to capture the views of staff and students on modules and programmes on an annual basis. In addition, all of the universities sampled had recourse to some form of staff/student liaison committee, which in turn reported discussions to programme boards or an education forum. These internal mechanisms tend to reinforce the individual and collective responsibility of academics for measures of student satisfaction. What is not so easy to grasp from the documentation is how central such activities are to the workings of particular universities.

That said, it is possible to theorise that these governance practices place academics under what Thiel (2019) calls a 'continuous panoptical gaze', since these practices set up a situation where two processes occur. The first is a form of *hierarchical observation* where managers access (in the name of transparency) the minutes of staff/student liaison meetings, module/course evaluation survey responses, module and programme evaluation forms and student attainment statistics that provide quantitative and qualitative data on the 'health' of a module or a programme. Thiel (2019: 544) suggests that hierarchical observation is an example of a pyramidal functioning of disciplinary power. In the case of module/course evaluation surveys, 'the students fulfil the panoptical gaze on behalf of university management'. The second process involves *normalising judgements* with regard to the quality of the teaching of particular academics. This is achieved through the ranking of student feedback from module/course evaluation surveys. This ranking sets up another evaluative process whereby university managers scrutinise the survey data for modules. In the event that reported levels of student satisfaction fall below a particular threshold, the staff concerned are asked to account for this and if necessary to develop a remedial action plan. They are then expected to implement this, and are subjected to further monitoring by management when the next student cohort evaluate that module. This form of normalising judgement can be thought of as a performative technology (Englund and Gerdin 2019) that emerges from the governmentality that underpins the technology of subjectification described above.

Performativity as seen through the prism of student satisfaction can be a double-edged sword, particularly within a highly marketised environment. This level of assessment of academic performance can be used to improve the student experience, but does not guarantee the production of graduates who are adequately prepared for the world of work – or indeed for the world. The net effect of a prevailing culture of performativity is that a situation arises whereby students sometimes do not trust the academic to guide their professional development and to enhance their critical faculties in order that they are better equipped to engage with issues of professional import. The professional judgement of academics is directed at designing learning experiences within teaching sessions that challenge, stretch and place intellectual or practical demands on students. The latter often use the framework of the staff/student liaison committee or module evaluation questionnaire to complain about certain aspects of teaching. Such complaints are often based on subjective judgements related to the teacher's personality rather than to their perceived professionalism. This can lead to a pervasive practice which can be summed up as a 'you said, we did' mentality. This connects with the discourse on student satisfaction in that the 'you' are the students and the 'we' are the academics. This form of 'customer satisfaction' behaviour is counterproductive, in so far as academics are in possession of particular knowledge and understanding of what the student is required to learn in order to meet the demands of a profession such as teaching. This can (and often does) run counter to what the students want in the moment, which is not to dismiss out of hand the perspectives of the latter.

It is this *transactional* view of teaching and learning that we argue runs counter to the *interactional* nature of teaching and learning within higher education. To reduce the student to the status of a customer, and the learning process to that of a transaction, is to demonstrate a lack of understanding of the purpose of higher education. What is often not considered within this discourse is the impact of such a culture of performativity on the professional identity of the academic. It is to this issue that we now turn.

Professional identity construction

Within the context our study, we subscribe to the view that professional identity construction is a complex and dynamic process that is mediated through socialisation and personal reflection. It revolves around an autonomous individual (the Self), who constantly moves between the need to connect and consult with colleagues, and the need to maintain a sense of individuality (Smith 1996). In this process, the Self is a coherent, bounded and intentional individual who is the locus of thought, action and belief, and has a unique biography (Rose 1998). From a Foucauldian perspective, the situatedness of the Self is problematised as a form of working subjectivity. According to this view, the Self is a polysemic product of the experiences and practices that constitute the Self in response to multiple meanings that need not converge upon a stable, unified identity (Holstein and Gubrium 2000).

When reflecting upon the findings of the directed content analysis and the nature of the governmentality and subjectification of academics working in higher education, we recognised that the professional discourses that exist within many HEIs create or support an environment where the academic must internalise these discourses in order to be fully integrated within the professional ecology of the institution. This is then reinforced through socialisation processes that influence academics' self-regulation. This is achieved by ensuring that the professional gaze is simultaneously turned inwards *as a responsibility* and outwards as a disciplinary mechanism of subjectification by rendering them *accountable to* proxy measures of quality such as student satisfaction.

The professional 'panoptical gaze' becomes a form of surveillance that produces normative coercion that may constrain academics' ability to develop their own working practices. It also has a potentially negative impact upon their professional identity by playing on their professional values by means of a process of self-censoring and self-disciplining. All this takes place within a culture where it is not only rules and routines that become internalised, but also the complex set of practices that provide the common-sense, self-evident experiences that contribute to the formation of personal identity. Professional identity thus resides in the complex interplay between strategies of normalising professional judgements developed and implemented by those in power and the level of compliance or resistance to the dominant governmental discourse on the part of those who are subjected to it.

Concluding remarks

The use of Foucauldian theory to support our stated aim 'to think differently' about higher education practice, and to make more explicit the prevailing governmentality of student satisfaction was enlightening in a number of ways. First, it provided a useful framework for the discussions we engaged in as part of the research process. Second, it provided a powerful discourse within which to describe routine practices that we encountered within our institution and to analyse the emerging themes arising from the data. Third, it created a liminal space within which we interacted with the artefacts gathered (as data) and each other. Fourth, it enabled us to frame our thoughts and the findings in a coherent way. An interesting by-product of our engagement with these Foucauldian concepts was the development of new lines of enquiry that this engagement with social theory has opened up to us. In particular, we were struck by how processes of subjectification relate to technologies of the self and how the prevailing governmentality permeates, and at times dictates, processes of subjectification and technologies of the self through self-governing practices. It is also possible to relate the Foucauldian notions of power, governmentality, processes of subjectification and technologies of the self with other areas of social theory, in particular Bourdieu's concept of habitus – the physical embodiment of cultural capital, to the deeply ingrained habits, skills and dispositions (Stahl 2018).

The argument pursued in this chapter is that academics face major challenges when it comes to upholding the purposes and values of higher education within contemporary society. This entails challenging the notion that higher education is a commodity that can be reduced to a series of transactions. It seems that there is a very real risk that the interactional nature of learning that is the hallmark of ethical academic practice is being suborned by the notion that it is good for students to be satisfied; and by the same token that it is good for staff to comply with rather than to challenge this new 'virtual reality'. We would argue that it is more important for students to be challenged and exposed to complex, real-world professional situations that take them out of their comfort zones. This provides the foundation for what might more meaningfully be described as professional satisfaction rather than the type of instant gratification promoted under the current 'regime of truth'. It transpires that the red pill is an elaborate compound medicine. We have embraced social theory by drawing upon the Foucauldian concepts – *governmentality*, *subjectification* and *technologies of self* – in order to diagnose how measures of student satisfaction fundamentally alter the relationship between academics and students and the nature of working practices in higher education.

It is unfortunate that the policy narrative surrounding measures such as TEF and the governmentality discourse found within most UK universities supports the entrenchment of marketisation within higher education. This is particularly evident within the English higher education system, where this discourse has been problematised and challenged (Neary 2016; O'Leary and Wood 2019). This is perhaps a positive unintended consequence of the political pressure currently being brought to bear on universities to justify charging high tuition fees.

Within the Scottish context, where there are no tuition fees for home students, our analysis suggests that the narrative is skewed towards universities being accountable for providing 'value for public money'. This refraction in focus, like that seen in England, has led to a form of governmentality that increasingly positions the student as customer/consumer, and where education is seen in transactional rather than in interactional terms. This subjects the academic to increased pressure to keep students satisfied. There is evidence to suggest that it has also resulted in increased pressure upon academics to alter their teaching and assessment practices so as to accommodate rather than challenge their students. We suggest that it is more important to view the notion of 'value for public money' from the perspective of the quality of public service demonstrated by those who graduate through the national higher education system. For it is ultimately these graduates who will find employment within the public sector, including as teachers in schools with the potential to influence future generations of learners.

Note

1   As the focus in this study is on Scotland, it should be noted that most Scottish universities do not participate in TEF.

References

Ball, S. J. (2019), 'A Horizon of Freedom: Using Foucault to Think Differently about Education and Learning', *Power and Education*, 11 (2): 132–144.

Bloor, M. and Wood, F. (2006), *Keywords in Qualitative Methods: A Vocabulary of Research Concepts*, London: Sage.

Collini, S. (2017) *Speaking of Universities*, London: Verso.

Cruikshank, B. (1999), *The Will to Empower: Democratic Citizens and other Subjects*, Ithaca, NY: Cornell University Press.

Englund, H. and Gerdin, J. (2019), 'Performative Technologies and Teacher Subjectivities: A Conceptual Framework', *British Educational Research Journal*, 45 (3): 502–517.

Foucault, M (1982a), 'Vorlesungen zur Analyse der Machtmechanismen 1978' (incomplete transcription of the lecture in 1978 at the Collège de France), in *Der Staub und die Wolke*, trans. A. Pribersky, 1–44, Bremen: Impuls.

Foucault, M. (1982b), 'The Subject and Power', in J.D. Faubion (ed.), *Power: Essential Works of Foucault 1954–1984*, 326–348, London: Penguin.

Foucault, M. (1988), 'Technologies of the Self', in L. Martin, H. Gutman and P. Hutton (eds.), *Technologies of the Self: A Seminar with Michel Foucault*, 16–49, Amherst, MA: University of Massachusetts Press.

Foucault, M. (1997), 'The Ethics of the Concern for Self as a Practice of Freedom' (trans. Robert Hurley and others), in P. Rabinow (ed.), *Michel Foucault: Ethics, Subjectivity and Truth: The Essential Works of Michel Foucault 1954–1984*, vol. 1, 281–301, London: Penguin.

Harrington, A. (2005), *Modern Social Theory: An Introduction*, Oxford: Oxford University Press.

Holstein, J. and Gubrium, J. (2000), *The Self that We Live By: Narrative Identity in the Postmodern World*, New York: Oxford University Press.

Kantola, A., Seeck, H. and Mannevuo, M. (2019), 'Affect in Governmentality: Top Executives Managing the Affective Milieu of Market Liberalisation', *Organization*, 26 (6): 761–782.

Lemke, T. (2002), 'Foucault, Governmentality, and Critique', *Rethinking Marxism*, 14 (3): 49–64.

Merlingen, M. (2011), 'From Governance to Governmentality in CSDP: Towards a Foucauldian Research Agenda', *Journal of Common Market Studies*, 49 (1): 149–169.

Miller, P. and Rose, N. (1995), 'Political Thought and the Limits of Orthodoxy: A Response to Curtis', *British Journal of Sociology*, 46 (4): 590–597.

Neary, M. (2016), 'Teaching Excellence Framework: A Critical Response and an Alternative Future', *Journal of Contemporary European Research*, 12 (3): 690–695.

O'Leary, M. and Wood, P. (2019), 'Reimagining Teaching Excellence: Why Collaboration, rather than Competition, Holds the Key to Improving Teaching and Learning in Higher Education', *Educational Review*, 71 (1): 122–139.

Ozga, J. (2009), 'Governing Education through Data in England: From Regulation to Self-evaluation', *Journal of Education Policy*, 24 (2): 149–162.

Pirrie, A. (2018), 'Subverting the Notion of Student Satisfaction', *Other Education: The Journal of Educational Alternatives*, 7 (2): 8–21.

Pirrie, A. and Day, S. (2019), 'Reflective Practice and Student Satisfaction: Never the twain shall meet?', *European Educational Research Journal*, 18 (4): 483–496.

Pirrie, A. and Fang, N. (2021), 'Venturing from Home: Writing (and Teaching) as Creative-Relational Inquiry for Alternative Educational Futures', *International Review of Qualitative Research* (forthcoming).

Radice, H. (2013), 'How We Got Here: UK Higher Education Under Neoliberalism', *ACME: An International E-Journal for Critical Geographies*, 12 (3): 407–418.

Rose, N. (1998), *Inventing Ourselves: Psychology, Power and Personhood*, Cambridge: Cambridge University Press.

Shore, C. and Davidson, M. (2014), 'Beyond Collusion and Resistance: Academic–Management Relations within the Neoliberal University', *Learning and Teaching*, 7 (1): 12–28.

Smith, D.G. (1996), 'Identity, Self, and Other in the Conduct of Pedagogical Action: An East/West Inquiry', *Journal of Curriculum Theorizing*, 12 (3): 6–12.

Stahl, G. (2018), 'Putting Habitus to Work: Habitus Clivé, Negotiated Aspirations and a Counter-Habitus?', in G. Stahl, D. Wallace, C. Burke and S. Threadgold (eds.), *International Perspectives on Theorizing Aspirations: Applying Bourdieu's Tools*, 68–83, London: Bloomsbury.

The Matrix (1999), [Film] Dir. The Wachowskis, USA: Warner Bros.

Thiel, J. (2019), 'The UK National Students Survey: An Amalgam of Discipline and Neo-Liberal Governmentality', *British Educational Research Journal*, 45 (3): 538–553.

University of Glasgow (2018), *Academic Quality Framework*. Available online: https://www.gla.ac.uk/media/media_127773_en.pdf (last accessed 18 September 2019).

University of Strathclyde (2019), *Assessment and Feedback Policy*. Available online: https://www.strath.ac.uk/media/ps/cs/gmap/academicaffairs/policies/assessment_and_feedback_policy_-_Effective_Sep_14.pdf (last accessed 18 September 2019).

5

What Does it Mean to Assess Quality? A Socio-historical Analysis of Quality Assurance Systems in Chilean Higher Education

Tomás Koch and Julio Labraña

Introduction

Higher education has undergone a dramatic transformation globally over the last few decades. The move from elite to mass access that started in the 1960s in the US has expanded worldwide, transforming many national higher education systems (UNESCO 2009). In addition, new areas for development have emerged within universities, together with economic transformation and transport and communication technologies that have helped to enhance inter-institutional and international connections, thus reflecting their status as a global trait (see Frank and Meyer 2007).

These transformations have highlighted the need for common standards among institutions and/or countries. In this context, several new 'technical instruments' have emerged to allow for institutions to be compared (e.g. transferable credits, quality assurance systems and international rankings). These new instruments have influenced universities' governance, funding and values. Not surprisingly, then, they have attracted increasing scholarly interest in recent decades (see Espeland and Sauder 2007; Tight 2012).

Higher education research has grown in both size and specialisation, partly motivated by the need to make sense of these transformations (Tight 2017). These developments have occurred together with a growing theoretical engagement of varying importance depending on the theme (Tight 2012). As Ball (2010) points out, theoretical engagement is key to questioning underlying assumptions, coming up with alternatives and making sense of the world of higher education, without being 'dazzled' by reality. Noticeably, theoretically informed research is particularly relevant to unveiling underlying patterns in seemingly technical areas, such as university governance or performance-based evaluation mechanisms.

This chapter contributes to this subject by proposing a hybrid framework for understanding quality assurance mechanisms in higher education. This framework aims to insert Niklas Luhmann's theory of social systems and Michel Foucault's discourse analysis into the dialogue. Unlike some previous works that have highlighted the possibilities of this dialogue (e.g. Pottage 1998; Borch 2005; Zamorano-Farías and Rogel-Salazar 2013), we do not propose to synthesise the two approaches, but rather to use some concepts highlighted by these authors to shed light on relevant aspects of a specific case. The combination of these approaches creates a framework that allows us to understand both long-term transformations and the mechanisms through which changes occur in higher education systems.

We applied this theoretical framework to the analysis of the evolution of the concept of quality in the Chilean higher education system and specifically to its operationalisation in current quality assurance mechanisms. In methodological terms, we designed a case study based on a content analysis of official documents. We undertook a literature review and conducted (formal and informal) interviews with scholars, university administrators and policy-makers to identify those documents. In line with our hybrid approach, we focused on two types of documents: (1) inspired by Luhmann's emphasis on semantic change, we selected official acts and decrees that allowed us to depict the normative orientation of the higher education system; and (2) following Foucault's analysis of power dynamics, we analysed guidelines, forms and protocols that manifest the subtle power mechanisms exercised through seemingly technical procedures of registration, evaluation and qualification. We examined 117 documents.[1] We developed a hypothesis-driven content analysis (Guest et al. 2013) oriented by the theoretically inspired hypothesis that quality and the mechanisms designed to ensure it change across time following the needs of a functionally differentiated society, with these changes taking place through the implementation of evolving mechanisms of control. Therefore, the coding process focused on the theoretically defined categories of quality definition, mechanisms to ensure it, and specific procedures to assess it.

The Chilean case is a good one to observe the evolution of the mechanisms to ensure quality for three main reasons: first, the relatively longstanding tradition of higher education institutions that can be traced back to the colonial period (seventeenth century); second, the relatively longstanding application of new public management inspired policies in higher education (since the 1990s); and third, the current technical trait of quality assurance and, more broadly, performance-based evaluation mechanisms, in higher education. Our approach provided a useful framework for the case study's methodology and was sensitive enough to identify transformations to both the definition of quality and the functioning of quality assurance mechanisms in higher education.

The chapter is divided into three sections. First, we present the theoretical background, paying attention to the concepts of observation and selection from Luhmann and power and truth from Foucault, which we adopted as the guidelines for the case study. Next, we look at the evolution of the idea of quality and the mechanisms that have ensured it, from early Chilean institutions up to the present day. We pay particular attention to the emergence and functioning of current quality assurance systems. Finally, we summarise the main results and reflect on the role of theory and methodology in higher education research.

Theoretical background

The approaches of both Luhmann and Foucault suggest insightful possibilities that shed light on the underlying complexities of quality assurance systems in contemporary higher education. Although these two theorists have rarely been considered together, their formulations shed light on different, yet intertwined, aspects of the social world. We argue that their combination is especially useful to socio-historical research aimed at a nuanced understanding of national higher education systems in the context of broader structural transformations.

Concepts from Luhmann's work such as observation and selection led us to acknowledge the historically contingent nature of the definition of quality in higher education and the importance of the historical mechanisms through which these definitions are set. The high abstraction of systems theory, however, makes its direct application as an empirical approach problematic. In contrast, Foucault's analysis on power and truth emphasises precisely the mechanisms through which certain practices and definitions became acceptable. These concepts direct our attention to the subtle mechanisms underpinning the rise and consolidation of specific ways of defining and assessing quality in higher education institutions. In this sense, our hybrid approach allows us to get away from evaluative approaches to higher education by focusing on the structural transformations and the historical mechanisms of implementation of quality assurance systems.

Moreover, the combination of the preferred empirical sources of these two theorists – Luhmann's focus on official acts and regulations, and Foucault's emphasis on seemingly technical documents and guidelines – is also useful to develop complex descriptions of higher education systems. While our focus on acts and documents allowed us to depict changes in the definition of quality derived, for example, from de-couplings from religious and political spheres, the analysis of technical documents allowed us to identify subtle, though influential, mechanisms of control such as the ongoing hierarchisation of university missions (i.e. teaching, research, public engagement). The combined analysis of these materials is, we believe, a good strategy to overcome official or technocratic accounts, and allows a theoretically informed understanding of seemingly technical aspects of higher education systems.

Observation and selection according to Niklas Luhmann

The concept of observation is essential to Luhmann's constructivist epistemology. This notion relates to how social systems distinguish between 'something' and 'everything else' (Luhmann 1995). Inspired by Maturana and Varela's developments (1980), Luhmann questioned the need for a shared ontology as the basis for differentiating between correct and incorrect descriptions of reality. Instead, he adopted a more radical social constructivism (Arnold 2010), proposing that the very concept of being is always specific to the observer since the observer is him- or herself the result of an act of observing (i.e. distinguishing between being and not-being).

In this light, reality can only be understood through observations whose value is assessed by the internal functioning of social systems, which use specific differences to define certain aspects of the world as relevant. As such, these differences determine what is considered important, true and/or appropriate in a specific context. As Luhmann (2012: 34) summarised, 'observing draws attention to the fact that "distinguishing and indicating" constitutes a single operation; we can indicate nothing that we do not, in so doing, distinguish; just as distinguishing makes sense only in that it serves to indicate one side or the other (but not both sides)'. Any observation, therefore, is always blind to its own base distinction.

Building upon this concept, Luhmann (2005) suggested differentiating between first- and second-order observations. While first-order observations take their direct relationship with reality for granted, second-order observations are instead oriented towards observing the distinctions through which observational systems construct their reality. As Luhmann (1995) highlighted, even second-order observations have their own blind spots, since they only pay attention to certain distinctions while ignoring the significance of other observations of reality. This acknowledgement led Luhmann to state that all descriptions of reality are necessarily selective. Thus, the plausibility of observations depends on the historical trajectory of the system and the characteristics of its social environment, and not on how the world is structured or a perceived-as-objective reality (Andersen 2003; Luhmann 2013).

The potential of second-order observations as an epistemological tool to explore reality is demonstrated throughout Luhmann's work (e.g. Luhmann 2002, 2010). Although he did not pay direct attention to analysing quality in higher education or to the institutionalisation of quality assurance systems, from our standpoint, his conceptualisation is particularly relevant to these fields. Adopting Luhmann's perspective allows us to abandon the idea that quality assessment represents objective standards of higher education institutions' desirable activities, as is often assumed in higher education studies. Rather, it directs our attention to the historical development and arbitrary selectiveness of quality (see Readings 1996).

The selective nature of such approaches has largely been criticised in specialised literature because of its rejection of the exclusion of content related to, for example, democratic ideals in the evaluation of quality (see Hyslop-Margison and Sears 2007; Olssen 2015). In contrast to these approaches, our analysis does not assess universities' (self-)observing methods according to how they comply with these institutions' expected activities or definitions. On the contrary, using Luhmann's approach, we consider these procedures as first-order observations that regulate the contingency of how they construct the world by ignoring these methods' historical origins. Building on this, the point of departure of our analysis will be to describe the contingency of quality assurance systems and to explore the key elements involved in their emergence, institutionalisation and change. By doing so, we will make use of some of Foucault's ideas on power and truth. We believe that these ideas provide a useful framework for a theoretical approach to explore the subtle mechanisms that underpin changes in the idea(l)s of quality in Chilean higher education in recent decades, without referencing ontological depictions of the world.

Power and truth according to Michel Foucault

Power has a long history as a key concept for understanding social organisations, particularly education systems. Most notably, since the 1970s, particular attention has been paid to the power mechanisms operating in educational systems (e.g.

Bourdieu and Passeron 1970; Althusser 1976; Willis 1977). Most of these approaches conceived of power as the active or potential capacity of individuals or institutions to influence the behaviour of others because of their position in the social structure. While these perspectives have helped unmask the connections between education and social structure, the *a priori* link they establish between structure and power has resulted, in our view, in a lack of attention being paid to the functioning of power itself as a selective mechanism.

In contrast to these approaches, Foucault developed a scheme for observing power that emphasises how it functions. Foucault's idea of power as something independent from individuals or institutions (e.g. Foucault 2005) led him to understand individuals as vehicles of power instead of its points of application (Foucault 1980: 98). This relational trait of power highlights the relevance of practices often depicted as marginal to analysing the kind of order created by familiar and seemingly neutral procedures and techniques. Therefore, based on Foucault's approach, in order to understand how power functions in higher education systems, we need to pay attention to the selectivity induced by the system's specific control mechanisms (i.e. registration, evaluation and qualification). Although these mechanisms are based on norms and restrictions, their most important trait is their productive nature. They induce certain forms of knowledge, behaviour and discourse (Foucault 1980: 119). In other words, power determines certain discursive conditions of possibility (Foucault 1977: 194).

By highlighting this performative trait of power as selectivity, Foucault considered power as 'action upon actions' and as the 'conduct of conduct' (Foucault 2007). In other words, he was referring to 'governmentality' mechanisms: the 'ensemble formed by institutions, procedures, analyses and reflections, calculation and tactics that allow the exercise of this very specific, albeit complex, form of power, which has as its target the population' (Foucault 2007: 144). The inherent connection between power and knowledge is important to this conceptualisation. While the exercising of power creates knowledge by creating new objects of knowledge and accumulating new bodies of information, knowledge engenders power by controlling the truth (Foucault 1980: 51).

Throughout his work, Foucault analysed how specific discursive formations authorised subjects to speak and then exercise power (e.g. Foucault 1972). By doing so, he highlights the relevance of the underlying distinctions that give meaning to statements, rather than their content or theoretical interpretation. The interplay of power and knowledge is constructed by fixing the gaze (i.e. surveillance) using observation, interpretation and classification. In this sense, transparency operates as a mechanism of power/knowledge, since 'power is exercised by virtue of things being known and people being seen' (Foucault 1980: 154).

According to this conceptualisation of power/knowledge, we can conceive the idea of quality in higher education systems in the same way as Foucault (2006) conceived madness – not as an object whose 'history' or 'truth' needs to be discovered but as the product of selective discourse. This non-ontological view of quality assurance mechanisms has much in common with Luhmann's approach, but highlights other aspects of the phenomenon. Following Foucault, we argue that observing measurement, interpretation and assessment procedures would shed light on the power/knowledge mechanisms that aim to be the 'knowledge of things, of the objectives that can and should be attained and the disposition one must employ in order to attain them' (Foucault 2007: 137).

Governmentality, then, is intimately tied in with truth or, more precisely, the fixation of truth. By analysing how truth depends on the conceptual system that is in operation, Foucault (1994) moved the question from the epistemological value of truth to the social and institutional historical conditions under which authorised statements can become true. In other words, power presupposes a system of ordered procedures for the production, regulation, distribution and circulation of statements. Scientific knowledge has gained a privileged position in the construction of truth in modern societies. In this context, relevant concepts to higher education – such as quality – become increasingly defined on the basis of disciplinary procedures and techniques, hiding their production mechanisms and inherent selectivity in the process (e.g. Foucault 1980: 94).

These truth construction processes are organised in relation to how power is exercised. In other words, each society has its own 'regime of truth': a system of discourses accepted as true; mechanisms and examples for distinguishing between true and false; techniques and procedures for acquiring truth and applying sanctions for non-adherence. New ways to define truth have gained ground in most societies. Instruments such as statistics have made these processes more technical, allowing governmentality by transforming the social world into data and then into something susceptible to government techniques (Foucault 2007). The expansion of performance-based mechanisms as criteria for evaluation both of and in higher education systems reflects this transformation. Examination has introduced individuals, actions and institutions into the field of documentation (Foucault 1977: 189). In this light, the emergence of performance-based evaluation mechanisms can be viewed as the technification of quality on the basis of calculating procedures that rest upon a contingent truth.

In summary, our brief outline offers a non-ontological approach to understanding the evolution of quality in higher education systems by bringing the contingent meaning of quality – as a result of immanent selectivity processes based on the exercise of power/knowledge – to the fore. This perspective raises relevant questions about the social conditions and systemic operation of quality assurance mechanisms, such as which social transformations have facilitated their emergence or which processes secure (or subvert) the system's current selectivity. In the following section, we address these questions by analysing quality assurance mechanisms in higher education in Chile.

State, prestige and technification – the formalisation of quality assurance mechanisms in Chile

Higher education has a relatively long history in Chile. The country's first higher education institutions were set up by Jesuit, Dominican and Franciscan orders during the seventeenth and eighteenth centuries. The doctrinaire principles adopted by these institutions as the basis for defining quality (Ponce et al. 2013) also had an influence on the first university, the Royal University of San Felipe, founded in 1747. Ideals such as obedience to the church, faithfulness to Christian dogmas and unbridled respect for ecclesiastical authorities heavily influenced the curriculum, teaching methods and graduation processes in these early institutions (Jobet 1970).

The link between religion and quality only began to lose its self-evidence after independence from Spain at the beginning of the nineteenth century. Intellectuals in this period strongly criticised the University of San Felipe because of its royal origins and religious orientation (Ruiz 2010). To replace it, a new institution – the University of Chile – was created in 1842 by merging the existing educational establishments, such as the Spanish University, the Convictorio Carolino and the Academy of San Luis. As its first rector – Venezuelan lawyer Andrés Bello – said, this institution's mission, inspired by modern ideas, was to enhance national progress by educating the elites.

Therefore, quality was conceived as being directly related to the national university's role as overseer. Thus, students at the non-state universities created during the following decades – the Pontifical Catholic University of Chile (1888), the University of Concepción (1919), the Federico Santa María Technical University (1926), the Catholic University of Valparaíso (1928), the Austral University of Chile (1954) and the University of the North (1956) – had to prove their proficiency to an ad-hoc commission of scholars from the University of Chile. Similarly, private institutions' study programme content had to be approved by the University of Chile.

The organisation of a higher education quality assurance system based on the University of Chile's role as overseer was recognised in law. Although Executive Order 7,500 (MINEDUC 1927) recognised the administrative autonomy of private and state universities in terms of their ability to define 'everything inherent to their organisation, location and operation' (Article 26), this regulation also established that education at private institutions was 'a cooperative activity for fulfilling the educational function, which is of the state's direction and responsibility and which, for this reason, is the only body qualified to grant degrees and higher education diplomas' (Article 12).

Similarly, Decree-Law 4,807 (MINEDUC 1929) explicitly indicated that the University of Chile was responsible for safeguarding the quality of Chilean higher education. This decree established that a University Council, which also included government and primary and secondary institution representatives, was responsible for deciding university admission criteria, the number of graduates (Article 14) and assessing the adequacy of private universities' curriculums (Article 78).

The University of Chile's role as responsible for overseeing and assessing the quality of higher education institutions became less feasible from the mid-1950s onwards. First, the number of university graduates increased significantly from 1.5 per cent of the relevant age group to 3.0 per cent in 1960, 7.0 per cent in 1970 and 8.1 per cent in 1980, exceeding the University of Chile's capacity to oversee them all (Braun et al. 2000). Second, the University of Chile lost its monopoly on the production and transmission of knowledge, since other universities had begun to perform similar activities (Levy 1986). Finally, the modernisation of the job market put professional training at the core of the university mission, regardless of whether it was a private or public institution (Gárate 2012).

In the second half of the century, the University of Chile's control of quality assurance mechanisms came to an end. From then on, quality began to be conceived as an attribute inherent to (all) Chilean university activities. Although this change was not reflected in new legislation encompassing all higher education systems, several small regulations helped this occur. These regulations relocated quality assessment within each university by providing them with the autonomy to grant professional degrees without state interference (see Campos 1960; Mellafe et al. 1992).

This situation remained largely unchanged until the neoliberal-inspired policies imposed in the 1980s during the military dictatorship (1973–1989). Along with enabling the creation of new private universities and organising a funding mechanism based mostly on students fees, Executive Order 1 (MINEDUC 1981) also created new quality assurance mechanisms based on the prestige and knowledge of 'traditional universities' (those founded before 1981). New universities had to obtain approval from the Ministry of Education and submit their study programmes for evaluation by scholars from traditional universities (Article 24).

The proliferation of new private universities in the late 1980s onwards, however, revealed that this was not enough to ensure quality. Increasing demands to certify new institutions (twenty-five between 1988 and 1990) exceeded the capacity of traditional universities to oversee them (Bernasconi and Rojas 2004). Then, at the end of the dictatorship, a further legislative act (MINEDUC 1990) was intended to both improve the evaluation system's capacity and secure the continuity of reforms. This regulation established a new licensing body called the Higher Education Council (CSE), which was responsible for evaluating new universities and assessing their development for a period of between six and eleven years.

The new evaluation system comprised three stages. First, the institutional project was analysed by the CSE, taking into consideration educational, didactic and technical-pedagogical aspects, as well as material and economic resources. Second, the Council reported annually on the institution's progress. These reports included the project's progress and a course evaluation by expert peers. Finally, the Council decided whether or not to grant autonomy to the university, based on this analysis.

The CSE continued to operate almost unchanged during most of the 1990s. However, its limitations became obvious with the rapid expansion of the higher education sector. New private university campuses sprang up all over the country. While in 1990 there were 60 universities and 70 campuses, in 1997 this number grew to 68 universities and 103 campuses (Zapata et al. 2003). However, it was not always clear how this expansion addressed the purposes the institutions had set out for themselves in the institutional project approved by the CSE. To tackle this problem, the National Commission for Undergraduate Teaching Accreditation (CNAP) was set up in 1999. This new body was responsible for drawing up a new accreditation system for higher education institutions that were already autonomous. Although their evaluations were not a condition for access to state funding, this initiative was the basis for creating a new quality assurance system based on independent bodies (Salazar 2013).

A few years later, Act 20,192 (2006) fully implemented a new quality assurance system for higher education in Chile. This piece of legislation emerged alongside a new student loan policy that aimed to provide mass access to higher education (MINEDUC 2005). These two instruments ended up becoming interconnected, since loans were only available to students enrolled in accredited universities. This move inaugurated a new form of higher education governmentality, in which the criteria for assigning resources moved gradually from structural elements such as universities' history or ownership to operational criteria (Sisto 2017). In other words, the state gradually came to replace the basis for university funding as an unspecified social contribution of the 'public good' with the efficiency of organisations, measured by their accreditation.

Since 2006, quality assurance for Chilean universities depended on a mechanism that combines the accreditation of undergraduate and master programmes by private agencies and the certification of institutions and PhDs by an independent body (the National Accreditation Agency), with different stakeholders involved (i.e. government, public and private universities, and scientific and professional organisations). In both processes, accreditation involves three consecutive steps (self-evaluation, peer-evaluation and assessment). This leads to the institution or degree's accreditation, graded on a scale of 0 to 7 years of validity (0 to 10 years for graduate programmes), according to how it adapts to the evaluation criteria. This grading method represents a major shift from previous ways of conceiving quality, by associating it with an assessment based on known parameters that have to be controlled regularly.

As far as institutional accreditation is concerned, the system established five areas of accreditation – institutional management, undergraduate teaching, research, public engagement and graduate teaching – only the first two of which are compulsory for accreditation purposes. In each of these areas, the regulations set out criteria based on both the 'fitness *to* purpose' and the 'fitness *of* purpose'. However, the lack of standard measures in most of these dimensions ended up mostly circumscribing fitness *of* purpose to the area of research. The system was consolidated during the following years, expanding its coverage and providing a ranking of universities that would soon become a marketing tool (Barroilhet 2019). This system, however, was strongly challenged at the beginning of the 2010s. A combination of social awareness about higher education – triggered by student demonstrations – and public exposure of corruption inside the National Accreditation Agency (CNA) publicly proved the system's inability to ensure quality. Since then, a series of reform proposals have been adopted through different regulations (e.g. MINEDUC 2016, 2018). Some of the most important reforms include excluding university representatives from the CNA, regulating its periodical evaluation by international bodies, including public engagement as a mandatory university function, and integrating undergraduate programme and institutional accreditation (except for highly sensitive areas, such as medicine and education).

Accreditation regulations and guidelines made it clear that the system's main goal was to ensure governmentality (observing, measuring and acting according to these measures) at different institutional levels. Then, while guiding the organisation of records that allow for comparisons to be made between past and present, the accreditation process attempted to transform institutional and individual practices. Setting up new technical offices and instruments reflected these institutional transformations (Rojas and Lopez 2016; Huerta-Riveros and Gaete-Feres 2018); institutions also promoted a series of actions to transform individual practices (Venables and Van Gaesten 2014). According to official regulations, this new rationality had to permeate all institutional levels and be aligned with its different spheres (e.g. scholarly hierarchisation and unit organisation). In other words, institutions maintained their traditions in terms of being able to define their impact and relevant areas of development, while standardising their practices. This apparent institutional autonomy, however, became increasingly dependent on the application of quality assurance mechanisms, as reflected, for example, by the transformation and hierarchisation of accreditation dimensions.

The transition of public engagement from an elective to a mandatory dimension of accreditation did not only involve the legal concept of university becoming more complex but also the formalisation of existing practices. Although the ranking of universities using accreditation mechanisms involves two elements (years of accreditation and the number of dimensions accredited), these elements are highly correlated[2] and institutions have started to include elective areas of accreditation sequentially, from public engagement to research and to graduate teaching. This could partially be explained by the use of standardised measures of productivity to accredit research and graduate teaching. This positioned public engagement as being in transit, with universities having the freedom to establish the meaning of 'public' (e.g. community, employers, government) and the sole requirement is to demonstrate actions. In this light, it comes as no surprise that many universities have created public engagement departments, replacing the old extension services offices (Dougnac 2016), which has resulted in a variety of practices (González et al. 2017). These practices construct the very notion of public engagement as a result of how they operate, paving the way to becoming an essential part of universities (and something considered mandatory for accreditation systems).

Along with this recursive definition of public engagement, the accreditation system structure has also been reinforced by the hierarchisation of teaching and research within universities. The use of standard productivity indicators to evaluate research has tended to homogenise the criteria for research evaluation and push for certain research process outputs (see Pineda 2015; Koch and Vanderstraeten 2019). Three parallel processes reinforced this performative effect of the instruments: (1) the growth of the use of university rankings, which qualify them in terms of their engagement with – and disciplinary coverage of – research and graduate training (e.g. Reyes 2016); (2) the ever-closer relationship between accreditation and funding, with years of accreditation even being extended as a measure of the value of the academic certifications awarded by the institution (e.g. CONICYT 2019: 9); and (3) the use of accreditation results as marketing tools to attract students.

The combination of these elements has helped redefine quality in Chilean higher education systems. In a higher education system highly dependent on students fees (state-subsidised or not), marketing became a primary strategy to attract students and obtain funding. These strategies are often based on 'demonstrating' the quality of the university and/or the programme. Rankings and accreditation results are key elements to this endeavour, with output-based measures increasingly gaining in importance. Quality is no longer considered as adapting to either religious doctrines or state-monitored or 'traditional university' traditions. Under the new regime of governmentality, what can be measured is technified, while other aspects tend to be forgotten or absorbed into efficiency indicators.

Critical reflections on social theory and methodology

This brief journey through the evolution of quality assurance mechanisms in Chilean higher education illustrates the evolution of both the idea of quality and the mechanisms used to assess and ensure it. Drawing on our theoretical framework, we can safely say that in regard to each of these definitions and practices, what is always at stake is the production of truth. In this process, the highly selective mechanisms that underpin the definition of quality become invisible and quality appears as a self-evident and shared concept. The evolution of quality from (religious or traditional) adequacy to the fulfilment of organisations' purposes illustrates Chilean society's transformation towards a decentralised or multi-central structure. Replacing tradition by performance as the criterion for assessing quality reflects the importance science has gained in modern societies and its role in the production of truth. In other words, our historical analysis showed the growing influence of governmentality and modern efficiency as control mechanisms in the way higher education is expected to work.

Our theoretically informed account helped us to identify patterns of change and draw meaningful conclusions. The combination of two different and seemly contradictory theories allowed us to consider different levels of methodological design and data interpretation. Whilst socio-historical analysis was important to both Luhmann and Foucault, they led us towards two different sources of information: official acts and regulations, and technical documents and guidelines that operationalised the path taken by regulations.

This duality also guided our analysis by directing our attention to the inherent selectivity in both the definition of quality and the material practices through which power operates. More importantly, it enabled us to avoid making *a priori* links between different areas of society (e.g. the economy, education or science). Indeed, Luhmann's non-ontological conceptualisation of these spheres brought their differentiation mechanisms and the evolution of their relationships to the fore, while also unmasking the decentred and productive nature of power identified by Foucault and expressed through registration, evaluation and classification processes.

Nonetheless, despite the fruitfulness of our approach, there are restrictions (partly) imposed by our theoretical and methodological strategies. These restrictions are derived from two sources: the inherent limitations of the methodological design as a case study and epistemological restrictions due to the second-order character of (social) sciences observation. As far as the first limitation is concerned, although it is wise to exercise caution in the face of generalisation, it is also reasonable to expect comparable developments in similar national contexts. The relatively long period of time covered allowed us to depict the general transformations likely to occur in quality assurance mechanisms in higher education in other Latin American countries, for example (see Brunner and Miranda 2016). Moreover, the broad reach of the transformations highlighted by both Luhmann and Foucault, also makes it reasonable to hypothesise that it is also likely that similar transformations have occurred in other spheres of society, such as politics, the economy or religion. Regarding the second limitation, it could be said that observing (social) reality is always observer-dependent since it relies on the selectivity of the observer. Thus, as a second-order observation, the emergence of blind spots in our observations – referring to the way we observe distinctions – is unavoidable. In other words, both our position as sociologists and the theoretical approach we adopted not only allowed us to observe certain elements but also made others invisible.

Stating an intimate relationship between theory and methods is nowadays commonplace in many methodology handbooks. However, questions such as the nature of this relationship, what ranks as a theory or method, or simply how to connect theory and methods seem to have received far less attention. Rather than proposing general answers to these questions, in this chapter we opted to present an example of this relationship. Far from proposing a universal framework, we intended to show the possibilities that hybrid frameworks can provide to both methodological design and data interpretation. Nonetheless, we would like to make two more broad observations on the relationship between theory and methods. First, intimate knowledge of local circumstances is needed to avoid theory being applied mechanically. It is also important to self-reflect on our theoretical background to avoid uncontrolled preconceptions and prejudices. From our standpoint, non-ontological theories such as those presented here might be a good tool for this, since they emphasise the contingent and power-laden nature of (social) reality. Second, as shown in the case study, the production of truth always depends on the social context. Therefore, assessing theories, methods and data is context-dependent. Far from discouraging us, this highlights the relevance of theoretically and empirically grounded reflections to understanding – and enhancing – higher education systems, while providing us with an antidote to the reification and deification of theories and methods.

Notes

1   On the one hand, we consulted different sources such as the websites of the Chilean government (http://www.gob.cl), Congress (http://www.congreso.cl), Senate (http://www.senado.cl) and the National Library, searching for laws, decrees and speeches (75 documents). On the other hand, we consulted the National Library, accreditation agency webpages and independent entities such as CNED (http://www.cned.cl), looking for guidelines, forms, reports and evaluations (42 documents). The selected documents display considerable variation in length, ranging from a few to more than 40 pages.

2   The correlation between the number of dimensions of accreditation and number of years of accreditation is quite high: 0.914 in 2010 (Cancino and Schmal 2014) and 0.76 in 2019 (based on data retrieved from CNA: www.cnachile.cl).

References

Althusser, L. (1976), 'Idéologie et appareils idéologiques d'État', in L. Althusser (ed.), *Positions (1964–1975)*, 67–125, Paris: Les Editions Sociales.

Andersen, N. (2003), *Discursive Analytical Strategies. Understanding Foucault, Koselleck, Laclau, Luhmann*, Bristol: Policy Press.

Arnold, M. (2010), 'Constructivismo Sociopoiético', *Revista Mad*, 23: 1–8.

Ball, S. (2010), 'Intellectuals or Technicians? The Urgent Role of Theory in Educational Studies', *British Journal of Educational Studies*, 43 (3): 255–271.

Barroilhet, A. (2019), 'Problemas estructurales de la acreditación de la educación superior en Chile: 2006–2012', *Revista Pedagogía Universitaria y Didáctica del Derecho*, 6 (1): 43–76.

Bernasconi, A. and Rojas, F. (2004), *Informe sobre la educación superior en Chile: 1980–2003*, Santiago de Chile: Editorial Universitaria.

Borch, C. (2005), 'Systemic Power: Luhmann, Foucault, and Analytics of Power', *Acta Sociologica*, 48 (2): 155–167.

Bourdieu, P. and Passeron, J.C. (1970), *La Reproduction. Éléments d'une théorie du système d'enseignement*, Paris: Les Editions du Minuit.

Braun, J., Braun, M., Briones, I., Díaz, J., Lüders, R. and Wagner, G. (2000), *Economía chilena 1819–1995: Estadísticas históricas: Documento de trabajo N° 187*, Santiago de Chile: PUC Ediciones.

Brunner, J.J. and Miranda, D.A. (eds.) (2016), *Educación superior en Iberoamérica: Informe 2016*, Santiago de Chile: CID.

Campos, F. (1960), *Desarrollo educacional 1810–1960*, Santiago de Chile: Universidad Andrés Bello.

Cancino, V. and Schmal, R. (2014), 'Sistema de Acreditación Universitaria en Chile: ¿Cuánto hemos avanzado?', *Estudios Pedagógicos*, 40 (1): 41–60.

CONICYT (2019), *Bases concurso becas de doctorado en el extranjero, Becas Chile convocatoria 2019*, Santiago de Chile: CONICYT. Available online: https://www.conicyt.cl/becasconicyt/files/2019/02/BASES-DOCTORADO-BECAS-CHILE-14-02-2019.pdf (accessed 4 November 2019).

Dougnac, P. (2016), 'Una revisión del concepto anglosajón public engagement y su equivalencia funcional a los de extensión y vinculación con el medio', *Pensamiento Educativo*, 53 (2): 1–19.

Espeland, W. and Sauder, M. (2007), 'Rankings and Reactivity: How Public Measures Recreate Social Worlds', *American Journal of Sociology*, 113 (1): 1–40.

Foucault, M. (1972), *The Archaeology of Knowledge*, New York: Pantheon Books.

Foucault, M. (1977), *Discipline and Punish*, New York: Pantheon Books.

Foucault, M. (1980), *Power/Knowledge: Selected Interviews and Other Writings by Michel Foucault, 1972–1977*, Brighton: Harvester.

Foucault, M. (1994), *The Order of Things*, New York: Vintage Books.

Foucault, M. (2005), *Histoire de la sexualité 1: La volonté de savoir*, Paris: Gallimard.

Foucault, M. (2006), *History of Madness*, London: Routledge.

Foucault, M. (2007), *Security, Territory, Population: Lectures at the Collège de France, 1977–1978*, Basingstoke: Palgrave Macmillan.

Frank, D. and Meyer, J. (2007), 'University Expansion and the Knowledge Society', *Theory and Society*, 36: 287–311.

Gárate, M. (2012), *La revolución capitalista de Chile (1973–2003)*, Santiago de Chile: Alberto Hurtado.

González, B., Saravia, P., Carroza, N., Gascon, F., Dinamarca, C. and Castro, L. (2017), *Vinculación con el medio y territorio. Heterogeneidad de modelos, prácticas y sentidos en las universidades chilenas*, Valparaíso: Universidad de Playa Ancha.

Guest, G., Namey, E.E. and Mitchell, M. (2013), *Collecting Qualitative Data: A Field Manual for Applied Research*, Thousand Oaks, CA: Sage.

Huerta-Riveros, P. and Gaete-Feres, H. (2018), 'Análisis de la dependencia de la acreditación institucional: Un estudio comparativo de universidades en Chile', *Actualidades Investigativas en Educación*, 18 (1): 1–30.

Hyslop-Margison, E.J. and Sears, A.M. (2007), *Neo-Liberalism, Globalization and Human Capital Learning: Reclaiming Education for Democratic Citizenship*, Dordrecht: Springer.

Jobet, J.C. (1970), *Doctrina y praxis de los educadores representativos chilenos*, Santiago de Chile: Universidad Andrés Bello.

Koch, T. and Vanderstraeten, R. (2019), 'Internationalizing a National Scientific Community? Changes in Publication and Citation Practices in Chile 1976–2015', *Current Sociology*, 67 (5): 723–741.

Levy, D.C. (1986), *Higher Education and the State in Latin America: Private Challenges to Public Dominance*, Chicago, IL: University of Chicago Press.

Luhmann, N. (1995), 'The Paradoxy of Observing Systems', *Cultural Critique*, 31: 37–55.

Luhmann, N. (2002), *Theories of Distinction: Redescribing the Descriptions of Modernity*, Stanford, CA: Stanford University Press.

Luhmann, N. (2005), *El arte de la sociedad*, México D.F.: Herder.

Luhmann, N. (2010), *Organización y decisión*, México D.F.: Herder.

Luhmann, N. (2012), *Theory of Society*, vol. 1, Stanford, CA: Stanford University Press.

Luhmann, N. (2013), *Theory of Society*, vol. 2, Stanford, CA: Stanford University Press.

Maturana, H. and Varela, F. (1980), *Autopoiesis and Cognition: The Realization of the Living*, London: Reidel.

Mellafe, R., Rebolledo, A. and Cárdenas, M. (1992), *Historia de la Universidad de Chile*, Santiago de Chile: Universidad de Chile.

MINEDUC (Ministerio de Educación) (1927), *Reforma educacional*, Santiago de Chile: MINEDUC.

MINEDUC (Ministerio de Educación) (1929), *Estatuto orgánico de la enseñanza universitaria*, 18 November 1929. Available online: https://www.leychile.cl/Navegar?idNorma=1028775 (accessed 4 November 2019).

MINEDUC (Ministerio de Educación) (1981), *Decreto con Fuerza de Ley N° 1. Fija normas sobre universidades*, 20 January 1981. Available online: https://www.leychile.cl/Navegar/index_html?idNorma=3621 (accessed 4 November 2019).

MINEDUC (Ministerio de Educación) (1990), *Ley Orgánica Constitucional de Enseñanza 18.962*, 10 March 1990. Available online: https://www.uchile.cl/portal/presentacion/normativa-y-reglamentos/8386/ley-organica-constitucional-de-ensenanza (accessed 4 November 2019).

MINEDUC. 2005. *Act 20027*. https://www.leychile.cl/Navegar?idNorma=239034 Accessed 15 April 2020.

MINEDUC (Ministerio de Educación) (2016), *Criterios acreditación de postgrado*, Santiago de Chile: MINEDUC.

MINEDUC (Ministerio de Educación) (2018), *Higher Education Act 21091 Ley Chile*, 29 May 2018. Available online: https://www.leychile.cl/Navegar?idNorma=1118991 (accessed 4 November 2019).

Olssen, M. (2015), 'Neoliberal Competition in Higher Education Today: Research, Accountability and Impact', *British Journal of Sociology of Education*, 37 (1): 129–148.

Pineda, P. (2015), *The Entrepreneurial Research University in Latin America: Global and Local Models in Chile and Colombia, 1950–2015*, New York: Palgrave Macmillan.

Ponce, M., Rengifo, F. and Serrano, S. (2013), *Historia de la Educación en Chile (1810–2010)*, Tomo II, Santiago de Chile: Taurus.

Pottage, A. (1998), 'Power as an Art of Contingency: Luhmann, Deleuze, Foucault', *Economy and Society*, 27 (1): 1–27.

Readings, B. (1996), *The University in Ruins*, Cambridge, MA: Harvard University Press.

Reyes, C. (2016), 'Medición de la calidad universitaria en Chile: La influencia de los rankings', *Calidad de la Educación*, 44: 158–196.

Rojas, J. and Lopez, D. (2016), 'La acreditación de la gestión institucional en universidades chilenas', *Revista Electrónica de Investigación Educativa*, 18 (2): 180–190.

Ruiz, C. (2010), *De la república al mercado. Ideas educacionales y política en Chile*, Santiago de Chile: LOM.

Salazar, J.M. (2013), 'Public policy for higher education in Chile: A case study in quality assurance (1990–2009)', PhD dissertation, Centre for the Study of Higher Education, Melbourne University, Victoria.

Sisto, V. (2017), 'Gobernados por números: El financiamiento como forma de gobierno de la Universidad en Chile', *Psicoperspectivas*, 16 (3): 64–75.

Tight, M. (2012), *Researching Higher Education*, Maidenhead: Open University Press.

Tight, M. (2017), 'Higher Education Journals: Their Characteristics and Contribution', *Higher Education Research & Development*, 37 (3): 607–619.

UNESCO (2009), *Trends in Global Higher Education: Tracking an Academic Revolution*, Paris: UNESCO.

Venables, J.P. and Van Gaesten, J. (2014), 'Radiografía de los modelos de acreditación: Organización, procesos y prácticas. El caso de las universidades Austral de Chile, de la Frontera y de los Lagos', *Calidad de la Educación*, 41: 51–81.

Willis, P. (1977), *Learning to Labour. How Working Class Kids Get Working Class Jobs*, London: Saxon House.

Zamorano-Farías, R. and Rogel-Salazar, R. (2013), 'El dispositivo de poder como medio de comunicación: Foucault – Luhmann', *Política y Sociedad*, 50 (3): 959–980.

Zapata, G., Rojas, F.L. and Fleet, N. (2003), *Evolución de las sedes de instituciones de educación superior en Chile*, Santiago de Chile: CNAP.

Part Two

Social Theory and the Politics of Academic Work

6

The Politics of Academic Work: Professional Identities and Intellectual Selves in Neoliberal Times

Cristina Costa

Introduction

This chapter is focused on the politics of academic work and different dimensions that impact, shape and inform academics' professional and intellectual selves. The chapter will start by providing an overview of the effects of neoliberal policies on the scholarly practices and identity (trans)formation of academics. More concretely, we will look at how the role of the academic has been weakened in favour of marketisation goals and how, in turn, the figure of the *Homo Academicus* (Bourdieu 1988) is increasingly being replaced with that of the *Homo Economicus*. This will lead us to examine how time and space are construed within the contemporary academy and the impact such notions have on academics' position and status with reference to emerging tensions between moral values and economic interests, a dilemma with a direct impact on academics' practices and sense of purpose. Next, we explore the emergent phenomenon of academic casualisation as well as the changing and immersive nature of intellectual work to accommodate neoliberal goals. In so doing, we will present evidence of movements that aim to resist the imperatives of the neoliberal academy, such as that of 'Slow Scholarship' and the 'Res-Sisters', movements that seek to reclaim an academic identity that mirrors the principles of knowledge work (Elias 1972). These movements have, to a great extent, stemmed from a need to fight off the hegemonic hand of academia and respect the nature of what academics produce (i.e. ideas). Such an approach shows the aspiration of academics in recovering their professional power as intellectuals. Lastly, such debates inspire a reflection on knowledge as a central activity of academic life. As 'carriers' and 'producers' of knowledge (Elias 1972) into, within and out of academia, academics are also faced with epistemological concerns regarding the production of knowledge (Murphy 2018), a monopoly that needs to be constantly interrogated to give way to a wide range of perspectives and approaches.

The effects of neoliberal policies on the scholarly practices and identity (trans)formation of academics

The growing body of literature focused on the (trans)formation of professional identities in contemporary academia is expressive of the pathologies of neoliberalism that currently affect knowledge work practices and academics. The critique has been targeted at the nefarious influence of neoliberalism measures on 'the nature, organisation and purpose of higher education' (Archer 2008: 265) that have a direct impact on the traditional sense of academic identity. Yet, the ramifications of the neoliberal hand do not stop here. Neoliberal policies have been weaved into academic life in such ways that they have had considerable implications for traditional forms of knowledge work and academics' sense of identity. This is particularly true to staff new to academia who are being presented with very limited options regarding the unwarranted present and future of higher education (Breeze et al. 2019; Courtois and O'Keefe 2015; McKenzie 2017), thus creating barriers to their full integration and sense of belonging within the academy.

What is more, the neoliberalisation of higher education has slowly but effectively triggered the restructuring of academia to serve symbolic imperatives, such as those of competitive advantage, prestige and (accumulated) reputation. This has been an ingenious ruse to pursue economic priorities that hide behind concerns of international representation, global reach and quality of academic work in the face of a changing society. However, it is not solely because of societal implications but especially because of economic ones that such changes have taken place. As such, the consequences of pursuing such goals have taken little notice of the implications on the ground, especially regarding academic staff who have seen the practice of intellectual inquiry being replaced with performative metrics (Olssen and Peters 2005) that do not reflect the essence of academic work as the independent pursuit for ideas and new knowledge. This inevitably has had a long-lasting impact on the lives of academics and their sense of worth as knowledge workers.

In line with other sectors of society, neoliberal policies have gained terrain in higher education and progressed to monetise the university. This process of *economification* of the university has become a dominant practice in academia in that higher education has become universally recognisable but economically undistinctive from other key economically driven industries. This process has been done with little regard for the core specificities on which knowledge work practices operate, such as freedom of inquiry as well as control over time and intellectual property rights (Marginson 2000). It can thus be said that academics' roles have progressed from the status of *Homo Academicus* to that of *Homo Economicus* given that the enterprise of knowledge production has become deeply implicated in the economic growth of the so-called knowledge societies (Kim 2017). Yet, perhaps, a more accurate account of the changes in higher education and its impact on the status of academic staff would be one of regression, not progression.

The traditional academic figure is not only going through a radical transformation to suit the restructure of higher education as a marketplace, but academics themselves are also seeing their sphere of influence shrink through the loss of intellectual clout (Enders and Kaulisch 2005). This can come across as ironic given that, as the role of the university becomes more preoccupied with serving the knowledge society, the figure of the academic seems to achieve less recognition. Underlining this reality is the expectation that academics, as intellectual workers, subject themselves to the economic structures that empower the university, but which in turn disempower their activity and with it their sense of self. Mechanisms of disempowerment within academia take on different methods that end up suppressing academic practice, of which time management, for example, through workload allocations and the setting of academic pace, has become an essential form of rationalising academic labour.

It is in this vein that academics feel the need to exercise reflexivity with regards to their own academic situation. Reflexivity is a critical methodological tool of analysis of one's position, as exemplified in Bourdieu's (1988) *Homo Academicus* monograph (see also Bourdieu 2003). It permits academics to distance themselves intellectually from the fields of power that currently command their professional lives (i.e. academia) and identify and fight off neoliberal imperatives that distort the core purpose of the university and their own professional identities. Questioning the ncoliberal doxa – now well ensconced in academia through the universalisation of academic conditions that compress time, repress intellectual work and affect working lives – serves to push back the barriers that institutionally, and increasingly publicly, devalue academic work and academics' sense of self. An implicit consequence of the neoliberal ideology in academia, it could be said, is that of depoliticising knowledge work and consequently degrading the role of knowledge workers to a money-making profession. The goal of academics in asserting their professional selves, on the other hand, is that of pushing back this process of universalisation of the higher education system as just another economic enterprise that academics are expected to embody as part of their professional lives. The result can be one of misrecognition (Bourdieu and Wacquant 1999) of the original purpose of the university with troubling consequences for the sense of identity of agents acting within that space, as their core values as knowledge and not money producers are being questioned.

This aspect can be further problematised when considering how and where the commodification of knowledge has impacted on the status of certain disciplines and their authors, especially those located in the social sciences and humanities. At first sight, such an approach may be considered a functionalist take on higher education that is usually enveloped in a rhetoric of employability and skill needs. Yet, a closer look at the socio-political contexts in which such stances are taken can also undercover a political project that compromises critical inquiry and discourse and harms academic freedom. In the last few years alone, the denigration of scholarship practices that are likely to – and often do – critique neoliberal rationalities and oppressive regimes has increased substantially. Well into the second decade of the twenty-first century, we have witnessed the banning of 'gender studies' in Hungarian universities by Orban's government (Petö 2018), the defunding of the social sciences and humanities in Brazil during Bolsonaro's leadership (Knobel and Leal 2019) and the silencing of academic voices in Turkey by Erdoğan's administration (Abbas and Zalta 2017; Özkirimli 2017). Such measures are direct attacks on the autonomy of higher education institutions and their agents. It is equally a strategic way of depoliticising the nations where these initiatives are taken.

Invitations to reflexivity are clearly present in this section of the collection, even if in implicit ways. Reflexivity as a tool needs to be methodologically aided by relevant theoretical traditions. For example, in Chapter 7 of this collection, Cannizzo debates academic temporal rhythms through Barbara Adam's sociology of time. Her work provide us with tools to explore how time is construed in academia and how it affects one's identities in contexts marked by a neoliberal agenda. In a similar fashion, Thomas's use of Massey's work invites us to explore gendered experiences of university through intersecting concepts of power and space as tools helpful for analysing one's sense of belonging (see Chapter 9).

Another aspect that is corroding academia from inside and which has a deep effect on the (trans)formation of one's academic identity and sense of belonging is the rise in precarious employment contracts that have become more and more prevalent in higher education and which ultimately affects academics in different ways, amongst which are issues pertaining to working conditions that tend to lead to physical, intellectual and emotional exhaustion and anxiety. Concerns over the well-being of academic staff have never been more prominent than in current times (Morrish 2019).

Academic casualisation and the changing nature of intellectual work

The casualisation of academic labour is an expanding problem in higher education worldwide. The first examples of casual contracts are from the 1990s as a form of flexible work offer, but have quickly become a growing trend in recruitment strategies for universities. The number of casual staff working at universities has reached unprecedented numbers. In 2018, the number of people employed at Australian universities on a casual contract was estimated to be just short of 100,000 (Norton et al. 2018), whereas in UK universities 69,000 staff are employed on atypical academic contracts, 23 per cent of which are employed on a zero-hours contract (see HESA 2019).

This has real consequences for the positioning of academic staff within the academic community, as casual work helps create a divide among academics that is underpinned by precarious pay and working conditions – these tend to undermine the possibilities of mobility within the higher education hierarchy. This divide also ensures that staff who take on casual work often 'find themselves voiceless in the workplace' (Brown et al. 2010: 169). This is usually so given the lack of representation. Jones et al. explore this aspect in Chapter 11 by drawing on Dorothy Smith's feminist sociology and Foucault's technologies of power to develop a perspective of 'othering' that is less akin to inclusive practices.

Nonetheless, movements against casualisation and the deterioration of working conditions have started to emerge. The most recent, official, example of this struggle was made apparent in the UK through the UCU general strike of December 2019, which amongst other issues, aimed to contest unreasonable workloads to which academic staff are subjected, low wages, unwarranted pension schemes and the casualisation of academic labour. This indicates that academic staff are being disregarded by their employers, but this cannot merely be conceptualised as a form of misrecognition à la Bourdieu where fields of power superimpose their rules on its agents; it is equally, in Honneth's terms, a form of disrespect towards academic staff, with serious implications to their self-esteem and self-respect as scholars (Honneth [1996] 2004).

Recognition – personal as well as general – is a key ingredient in the construction of one's identity. It is in this vein that Honneth ([1996] 2004) provides us with two concepts from which to work:

1. 'recognition' (personal, legal and communal) that acts as a form of identity confirmation, and
2. 'reification' that works as a social pathology that is forgetful of 'recognition' and where the 'relation between people has taken on the character of a thing' (Honneth 2012: 96), as if depriving the individual of their own humanity.

Lukács ([1923] 2011), from whom Honneth takes inspiration for this concept, asserts that reification is at the base of many social problems, especially when 'commodity exchange' is a key activity. In the case of higher education, knowledge transmission (teaching) and knowledge production (research) have become two of the most prized commodities produced by academia. Knowledge as a commodity places academia in a key strategic position within a capitalist society that has information and a graduated workforce as two of its main currencies. It is thus no surprise that academic knowledge has become 'something objective', of value, but able to stand independently of its makers (Lukács [1923] 2011). Reification's role here is thus that of suppressing the relationship between product and producer, which in the case of academia – one could say – means to remove the academic soul from the academy. This is an issue that is not just financial, spatial or temporal, but also ethical and moral. In Chapter 10, Winter Pereira makes a good point in this regard in that she calls for acts of care in an attempt to restore some sense of justice to academics and their work, at the same time as it aims to destabilise what has become the norm of academic performativity.

In this vein, several forms of resisting neoliberal academia have begun to emerge, with academics organising alternative scholarship movements that aim to return dignity to academic work and recapture the sense of self of knowledge workers as intellectuals. For example, the Res-Sisters, a group of female academics based in the UK, is a response to the 'academic jungle where neo-liberal values and processes permeate academic life' (2017: 268). The Res-Sisters' goal is to resist the system by putting feminism to work. At the heart of their tactical approach is the intent of self-preservation as an identified need and collective responsibility of the collegiate; a form of solidarity that recognises joint struggles and which aims to promote change against neoliberalism and the individualistic approaches that it incites. This proposal is different from those who suggest a form of 'slow scholarship', not because the fast pace of academic work should not be challenged, but because behind questions of time are concealed issues of privilege that epitomise the unequal structures of academia. Be that as it may, 'slow professor' (Berg and Seeber 2017) or not, what such movements aim to do is to challenge and change a working culture that is threatening the substance and shape of intellectual work when subjected to a neoliberal ideology. In doing so, such movements aim to incite a spirit of shared meaning and rescue the core principles of knowledge work (Elias 1972) that place importance on long-term processes of knowledge growth.

Such processes are at odds with the dynamics of knowledge production within current economic developments (Elias 1972: 122) that characterise contemporary academia and which, to a certain degree, are likely to affect the relationship of academics and their work in relation to society. In current times, this aspect is perceptible through the ways in which academic knowledge is often ignored or regarded with suspicion by the general public. The discrediting of scientific consensus over global warming issues is a good example of how academia has lost political relevance in society. The rise of public anti-intellectualism and distrust on academic work is further exacerbated by the mainstreaming of social media, which is partly free of critical knowledge gatekeepers, and the slow uptake of academics to digital scholarship practices as a form of devolving academic knowledge to the public realm (Murphy and Costa 2019). At the centre of the transformations brought about by the neoliberalisation of higher education is a serious epistemic crisis that threatens academics' professional identity. It is in this vein that Hodgson and Watts (see Chapter 8) interrogate the possibilities of maintaining the notion of the academic scholar under the predicaments that currently shape higher education by engaging with existential and stoic philosophy.

In short, the politics currently surrounding academia have incited a crisis of meaning that is reflected in how academics feel the need to constantly examine and redefine their identity with implications not only for their professional practice but also their well-being and job stability.

References

Abbas, T. and Zalta, A. (2017), 'You cannot talk about academic freedom in such an oppressive environment': Perceptions of the *We Will Not Be a Party to This Crime!* petition signatories, *Turkish Studies*, 18 (4): 624–643.

Archer, L. (2008), 'The new neoliberal subjects? Young/er academics' constructions of professional identity', *Journal of Education Policy*, 23 (3): 265–285.

Berg, M. and Seeber, B. (2017), *The Slow Professor: Challenging the Culture of Speed in the Academy*, reprint edition, Toronto: University of Toronto Press.

Bourdieu, P. (1988), *Homo Academicus*, trans, P. Collier, Stanford, CA: Stanford University Press.

Bourdieu, P. (2003), 'Participant objectivation', *Journal of the Royal Anthropological Institute*, 9 (2): 281–294.

Bourdieu, P. and Wacquant, L. (1999), 'On the cunning of imperialist reason', *Theory, Culture and Society*, 16 (1): 41–58.

Breeze, M., Taylor, Y. and Costa, C. (2019), 'Introduction: Time and space in the neoliberal university, in M. Breeze, Y. Taylor and C. Costa (eds.), *Time and Space in the Neoliberal University: Futures and Fractures in Higher Education*, 1–14, Dordrecht: Springer.

Brown, T., Goodman, J. and Yasukawa, K. (2010), 'Academic casualization in Australia: Class divisions in the university', *Journal of Industrial Relations*, 52 (2): 169–182.

Courtois, A.D.M. and O'Keefe, T. (2015), 'Precarity in the ivory cage: Neoliberalism and casualisation of work in the Irish higher education sector', *Journal for Critical Education Policy Studies*, 13(1): 43–66.

Elias, N. (1972), 'Theory of science and history of science', *Economy and Society*, 1 (2): 117–133.

Enders, J. and Kaulisch, M. (2005), 'Vom Homo Academicus zum Homo Oeconomicus? Die doppelte Kontextualisierung der Forschung und ihre (möglichen) Folgen für die Wissenschaft als Beruf', in M. Pfadenhauer (ed.), *Professionelles Handeln*, 207–220, Wiesbaden: VS Verlag für Sozialwissenschaften.

Higher Education Statistics Agency (HESA) (2019), *Higher Education Staff Statistics: UK: 2017/18*. Available online: https://www.hesa.ac.uk/news/24-01-2019/sb253-higher-education-staff-statistics.

Honneth, A. ([1996] 2004), *Struggle for Recognition: The Moral Grammar of Social Conflicts*, reprint, Cambridge: Polity Press.

Honneth, A. (2012), *Reification: A New Look at an Old Idea*, Oxford: Oxford University Press.

Kim, T. (2017), 'Academic mobility, transnational identity capital, and stratification under conditions of academic capitalism', *Higher Education*, 73 (6): 981–997.

Knobel, M. and Leal, F. (2019), 'Higher education and science in Brazil: A walk toward the cliff?', *International Higher Education*, 99: 2–4.

Lukács, G. ([1923] 2011), 'Reification and the consciousness of the proletariat', in I. Szeman and T. Kaposy (eds.), *Cultural Theory: An Anthology*, 172–187, Chichester: Wiley.

Marginson, S. (2000), 'Rethinking academic work in the global era', *Journal of Higher Education Policy and Management*, 22 (1): 23–35.

McKenzie, L. (2017), 'A precarious passion: Gendered and age-based insecurity among aspiring academics in Australia', in R. Thwaites and A. Pressland (eds.), *Being an Early Career Feminist Academic: Global Perspectives, Experiences and Challenges*, 31–49, London: Palgrave Macmillan.

Morrish, L. (2019), *Pressure vessels: The epidemic of poor mental health among higher education staff*, Occasional Paper no. 20, Oxford: Higher Education Policy Institute. Available online: https://www.hepi.ac.uk/2019/05/23/pressure-vessels-the-epidemic-of-poor-mental-health-among-higher-education-staff/.

Murphy, M. (2018), 'The legacy of postmodernism in educational theory', *Educational Philosophy and Theory*, 50 (14): 1332–1333.

Murphy, M. and Costa, C. (2019), 'Digital scholarship, higher education and the future of the public intellectual', *Futures*, 111: 205–212.

Norton, A., Cherastidtham, I. and Mackey, W. (2018), *Mapping Australian higher education 2018*, Report no. 2018-11, Grattan Institute. Available online: https://grattan.edu.au/wp-content/uploads/2018/09/907-Mapping-Australian-higher-education-2018.pdf.

Olssen, M. and Peters, M.A. (2005), 'Neoliberalism, higher education and the knowledge economy: From the free market to knowledge capitalism', *Journal of Education Policy*, 20 (3): 313–345.

Özkirimli, U. (2017), 'How to liquidate a people? Academic freedom in Turkey and beyond', *Globalizations*, 14 (6): 851–856.

Petö, A. (2018), 'Attack on freedom of education in Hungary: The case of gender studies', *Engenderings*, 24 September. Available online: https://blogs.lse.ac.uk/gender/2018/09/24/attack-on-freedom-of-education-in-hungary-the-case-of-gender-studies/.

The Res-Sisters (2017), '"I'm an early career feminist academic: Get me out of here?" Encountering and resisting the neoliberal academy', in R. Thwaites and A. Pressland (eds.), *Being an Early Career Feminist Academic: Global Perspectives, Experiences and Challenges*, 267–284, Basingstoke: Palgrave Macmillan.

7

The Experimental Rhythms of Academic Work

Fabian Cannizzo

Introduction

This chapter draws on Barbara Adam's sociology of time to develop a time-sensitive perspective of academic identity and governance. Austere funding climates and managerialism within universities have encouraged attempts to rationalise education and research in universities, leading many sociologists of university life to decry the colonisation of science by the imperatives of capital. However, unlike the bodily movements of pig iron workers, famously captured in F.W. Taylor's time-motion studies, academic work is often organised around craft principles that prevent its precise measurement and the application of rational time management. The devolution of responsibility for the efficiency of academic labour to department managers, teachers and researchers has nevertheless incentivised experiments and attempts to take control of the rhythms of craftwork by academics.

The chapter explores (1) the chronopolitics that characterises academia and the rhythms of scholarship, and (2) the strategies that academics have developed to produce those rhythms, such as blogging and writing groups. While past research often points towards the political rationality of academic governance (neoliberalism, managerialism, new public management, marketisation) as driving the internalisation of a new work ethos (sometimes described as an enterprising self), this top-down focus is insufficient for understanding the organisation of time and work patterns in academia. I argue that academic labour researchers may develop a less deterministic perspective through seeking to understand academics' roles in producing the appearance of temporal order and 'efficiency'. The experience and organisation of time in academia is not a top-down directive, but rather a dialectic of organisational change management and experiments with self-regulation that ordinarily emerge in social life. A sociology of academic time provides a methodological tool to explore the production of temporal regimes in academia and identify the practices through which temporalities are embedded in academic identities and governance.

Popular discourses surrounding the transformation of academia around the globe often draw on a set of dichotomous discourses, characterising organisational change as inciting a clash or struggle between opposing conceptions of the academy and its workers: scientific versus corporate values (Winter 2009); collegial versus managerial work control (Parker and Jary 1995); fast versus slow productivity (Berg and Seeber 2017; Pels 2003a); instrumental versus substantive goals (Osbaldiston et al. 2019); and high modern versus postmodern knowledge orders (Delanty 2001). In this chapter, I narrow in on a key battleground for the politics of academia – that is, the temporal ordering of scholarly work. The perception that academic workers are under more pressure than they have been in the past and that this pressurisation is leading to widespread negative consequences has become near doxic among critical higher education scholars. Here, I interrogate the study of time ordering in academia, which I describe as a chronopolitics of academic work (see Vostal 2016: 170ff). I begin by outlining how a large segment of studies of socio-temporalities in academia have tended to mirror the dichotomies described above. I situate these studies within a political economy of academic work and policy developments that have imparted productivity imperatives upon academia through performative metrics (Ball 2003) in order to produce auditable subjects (Power 1999). Best captured in the slow scholarship movement (Berg and Seeber 2017; Mountz et al. 2015; Treanor 2008), the study of academic temporalities is seldom divorced from analysis of the transformation of the university and its implications for the kind and degree of work autonomy experienced by scholarly professionals.

I offer an alternative way of approaching the chronopolitics of academic work through elaborating on a key assumption within much of the current literature: that broad social transformations to the policy and organisational infrastructure of global academia have a deterministic relationship with academic work temporalities. I seek to problematise the assumption that neoliberal and managerial interventions into the organisation of academic life have systemic, logically inferable influences over the temporal experience of academic work through drawing on insights from Barbara Adam's (1990) social theory of time. In place of the neoliberal assumption, I advocate for empirical scrutiny of the relationship between policy infrastructures, managerial programmes for intervening on academic productivity, and the responses that academics produce within a transforming work environment. Central to my invocation here is the significance of ongoing socialisation rituals to the development of time-management practices in academia. Much past research has offered a synchronic analysis of academic power relationships, which idealised academics as already-socialised personalities. These studies have been useful for outlining underlying governmental rationalities within academia, but less helpful for describing how a chronopolitics is (re)produced through the agentic conduct of academics themselves. By focusing on the socialisation of academics to time-management practices, scholarly work can begin to describe how academic staff become complicit in the reproduction of timescapes felt to produce undesirable consequences, without resorting to the self-defeating mantra, 'there is no alternative'.

The chronopolitics of academic work

Academic work is produced through temporal demands and rhythms that stem from several sources: the necessary duration of work activities, the politics of academic capitalism, organisational imperatives, and national governmental strategies that frame universities as economic entities. The study of academic work temporalities has been underscored by an often-repeated dichotomisation of temporal experiences that can roughly be designated as the 'fast', which is deemed to properly belong to the realm of capitalism and ensuing economic rationalities, and the 'slow', which is the purview of science, bureaucracies and the idealised academic *lebensführung*, or ethical lifestyle choices (Abel and Cockerham 1993; also see Vostal et al. 2019). Each concept is – as all dichotomies are – relational, bifurcating and hence a means of limiting analytic focus to a boundary within social life (Adam 1990: 155).

Since the turn of the century, studies of academic temporalities have been mobilised to explore issues of accelerationism (Müller 2014; Vostal 2016), experiences of work intensification (Menzies and Newson 2007; Ylijoki 2013; Ylijoki and Mäntylä 2003), projectification (Ylijoki 2014), career governance (Hey 2001), academic freedom and autonomy (Pels 2003a, 2003b; Noonan 2015), and the marketisation of time (Guzmán-Valenzuela and Barnett 2013). What these studies share is a concern for the temporal experiences that result from the governance of scholarly work. Nicola Spurling (2015) has pointed out that academic work occurs within qualitatively different experiences of time that stem from both organisational and personal attempts to order the rhythms of academic work (also see Murphy 2014).

Academics order their time through different temporal rationalities (Osbaldiston et al. 2019). While many daily tasks will be conducted because of bureaucratic requirements (lending to experiences of 'instrumental times'), other activities, such as writing, reading for research and deliberation are conducted with a vision of an idealised future self in mind, producing value-rational action or 'substantive times' (Osbaldiston et al. 2019: 755). While these temporal categories are ideal-types (and not mutually exclusive), they objectify aspects of academic life which are processual, leading to the appearance of distinct social phenomena with marked boundaries. Whereas, *in situ*, an act of writing may be directed towards both the contemplation of knowledge for its own sake (a value-rational action) and also contribute to a scholarly publication, which helps the faculty maintain its research assessment score (a means-ends rational action). While instrumental times are experienced as increasing in tempo and intensification for early-career academics, substantive times are associated with slower-paced activities, which there are decreasing amounts of time to experience. Therefore, our use of the Weberian concept of rationality implies a binary of temporal rationalities in everyday academic life, between faster and slower work trajectories. Osbaldiston et al. (2019) are not alone in drawing on this dichotomy.

Studies drawing on analytic lenses that aim to demonstrate different 'qualities' of time may similarly reproduce this dichotomy of faster/slower. Oili-Helena Ylijoki and Hans Mäntylä (2003) distinguish four perspectives that academics use to account for their work: scheduled time, timeless time, contracted time and personal time. Although these perspectives are grounded in their participants' accounts, the constructs are discussed in terms of their relative pace to one another. Scheduled time has an 'accelerating pace' and is characterised by 'time pressure' (2003: 60), which contrasts with timeless time, which 'is not subjected to any kinds of external pressures and demands' (2003: 62) and requires that academics 'break away from the firm grip of scheduled time' (2003: 63). Meanwhile, contracted time, which is the temporal experience of working on a project-based contract that is always coming closer to terminating, is characterised as a harried experience that encourages thinking about 'short-term survival' (2003: 66) and contrasts with personal time, which Ylijoki and Mäntylä claim is 'grounded in the inescapable finitude of human existence' (2003: 67) through which academics reflect on the longest duration of their living experience. These temporal categories are bifurcated by the experience of time pressure, which is imposed by scheduled and contracted time and takes away from slower experiences, such as the enjoyment of research (2003: 70) and sharing time with colleagues (2003: 73).

Research premised on Rosa's (2013) social acceleration thesis similarly reproduces this distinction. Noonan's (2015: 111) concept of thought-time, which is 'free from externally imposed routines and deadlines' and central to academic work is contrasted to money-time, which is 'determined by the generic goal of capitalist productivity' and hence prone to accelerationism. Filip Vostal (2016) has similarly identified slow and fast sites within universities that are largely indicative of how embedded economic rationality has become in some areas of academic life, encouraging entrepreneurialism and time discipline from academics. I will come back to discuss Vostal's work, as it does aim to directly address temporal reductionism (Vostal 2016: 196; Vostal et al. 2019). Despite an expansion of theorising towards a plurality of time-ordering practices and mechanisms, scholarship of academic times is drawn back to the temporal binary of 'faster' and 'slower' times.

Critical reflections on social theory and methodology

In attempting to create a methodology for understanding temporality in academia, the social time theory of Barbara Adam is a valuable approach for moving beyond limiting dichotomous thinking. Drawing on Giddens, Adam defines temporal dichotomies (such as slow/fast, linear/recurring, traditional/ modern rates of change) as dependent upon 'the observer's frame of reference' (Adam 1990: 29). The perception of fast, linear or traditional rates of social change, for example, hence depend upon the recognition of rhythms, flows and repetitions of events characterised as normative from a particular point of reference. This section outlines the point of reference produced in academia from which evaluations of 'fast' and 'slow' academic times have derived, as well as outlining methodological implications and challenges in moving beyond dichotomous temporal thinking.

The study of the socio-temporal order was not destined to become concerned with the experience of 'fast' and 'slow' times. For most of its history, sociology has treated time as 'a contingent feature' of research, with synchronic analysis and motionless 'state perspectives' taking pride of place on the canonical mantel (Hassard 1990: 1). Early conceptualisations of social time, in the Durkheimian tradition and the work of Pitirim Sorokin and Robert Merton ([1937] 1990), drew distinctions between objective temporalities, such as clock time and astronomical time, and the qualitatively distinct temporalities that form within communal life. As a notable theorist of the socio-temporal order specific to modernity, Eviatar Zerubavel ([1981] 1985: 2) focuses his investigation on the production of 'temporal regularity', or 'the temporal rigidification of social situations, activities, and events'. Adopting a Weberian theoretical framework, his method is concerned with elaborating the human endeavour to order and fix social life in the process of rationalisation, involving temporal rigidification, conventionalisation, scheduling and the production of social rhythms. While the machinations of industrialisation have produced quantifiable 'clock time' and 'calendar time', Zerubavel argues that these apparent quantifications also delineate the 'social, intellectual and religious significance' of temporalities ([1981] 1985: 101). The duality of time in modernity, as both quantitatively divisible into days, months and years (via the calendar) and seconds, minutes and hours (via the clock) and also qualitatively differentiated because of the social significance of events, allows Zerubavel to produce temporal dichotomies that reflect the social significance of time: such as sacred/profane time and private/public time. More recently, Judy Wajcman (2015) has argued that the seemingly quantitative temporal experience of time-pressure (or loss of time) is socially produced; that is, time spent answering emails does not overload academics, but rather work cultures that diminish the significance of office hours to work routines do. In this framing, time-pressure is a function of the norms of time use, rather than a specific quantity of time used to engage in some activity. As distinct from the physio-temporal order of the celestial bodies and physical mechanics and the bio-temporal order of living organisms and ecosystems, the socio-temporal order is built upon the rhythms, duration and sequencing of social events. Zerubavel's method presents a powerful analytic tool alongside social theories of modernity, precisely because it demonstrates that the social production of a rationalising world requires meaningful practices, methods and technologies of temporal ordering. The dichotomisation of fast/slow times in studies of academia emerged later on.

When applied to the study of academic work, analysis of socio-temporalities became inflected with the longstanding belief that academic life is and ought to exist beyond the worlds of economics, politics and popular media. In *Homo Academicus*, Bourdieu defends the autonomy of the scientific field, claiming that the cultural hierarchy of 'scientific and intellectual renown' competes against the broader social hierarchy of 'economic and political capital' (1988: 48). This competition between hierarchies links them in a temporal economy, or as Bourdieu (1988: 95) claims, the political and economic advantages that form 'academic power can only be accumulated and maintained at the cost of constant and heavy expenditure of time'. Investment in bureaucratic power therefore tends 'to compromise the accumulation of a capital of scientific authority and vice versa' (Bourdieu 1988: 96). Dick Pels has pointed out that Bourdieu's apparently neutral descriptions of the field of intellectual struggle lack a degree of self-reflexivity in that they fail to acknowledge that they are in fact part of that field of struggle. In attempting to define the intellectual field and its social logic, Bourdieu presents '*performative* definitions that (re)describe their object in such a manner that the description simultaneously (re)creates what it purports to describe' (Pels 2003a: 117). The implication here is that 'scientists *should* actually recognize no other clients than their [scientific] competitors, and *should* in fact exclude as illegitimate all exchanges that are not considered legal tender in the field' (Pels 2003a: 118).

Pels embraces this performativity, describing scholarly autonomy as producing a 'self-interested science' (2003a: 112) that is distinguished from other domains of life by its unique anti-politics and anti-economics. For Pels, scientists necessarily traverse both domains of slow scholarship and fast politics, but in doing so 'continue to represent *the interests of slowness*', as ambassadors of a 'slow corporation' with interests in 'a secluded and unhastened culture of research that delivers a specifically detached or estranged perspective on the world' (2003a: 128). Despite Pels' more advanced conception of science as a moral and performative organisation, his perspective also embraces the dichotomisation of faster and slower times through implicating time in the social action appropriate to different areas of social life – fast politics and economy against slow science and scholarship.

The study of academic temporality has hence been largely concerned with not only asynchronicity, but a fact and value claim that the rhythms of both science and scholarly life are of and require a slower pace than society more broadly, especially slower than politics and economy. This approach embraces Barbara Adam's (1990) perspectival framework, as fastness and slowness are not binary concepts, but rather relational features of domains of social life that are only sensible when one domain is compared to another. A centring of the comparison of faster/slower times is the outcome of the intersection of two processes that underlay the chronopolitics of academic work: the modernisation of temporality and the idealisation of academic work as a craft practice. I will describe each process in turn before returning to how these help centre the dichotomy of faster/slower times in current research.

First, in modern life, time is commonly defined by mechanical duration, as if it is a substance that can be divided and exchanged, rationally organised through planning the future, but never accessible once in the past. Weber ([1930] 2001: xxxix) argues in *The Protestant Ethic* that the development of economic rationalism as much as ascetic Protestantism depended on the disposition of workers to adopt 'certain types of practical rational conduct'. Centring Benjamin Franklin's essay in which he advises, 'Remember that *time* is money' (cited in Weber [1930] 2001: 14), Weber underlines that the moral imperative to rationally use capital implies the rational organisation of time itself. The development of industrial capitalism enabled the hegemony of a linear time perspective in society at large as time became conceptualised as a divisible, homogeneous, quantifiable commodity to be consumed at the discretion of its possessor (Hassard 1990: 12–13). The metaphors of possessing time and dispossessing oneself of time are central to the chronopolitics of capitalist modernity, as the ability to rationally organise time is not distributed arbitrarily. Steven Ward (2012) has noted that the emergence of new public management and similarly output-oriented forms of academic governance have resulted in the perception of an intrusion of external interests into the reproduction of the academic profession and the conduct of work. The shift from bureaucratic rule-driven governance to output-driven quasi-corporate governance in a sense modernised the perception of time in universities, as a growing body of administrators and senior managers have spread the impetus to rationally organise science and scholarship. A chronopolitics can hence be seen to form at least between scholarly labourers and the university as an increasingly corporatised entity. I have argued elsewhere that the neoliberalisation of national policy agendas has devolved into 'tactical evaluations' (Cannizzo 2018) on the part of scholars as they come to embody what Mirowski (2013) has described as the experience of 'everyday neoliberalism' – that is, a propensity to see one's self as a self-managing enterprise within a web of value-judgements. Within the minds of many academics, time is felt to be fragmented between the desires of their employers, clients, funding committees and others who jostle for control over the expenditure of time.

Second, however, the dominance of a modernist conception of time is not enough to explain how a chronoeconomy becomes a chronopolitics, nor why academic work is ostensibly a slower affair than other areas of life. Following Pels, I argue that we need to exercise reflexivity and take account of the performativity of descriptions of academic work, which 'mix normative and empirical judgements' (Pels 2003a: 117). A central performative category in the production of a chronopolitics is that of craftwork. In their polemic, *The Slow Professor*, Berg and Seeber (2017: 17) claim that the time-pressures in contemporary universities are 'detrimental to intellectual work, interfering with our ability to think critically and creatively'. This sentiment is often repeated within the slow university literature, centring cognitive and communicative temporalities in academic work. Elsewhere (Cannizzo 2019), I have described how craftwork in academia is characterised not only as slow work, but also as deeply personal work. C. Wright Mills describes this work as 'a choice of how to live as well as a choice of career':

> whether he [*sic*] knows it or not, the intellectual workman forms his own self as
> he works toward the perfection of his craft; to realise his own potentialities, and
> any opportunities that come his way, he constructs a character which has as its
> core the qualities of the good workman.
>
> Mills 1959: 196

The moral evaluation of the craftsperson present in Mills' account of academic work resonates with common assumptions about science and scholarship as time-consuming and 'unhastened' (Pels 2003b) practices. Claims that academic work require standards set by the academic profession are hence not merely descriptive, but often performative statements through which academic work routines and control are contested and legitimated. With control of labour placed at the centre of analysis, the dichotomisation of temporalities into faster/slower categories are revealed as political tactics. The modernist conception of time as a linear, divisible phenomenon is consequently reified as a commodity to be exchanged or fought over.

Once we mobilise Barbara Adam's (1990) perspectival framework and recognise the conflict over the speed of social action, between faster and slower times, as a performative chronopolitics aimed at achieving control over areas of social life, the temporal attributes of scientific and scholarly work become more apparently about scheduling *per se* than the pace of scheduled events. This perspective introduces methodological challenges in understanding how academics seek out control over the scheduling of their work. This discussion centres largely around the rationalisation of time in modern societies, but with a specific focus on the consequences of the 'scientific management' (Taylor [1911] 1919) of labour that has developed throughout the twentieth century. Adam (2009) notes that sociologists of modernity have been long concerned with futurity and temporality in an implicit way, as in Max Weber's methodological writings, which are concerned with how individuals imagine futures in the rational pursuit of social action (also see Zerubavel [1981] 1985). The Weberian call to not only document the empirical facts about society, but also understand the cultures of social actors stems from the view that imagining futures are central to social action (Adam 2009: 13). Scientific management and the ideology of managerialism make a claim on the future, as authorities of social action and industrial rationality. But a relational approach to understanding social time (Adam 1990) reveals perspective-dependent rationalities for organising time into our understanding of academic life. I aim to demonstrate that methodological difficulties produced by a relational approach to studying academic time presents a promising advancement in the field of academic labour studies, as academic identities and groups become produced through experiences of temporal asynchronicity and agency. Methodologically, we can trace the foundations of academic identity formation partially through temporality, as is described in the following section.

Temporal complexity and agency in academia

Scientific discovery and educational work are both temporally complex. Vostal et al. have recently begun to map these complexities, noting that scientific production contains a mixture of temporal dynamics that require scientists to engage in 'agentic synchronisation' to conduct knowledge work successfully (2019: 17). Scientific work is unpredictable: discoveries are produced unreliably and often irregularly through experimental methods; scientists' expectations of their work shift over time; and scientific work is negotiated among several actors existing within their own temporal norms. Teaching and learning may similarly require long trials of testing and revising methods and assumptions before a reliable curriculum and means of communication are established between educator and student, as students exist within their own socially differentiated timescapes (Bennett and Burke 2018). Descriptions of the acceleration of scholarly work (see Vostal 2016) must hence take account of the role played by academics themselves in producing either the self-governance necessary for predictable work rhythms or else describe how arrhythmicity results in acceleration.

Melissa Gregg (2017) has documented an example of such worker-driven work acceleration in the work of Silicon Valley technology companies. Gregg claims that, in a genealogy that can be partially traced back to F.W. Taylor's time-motion studies, technology company workers adopt technological means of monitoring and acting on their work though a culture where speed 'became a measure of accomplishment' (Gregg 2017: 105). Scientific managers from Taylor to Henry Ford to Elton Mayo have described industrial management as a form of art in which managers would craft 'the political, social, industrial, and moral mass into a sound and shapely whole' (Ford, in Mannevuo 2018: 1253). The user of self-management technologies is simultaneously their own manager (their own 'artist') and subordinate, internalising the desire to rationalise labour.

However, as noted by Vostal et al. (2019), not all scholarly activities are able to be cast within the techniques of measurement and representation described by Gregg. The time taken to make a scientific breakthrough cannot be improved upon if discovery is not reliably predictable. But more than serendipity, academics can and do seek out means to organise their work habits beyond the productivism that characterises performative evaluations and self-management technologies – to assert their own forms of control over time (Adam 1990: 110). I briefly outline two practices here to demonstrate that academics are seeking out means of taking control of their work in ways that shape their temporal experiences and that while these practices are partially a response to the athletic pace of university productivism, they also produce their own temporalities and group identities beyond the managerial logic of acceleration. These practices are academic blogging and writing groups. I have chosen to focus on practices associated with writing because this genre of practice is commonly identified as a candidate for temporal acceleration and intensification (see Gregg 2017).

Academic blogging is a widespread practice that is still largely beyond the ordinary institutional performance measuring and monitoring of universities. In an analysis of 100 academic blogs, Mewburn and Thomson (2013) found that blogs were often directed towards persons with similar interests to the author, suggesting that rather than means of communicating with the 'general public' (i.e. Bourdieu's speedy field of media), there exists 'a loose academic blogging community of practice' (2013: 1114) with the characteristics of a 'virtual staffroom' (2013: 1116) or 'conversational scholarship' (Gregg 2006; also see Carrigan 2016). While academic blogging can be used to create a heightened scholarly profile, Mewburn and Thomson claim that bloggers were more often engaged in a 'gift economy' of exchange without the expectation of reward (2013: 1115). Although some blogs have been inscribed into publication metric platforms, such as GoogleScholar, the majority of academic blogging is largely beyond the quantification of academic promotion and hiring committees. The blogging communities of practice impart temporal relations that are estranged from the productivist drive towards the efficient control of labour. First, the production of blog posts is not incentivised in the same way that scholarly journal or book publishing is, as scholarly reward systems render blogging invisible unless it is part of an impact statement related directly to project outputs. Second, the community of practice around bloggers is often geographically dispersed and networked, adding a real-time temporal dimension to both long-form blogging (i.e. through Wordpress.com) and especially to micro-blogging platforms such as Twitter. Blogging is hence neither an inherently 'fast' nor 'slow' practice, but rather one in which the disconnection from academic reward systems allows for a more prominent sense of control over writing and publishing pace, frequency and rhythm, which may be more attuned to the norms of a community of practice than its relationship to the pace of capital. This research effectively mobilises a perspectival temporal framework (Adam 1990), as the production of a virtual academic community is developed through the production of shared temporalities.

Academic writing groups similarly escape the evaluative measures and rewards systems within universities, but are often used by participants as opportunities to create time-management habits (Myatt et al. 2014). However, the design and uses of writing groups are not singularly productivist. Fegan notes that, as funding is cut for doctoral support programmes, writing groups such as the Shut Up and Write (SUAW) initiative can act as communities of practice that offer students an opportunity to be 'effective agents in their own training' (2016: A25). Mewburn et al. (2014), in their analysis of two SUAW groups in metropolitan Australia, argue that SUAW is valuable to participants because of a unique alchemy of affective states. First, SUAW meetups are structures around several 'Pomodoros' – a combination of writing 'sprints' of around 25 minutes, with break times in between of around five minutes or so. The obligation formed among SUAW group members to 'just write' during the Pomodoros may produce discomfort or anxiety in participants, which is used to motivate their writing in a similar fashion to the self-quantifying productivity technologies described above. But in addition to these writing sprints, SUAW sessions also include time for socialisation, which Mewburn describes as 'the key "informal learning space" as it allows the exchange of ideas and thoughts about workplace practice, that is, "shop talk"' (Mewburn et al. 2014: 410). Through SUAW, participants work together to communally produce anxiety, relief and joy. The sense of anxiety reported by SUAW participants is characteristic of what Vostal (2016: 124) describes as 'acceleration embraced' as a pleasurable experience. This model for the affective regulation of writing has been replicated in regular virtual meetings, such as Shut Up and Write Tuesdays (SUWT), a network of three Twitter accounts that conduct virtual meetings across Australia, the UK and the USA. These online sessions, similarly to their real-life counterparts, 'make the process [of writing] visible to others' (O'Dwyer et al. 2017: 258) and thereby enable the socialisation of writing practices, most notably through time scheduling (2017: 262).

The examples of academic blogging and writing groups demonstrate two distinct practices for the socialisation of academic time-management that do not derive from organisational directives or command structures. Yet, both practices may assist in helping academics to integrate into the existing systems of scholarly production and evaluation. Both blogs and writing groups offer the opportunity to learn scholarly norms and techniques, build networks, and gain access to tacit knowledge and myths about academia. Also, more than merely exposing scholars to a pre-existing logic of acceleration, these spaces allow for *agentic experimentation* with different rhythms, paces, senses of pressure and relief, social and technological infrastructures, enabling space for the formation of scholarly communities and non-organisational identities. Conceptualising these time-management experiments as responses to the organisational transformation of universities towards massified, managerialised entities begs caution in drawing hard conclusions about the relationship between organisational rationalities, time-management and identity formation in academia.

Temporal agency is not equally distributed throughout society, which, as Dörre has claimed, has been transformed since the Fordist era's focus on linear, organisable time, into an era of flexible production and the 'introduction of a regime of discontinuous time' (2011: 84) to which lower-status workers are more exposed. The disposal of linear Fordist work time (i.e. clock-in, clock-out) makes 'extra-curricular' activities such as blogging and writing groups a possible means of work governance, as these activities may be used to socialise early-career academics into the long-hours culture that has developed within the 'trust-based working hours' (Dörre 2011: 85) of academic workplaces. Ylijoki's claim that the rationality of 'project time gradually penetrates into all kinds of activities and subordinates other temporalities' (2014: 99) is suggested here to overlook the value of worker-managed forms of time-management for the reproduction of academia. Ylijoki does state that 'academics are active agents who can learn to navigate skilfully within the project format, negotiate its temporal terms and reshape the schedules' (2014: 104), but limits this agency to forms of quantitative 'bargaining time' among competing activities, rather than discussing the development of social norms and identities through different temporal experiences. Positions that contrast the psycho-temporal experiences of scientific discovery with more procedural academic work, such as Peter Murphy's distinction between 'discovery' and 'delivery' university functions (2014: 150), risk reifying the movement of academic times through confusing ideal-types with mutually exclusive experiential phenomena. Literature emphasising the conflict between accelerated society and 'slow' academic spaces (Pels 2003a, 2003b) needs to make space for the socialisation of habit and rational action, between broader temporal rationalities and the experiences of academics working within anxious, harried timescapes.

Socialised rhythms: Notes towards a research programme

The study of socialisation invites diachronic analysis back into the study of social life. When conceptualised synchronically, as part of a social structure of power relationships, temporality is reduced to a factor of structure itself. In the case of growing managerialism within universities, harried working practices are seen as a logical outcome of the imposition of the efficiency principle upon the structure of work. However, a focus on how academics develop time-management practices reveals the processual development and reproduction of managerial norms, which require the agency of academics. A greater understanding of how everyday, routinised procedures for organising work and life activities are reconciled with other orders of time, including lifetime (Rosa 2013: 8), would place agency back at the centre of analyses of academic work and living. Rather than reifying time-management under the power structure of managerial governance, in which the 'fast' times of productivity, media and economics are juxtaposed to the 'slow' times of thinking, learning and crafting, we might instead ask what practices academics find to cope with the myriad expectations, hopes, and commitments made of their bodies and presence by employing Adam's (1990) perspectival approach. The answers found might not necessarily entail competition between different conceptions of time, but rather the development of a skill set that Vostal et al. (2016) have described as 'agentic synchronisation', or which Erikson and Mazmanian (2017) call 'temporal entrepreneurship', rather than a retreat into an 'oasis of deceleration' (Rosa 2013: xxxvii). Such a perspective may help to identify how performative descriptions of academic 'productivity' intersect with the socialisation of academics and the development of time-management practices.

Further to the study of the socialisation of time-management itself, a diachronic method invites an exploration of the ongoing transformation of temporalities across the academic careers. Academics on casual contracts develop different career planning and informational desires to others, as changing identities alter their perceived relationship to the industry around them (Brown et al. 2013; Rothengatter and Hil 2013). A diachronic analysis could trace the development of an idealised sense of future self and its relationship to the everyday temporalities and the mid-term horizons of project-time (Ylijoki 2014) and performance evaluation cycles. Adam (2009) has identified the value of expanding on Max Weber's methodological writings to situate future selves in sociological analysis. Because 'futurity', including projections of life/career trajectories, for Weber is inferred rather than observed, yet may still form part of the explanation of observable phenomena (values, morals, ideals, motives, reasons), the envisioned future is observable through its transformation of sociality – 'real in its consequence' (Adam 2009: 18). Taking this approach necessitates investigations of how academics use ideas about temporal sequencing, boundary-making, 'slowing', acceleration and synchronisation as part of ongoing practices of experimentation with time-management. Such an approach is proposed in the hope that it might avoid overly deterministic readings of the transformation of academic work and its identification with 'slowness'. The pace of scholarship is as variable as its environments.

References

Abel, T. and Cockerham, W.C. (1993), 'Lifestyle or Lebensführung? Critical Remarks on the Mistranslation of Weber's "Class, Status, Party"', *The Sociological Quarterly*, 34 (3): 551–556.

Adam, B. (1990), *Time and Social Theory*, Cambridge: Polity Press.

Adam, B. (2009), 'Culture Future Matters: An Exploration in the Spirit of Max Weber's Methodological Writings', *Time and Society*, 18 (1): 7–25.

Ball, S.J. (2003), 'The Teacher's Soul and the Terrors of Performativity', *Journal of Education Policy*, 18 (2): 215–228.

Bennett, A. and Burke, P.J. (2018), 'Re/conceptualising Time and Temporality: An Exploration of Time in Higher Education', *Discourse: Studies in the Cultural Politics of Education*, 39 (6): 913–925.

Berg, M. and Seeber, B.K. (2017), *The Slow Professor: Challenging the Culture of Speed in the Academy*, Toronto, ON: University of Toronto Press.

Bourdieu, P. (1988), *Homo Academicus*, trans. P. Collier, Stanford, CA: Stanford University Press.

Brown, N.R., Kelder, J.-A., Freeman, B. and Carr, A.R. (2013), 'A Message from the Chalk Face – What Casual Teaching Staff Tell Us They Want to Know, Access and

Experience', *Journal of University Teaching and Learning Practice*, 10 (3): Art. 5. Available online: http://ro.uow.edu.au/jutlp/vol10/iss3/6 (accessed 30 June 2019).

Cannizzo, F. (2018), 'Tactical Evaluations: Everyday Neoliberalism in Academia', *Journal of Sociology*, 54 (1): 77–91.

Cannizzo, F. (2019), 'Academic Craftwork: On Authenticity and Value in Academia', in F. Cannizzo and N. Osbaldiston (eds.), *The Social Structures of Global Academia*, 91–106, London: Routledge.

Carrigan, M. (2016), *Social Media for Academics*, London: Sage.

Delanty, G. (2001), *Challenging Knowledge: The University in the Knowledge Society*, Buckingham: The Society for Research into Higher Education and Open University Press.

Dörre, K. (2011), 'Capitalism, *Landnahme* and Social Time Regimes: An Outline', trans. M. Booth and M. Dressler, *Time and Society*, 20 (1): 69–93.

Erikson, I. and Mazmanian, M. (2017), 'Bending Time to a New End: Investigating the Idea of Temporal Entrepreneurship', in J. Wajcman and N. Dodd (eds.), *The Sociology of Speed: Digital, Organizational, and Social Temporalities*, 152–168, Oxford: Oxford University Press.

Fegan, S. (2016), 'When Shutting Up Brings Us Together: Some Affordances of Scholarly Writing Groups in the Neoliberal University', *Journal of Academic Language and Learning*, 10 (2): A20–A31.

Gregg, M. (2006), 'Feeling Ordinary: Blogging as Conversational Scholarship', *Continuum*, 20 (2): 147–160.

Gregg, M. (2017), 'The Athleticism of Accomplishment', in J. Wajcman and N. Dodd (eds.), *The Sociology of Speed: Digital, Organizational, and Social Temporalities*, 102–116, Oxford: Oxford University Press.

Guzmán-Valenzuela, C. and Barnett, R. (2013), 'Marketing Time: Evolving Timescapes in Academia', *Studies in Higher Education*, 38 (8): 1120–1134.

Hassard, J. (1990), 'Introduction: The Sociological Study of Time', in J. Hassard (ed.), *The Sociology of Time*, 1–18, New York: Palgrave Macmillan.

Hey, V. (2001), 'The Construction of Academic Time: Sub/contracting Academic Labour in Research', *Journal of Education Policy*, 16 (1): 67–84.

Mannevuo, E. (2018), 'The Riddle of Adaptation: Revisiting the Hawthorne Studies', *The Sociological Review*, 66 (6): 1242–1257.

Menzies, H. and Newson, J. (2007), 'No Time to Think: Academics' Life in the Globally Wired University', *Time and Society*, 16 (1): 83–98

Mewburn, I. and Thomson, P. (2013), 'Why do Academics Blog? An Analysis of Audiences, Purposes and Challenges', *Studies in Higher Education*, 38 (8): 1105–1119.

Mewburn, I., Osborne, L. and Caldwell, G. (2014), 'Shut Up & Write! Some Surprising Uses of Cafés and Crowds in Doctoral Writing', in C. Aichison and C. Guerin (eds.), *Writing Groups for Doctoral Education and Beyond: Innovations in Theory and Practice*, 399–425, London: Routledge.

Mills, C.W. (1959), *The Sociological Imagination*, Oxford: Oxford University Press.

Mirowski, P. (2013), *Never Let a Serious Crisis Go to Waste: How Neoliberalism Survived the Financial Meltdown*, London: Verso.

Mountz, A., Bonds, A., Mansfield, B., Loyd, J., Hyndman, J. and Walton-Robers, M. (2015), 'For Slow Scholarship: A Feminist Politics of Resistance through Collective Action in the Neoliberal University', *ACME: An International Journal for Critical Geographies*, 14 (4): 1236–1259.

Müller, R. (2014), 'Racing for What? Anticipation and Acceleration in the Work and Career Practices of Academic Life Science Postdocs', *Forum Qualitative Sozialforschung / Forum: Qualitative Social Research*, 15 (3): art. 15. Available online: http://nbn-resolving.de/urn:nbn:de:0114-fqs1403150 (accessed 30 June 2019).

Murphy, P. (2014), 'Discovery and Delivery: Time Schemas and the Bureaucratic University', in P. Gibbs, O.-H. Ylijoki, C. Guzmán-Valenzuela and R. Barnett (eds.), *Universities in the Flux of Time: An Exploration of Time and Temporality in University Life*, 137–153, London: Routledge.

Myatt, P., Edwards, A. and Bird, F. (2014), 'Achieving Greater Productivity with a Peer Writing Group', in *Proceedings of the Australian Conference on Science and Mathematics Education*, University of Sydney, 29–30 September 2014, pp. 140–148.

Noonan, J. (2015), 'Thought-time, Money-time, and the Temporal Conditions of Academic Freedom', *Time and Society*, 24 (1): 109–128.

O'Dwyer, S.T., Jefferson, R., McDonough, S.L., Goff, J.A. and Redman-MacLaren, M. (2017), 'Writing Groups in the Digital Age: A Case Study Analysis of Shut Up & Write Tuesdays', in A. Esposito (ed.), *Research 2.0 and the Impact of Digital Technologies on Scholarly Inquiry*, 249–269, Hershey, PA: IGI Global.

Osbaldiston, N., Cannizzo, F. and Mauri, C. (2019), '"I Love My Work but I Hate My Job" – Early Career Academic Perspective on Academic Times in Australia', *Time and Society*, 28 (2): 743–762.

Parker, M. and Jary, D. (1995), 'The McUniversity: Organization, Management and Academic Subjectivity', *Organization*, 2 (2): 319–338.

Pels, D. (2003a), *Unhastening Science: Autonomy and Reflexivity in the Social Theory of Knowledge*, Liverpool: Liverpool University Press.

Pels, D. (2003b), 'Unhastening Science: Temporal Demarcations in the "Social Triangle"', *European Journal of Social Theory*, 6 (2): 209–231.

Power, M. (1999), *The Audit Society: Rituals of Verification*, Oxford: Oxford University Press.

Rosa, H. (2013), *Social Acceleration: A New Theory of Modernity*, trans. J. Trejo-Mathys, New York: Colombia University Press.

Rothengatter, M.R. and Hil, R. (2013), 'A Precarious Presence: Some Realities and Challenges of Academic Casualisation in Australian Universities', *Australian Universities Review*, 55 (2): 51–59.

Sorokin, P. and Merton, R. ([1937] 1990), 'Social-time: A Methodological and Functional Analysis', in J. Hassard (ed.), *The Sociology of Time*, 56–66, New York: Palgrave Macmillan.

Spurling, N. (2015), 'Differential Experiences of Time in Academic Work: How Qualities of Time are Made in Practice', *Time and Society*, 24 (3): 367–389.

Taylor, F.W. ([1911] 1919), *The Principles of Scientific Management*, New York: Harper and Brothers.

Treanor, B. (2008), 'Slow University: A Manifesto', *LMU Faculty Website*. Available online: http://faculty.lmu.edu/briantreanor/slow-university-a-manifesto/ (accessed 30 June 2019).

Vostal, F. (2016), *Accelerating Academia: The Changing Structure of Academic Time*, Basingstoke: Palgrave Macmillan.

Vostal, F., Benda, L. and Vortová, T. (2019), 'Against Reductionism: On the Complexity of Scientific Temporality', *Time and Society*, 28 (2): 783–803.

Wajcman, J. (2015), *Pressed for Time: The Acceleration of Life in Digital Capitalism*, Chicago, IL: University of Chicago Press

Ward, S. (2012), *Neoliberalism and the Global Restructuring of Knowledge and Education*, New York: Routledge.

Weber, M. ([1930] 2001), *The Protestant Ethic and the Spirit of Capitalism*, trans. T. Parsons, London: Routledge.

Winter, R. (2009), 'Academic Manager or Managed Academic? Academic Identity Schisms in Higher Education', *Journal of Higher Education Policy and Management*, 31 (2): 121–131.

Ylijoki, O.-H. (2013), 'Boundary-work Between Work and Life in the High-speed University', *Studies in Higher Education*, 38 (2): 242–255.

Ylijoki, O.-H. (2014), 'Conquered by Project Time? Conflicting Temporalities in University Research', in P. Gibbs, O.-H. Ylijoki, C. Guzmán-Valenzuela and R. Barnett (eds.), *Universities in the Flux of Time: An Exploration of Time and Temporality in University Life*, 94–107, London: Routledge.

Ylijoki, O.-H. and Mäntylä, H. (2003), 'Conflicting Time Perspectives in Academic Work', *Time and Society*, 12 (1): 55–78.

Zerubavel, E. ([1981] 1985), *Hidden Rhythms: Schedules and Calendars in Social Life*, Berkeley, CA: University of California Press.

8

Exploring Academic Identities in the Neoliberal University

David Hodgson and Lynelle Watts

Introduction

What has being an academic come to mean in the neoliberal spaces of the modern university? In the last two decades, this question has formed the basis of an ongoing dialogue between us about the possibilities and constraints with regard to attaining and maintaining an identity as a scholar. As the spaces around us have undergone multiple transformations through processes of restructuring, managerialism, changes in staff and students, and the impact of digital technology, we have engaged with, resisted and transformed the various imperatives and pressures to become instrumentally focused in our work. In doing so, we have asked, and continue to ask, if it is possible to maintain the notion of academic scholar within the conditions of the modern neoliberal university.

A reflexive methodology (Alvesson and Sköldberg 2009) and a method of pair-interviewing adapted from Gilmore and Kenny (2015) guided discussions and personal reflections and conversations over a twelve-month period, where we reflected on the meaning and struggles associated with academic identity and the pursuit of scholarly work. We drew from Archer (2000), who suggests that social change calls into operation the reflexivity of agents as they engage with the conditions in which they find themselves. Other informing ideas came from two distinct philosophical sources: existentialism, in particular Simone de Beauvoir ([1947] 2018), and stoicism (Aurelius 2003; Pigliucci 2017). Our reflexive engagement with existential and stoic philosophy involved an ongoing dialogue and critical examination of the tensions and felt experience of pursuing academic work in the shifting terrains of the neoliberal university. The chapter demonstrates how reflexive methodological inquiry can be utilised to investigate contemporary institutional conditions.

Background

Our interest in this topic begins with our felt experience and observations of *being* academic workers in the context of the neoliberal corporate university. There is widespread acceptance that universities globally are undergoing profound transformation and change, increasingly defined by and subjected to the economic imperatives associated with global market forces, fiscal austerity, and rapid technological and digital transformation (Beilharz 2014; Rustin 2016; Thornton 2014). As discussed below, these changes pose serious challenges for the attainment of intellectual and moral flourishing and well-being, for students and educators alike.

The contemporary forces that shape and constrain the university have been described as 'neoliberal corporate capitalism' (Rustin 2016: 4). Freeman (2018) argues that it is not so much neoliberalism that has swept its way through the academy, but technocratic corporatism with neoliberal tendencies. For many commentators, this neoliberal *plus* corporatist turn of events is a travesty, turning universities into money-making enterprises at the mercy of market forces and government austerity, turning students into user-paying customers, rendering learning and knowledge production into narrowly instrumental forms, culminating as 'academic capitalism' (Thornton 2014: 3). This space/time compression and the sheer accelerated pace of change of modernity has led to recurring rounds of digital and technological change in the academy, an explosion in information, the measurement and ranking of everything, audit cultures, endless restructuring, and a constant drive to do more with less. These macro social, economic and cultural forces of neoliberal corporatism drive a path-dependent logic for an on-demand culture of 'nowism' (Beilharz 2014: 40).

It is our view that this broader context has a profound and not wholly positive effect on the nature of academic work: transforming relationships and distorting academic values; constructing and reconstructing identities; and introducing doubt and uncertainty into the meaning and purpose that people invariably bring to their work. Neoliberal policy, ideology and discourse filters its way into the fibres and tentacles of academic workplaces and, notwithstanding obvious exceptions, what emerges at a systemic level is an overall indifference to the state of people's work environments, the intensification and narrow instrumentality of labour towards economic ends, the objectification of bodies and emotions as cogs in an academic machine, and the contraction of intellectual creativity (Schofield 2005).

There is now widespread evidence – both anecdotal and as reported in the research literature – of high levels of stress, anxiety and mental distress amongst faculty, driven by the intensification and economic rationalisation of intellectual labour, competitive individualism and rankings, job precarity and uncertainty, bullying and a culture of overwork (Berg et al. 2016; Zabrodska et al. 2011). For example, individualised research performance assessments and rankings as reported in our neighbouring New Zealand drive performance anxiety (Stahl 2015). Berg et al. (2016) explain that academics are increasingly pushed to become more entrepreneurial in their outlook and in their identity, to guide their own conduct and performance towards the capitalist enterprise. So pervasive and widespread are these conditions that Maldonado and Guenther (2019) describe how some – especially those working within a critical theoretical tradition (e.g. feminist, critical cultural studies) – find themselves marginalised and devalued, forced into exiting academia altogether.

Neoliberal discourse is an institutional practice, but it also 'works on us without our consent and despite our motivations as well as being actively taken up by us in conscious ways, constraining us as well as constructing us and being constructed through our responses to it' (Heath and Burdon 2013: 386). As Berg et al. (2016) note, academics are producers and transmitters of knowledge value, but they do not own or control the means of knowledge production and, following Marx, may experience alienation from their labour, from each other and, ultimately, from themselves. Labour is key to how human beings express and realise themselves, insofar as they may see themselves and derive meaning and form attachments to their work. When academic labour and knowledge is commodified, packaged and sold, heavily routinised and cut up in piecemeal fashion, workers 'can become alienated through the estrangement from their subjectivity because workers must subordinate their *human nature* in the process of working for others' (Watts and Hodgson 2019: 103, original emphasis). This estrangement from one's subjectivity is important to recover, because a practice towards freedom and meaning can be constituted as an ethical antidote to the alienation that can be so undermining and demoralising in the academy. The stoic and existential framing that we elaborate below is intentionally posited here as a route to examine and reconceptualise academic work within a framework of freedom and purpose. It is within this particular context that we situate our inquiry into what it means to be an academic worker in the neoliberal university.

Methodology and methods

To explore our own experience, we utilised a reflexive methodology (Alvesson and Sköldberg 2009) to engage in a series of reflective dialogues utilising a pair-interviewing approach which we had successfully adapted from Gilmore and Kenny (2015) in previous work (Hodgson and Watts 2016). The method involved conducting six audio-taped unstructured reflective discussions between ourselves across a twelve-month period in 2017. During these reflective discussions, each of us took turns opening the dialogue usually with some event or aspect of academic life that we had been considering or which had caught our attention. The dialogue would then explore the event or aspect. Dialogues ranged from 30 to 60 minutes with an average of 45 minutes.

At the time of our reflective dialogues, we had been separately reading and thinking about two major bodies of thought: existentialism and stoicism (Pigliucci 2017). The audio recordings of our dialogues were transcribed by a transcription service and each of us read and coded all the dialogues separately using an open coding process (Saldaña 2012), which was guided by sensitising concepts drawn from our readings of existential and stoic philosophy. After this stage, we engaged in further reflective dialogue, which involved each of us discussing our thoughts while the other took extensive notes. The coding and the extensive notes of this second stage of discussion form the basis for the three main themes discussed below, and in relation to our question: 'What has being an academic come to mean in the neoliberal spaces of the modern university?'

The use of these different philosophical worldviews provided important contrasts to the neoliberal academic environment we were grappling with. The theory gave us a way to try to free ourselves 'from the horizons of the practices and problematisation' (Tully 2008: 31) of the neoliberal environment. On the face of it, our choice of theories has emerged from different traditions: existentialism, stoicism and, methodologically speaking, public philosophy and critical realist social theory. However, methodologically there is a common thread between them: each supports the use of deliberative thinking and reflection. Reflection in existentialism involves navigating the ambiguity inherent in life in order to free oneself and locate meaning and purpose. For stoicism, reflection is the faculty through which one engages in mastery of oneself. Likewise, the species of political philosophy, outlined by James Tully, incorporates reflection and dialogue where 'participants exchange practical reasons over the contested criteria for the application of concepts in question ...' (Tully 2008: 26). Tully's point aptly describes the form and function of our dialogues, and we elaborate these ideas further below in the context of our discussion.

Constructing meaning, resilience and identity in the academy

Our reflective dialogues with each other illustrate grappling with our ethical subjectivity, and the struggle over what it means to work in the context of the neoliberal university – that is, what it might mean to *be* and *become* an ethical subject as academics. There were three main themes that our conversations cycled around: the pursuit of virtue; the struggle over meaning and purpose; and the emergence of a neoliberal academic subjectivity.

The pursuit of virtue

Neoliberalism involves a radical and hegemonic reconfiguration of institutional norms, practices and subjectivity towards market and economic ends (Watts and Hodgson 2019). This presents somewhat of a problematic challenge to historically derived normative scholarly virtues. While obviously contested, and in no small part varying by context, scholarly virtues may include, for example: the pursuit of wisdom (practical wisdom, or *phronesis*); courage and conviction (risk of having one's ideas publicly critiqued); collegiality (working with others, supporting others, involving others); truth and justice (the twin and sometimes competing academic *telos*); intellectual freedom and learning (creating new ideas and sharing them); teaching; community; and, quite literally, the time and space to think and reflect (the mental space and time for contemplation). We are not saying that these virtues are entirely dissolved under the weight of neoliberalism, but they are called into question by forces that emphasise market values: productivity; instrumentalism; conformance as a proxy for performance; a growth telos; responsibilism; competitive individualism; the rationalisation of resources; and the metrification and quantification of value (for example, the metric calculus on research output, university rankings).

How to go about maintaining virtue (whatever virtue means) and a sense of oneself as an academic under the conditions of neoliberalism seems to be important. In the exchange below, we are calling into question a transcendental notion of academic virtue, noticing that as academics we experience ourselves in a painful nexus between an idealised notion of academic work, and the *realpolitik* of neoliberal ethics, which is (re)constructing and (re)calibrating notions of virtue. Here we are discussing academic virtue as something circulated in a moral economy:

> **LW**   So if you think about it as a moral economy, I think historic virtues are supposed to be kind of context-independent virtues.
>
> **DH**   And I think that's problematic.
>
> **LW**   That's the problem.
>
> **DH**   That's a limit to me because I'm more in the line of . . . that –
>
> **LW**   Yeah, your ethics comes out of your practice.
>
> **DH**   Yeah and it's historically conditioned.
>
> **LW**   Yeah. Well we've experienced that haven't we, because what was ethical six years ago, the moral economy that existed six years ago, is completely different to the moral economy now –
>
> **DH**   Here's a bit of a question, can virtues be altered or changed or burnt out or destroyed by a [workplace] environment?
>
> **LW**   Yeah, I reckon.
>
> . . .
>
> **DH**   So what's the virtue?
>
> **LW**   That's the behaviour. I don't know. In that case –
>
> **DH**   Helping?
>
> **LW**   Maybe it is the wisdom . . . because I don't think cooperation under every circumstance is a virtue.
>
> **DH**   No, because you need a mean, like Aristotle's mean?
>
> **LW**   Yeah, that's right. I think it [cooperation as virtue] can be killed for sure . . . I think it can be extinguished as a behaviour.

There is a certain ambiguity underlining this exchange, a grasping for some foundation or grounding upon which one might build a basis for one's work and life projects in the academy. Does the context of neoliberalism call into question some foundational assumptions, values and beliefs? We think it does. Is this why academic work in neoliberal institutions can sometimes feel instrumental, and as though there quite simply is no time to actually meet the requirements of the job (Davies and Bansel 2005)? We have found the existentialism of Simone de Beauvoir helpful in untangling some of these concerns, particularly her book *The Ethics of Ambiguity*, first published in 1947.

In *The Ethics of Ambiguity* ([1947] 2018), de Beauvoir offers a critique of the universalism in utilitarian ethics and of the transcendentalism in Kantian deontology. For de Beauvoir, ethics are best seen as both individual and relational. We found some comfort in her argument that the context and experience of being human is ambiguous. Hence, we can say that the context and experience of working and inhabiting the neoliberal university is one of perpetual ambiguity over its condition and its meaning. In the Sartrean existential view, existence is absurd and inherently meaningless. de Beauvoir ([1947] 2018) offers a more nuanced distinction by contending that existence is not absurd, but instead it is ambiguous. By ambiguity, she means that existence is not meaningless, rather, meaning is not fixed. This is a more hopeful and optimistic vision, suggesting that the meaning and joy in academic work may be found in the playful use of freedom and possibility (Sims 2012), a challenging position to maintain in the face of the neoliberal onslaught we might add. However, it was clear from our conversations that we saw academic work as an important and worthwhile venture. Moreover, we were attempting to work on ourselves inasmuch as working on our context so as to circumvent the narrow instrumentalism of academic work. We were attempting to locate spaces for freedom and possibility.

At first glance, de Beauvoir's proposition about ambiguity might seem uncomfortable, and for anyone looking for or clinging to certitude about absolute moral values it probably is. This reflected much of our discomfort and disquiet over the state of neoliberal academic work. We realised we were looking for certain moral values, and were appealing to a fixed and somewhat normative view over what an academic job *should* look like, and then feeling disappointed when our expectations failed to manifest themselves. Amidst this sense of disappointment, we wrestled with and tried to resist the seductive pull of endless rounds of complaining about how bad the neoliberal university has become. By accepting a state of ontological ambiguity, we can allow for seeing things from different perspectives, thereby avoiding a foreclosing of thought into binaries, certitude or appeals to final universal ethical norms. It was helpful to us in closing the 'is/ought' gap that was lodged in our negative perceptions over the state of the neoliberal university.

It should be pointed out that this is unequivocally *not* a descent into solipsism or nihilism, even though we did enter into thought experiments about where a solipsistic and nihilistic position might take us. We rejected these positions, however, having been more persuaded by de Beauvoir's promise that this state of ambiguity 'leads to an ethic of liberation' (Slattery 1999: 24). Clinging to a position that seeks to erase this ambiguity is a path to oppression and domination, whereas her ethics outlines a position that involves facilitating the freedom of others, recognition of their humanity, not treating people as objects to be used for other ends, and critical self-reflection of the inherent ambiguity of our lives and the lives of others (Sims 2012). Fixed and certain judgements built out of formulaic ethical principles run the risk of being oppressive and dominating (Slattery 1999). As Slattery suggests:

> Unambiguous goals actually eliminate the possibility of freedom when they infuse schooling [or in our case, academic work] with the lifeless drudgery of repetition.
>
> 1999: 30

In the neoliberal context that can readily feel devoid of meaning, de Beauvoir's ethics encourage us to work towards a particular good, such as reciprocity, cooperation, trust and relations of virtue. Such goods require 'conscious decisions about which relationships to prioritize and which to subordinate or eliminate' (Archer 2013: 162). Having a philosophical framework to draw on helped us escape our horizons of thinking just long enough to begin to think critically about the relations of governance that characterise the academy. For de Beauvoir, ethics is concerned with recognition of the *other*, and recognition that people are not simply individuals, but exist in relationships with others, which demands their care and concern (Sims 2012). This is a movement away from the existential concern with the self, and away from a descent into solipsism, towards a position that is based in 'solidarity, intersubjectivity and collectivity' (Sims 2012: 681). In following, we consider that any concern with academic freedom must situate recognition of others as an ethical enterprise (Slattery 2008). Teaching and research that is subjected to the instrumentality and governmentality of neoliberalism undermines democratic freedom in the name of instrumental ends – such as industry, accreditation or employer-driven demands for a certain kind of curriculum leading to a certain kind of graduating worker (Slattery 2008). In our view, this can be ethically problematic as a guiding frame for academic work.

Working in the neoliberal academy means finding ways to contend with one problematisation (i.e. neoliberalism) by reflexively comparing this with other frameworks of meaning. In short, our dialogues were small spaces of resistance to the absurdity and apparent meaning vacuum generated by the conditions of neoliberalism on the academy. We were seeking to sketch out an ethical framework that is comfortable with ambiguity, focusing our sense of identity and work as part of a broader struggle for meaning and purpose.

The struggle over meaning and purpose

In our conversations, existentialism helped us pose some critical questions. What does academic work mean? And how can we find meaning in our work within the confines of the neoliberal university? The answer, it seems, is that there is no objective transcendental meaning to these questions at all. As mentioned, de Beauvoir argues for ambiguity and against transcendental idealism. We settled on a view that accepts there is no *arriving*, no final destination or end point, no ideal state that we may return to or find. Instead, de Beauvoir suggests that flourishing means to work to support creativity and freedom in oneself *and* in others. Applied to the context of academia, this means actively working against falling into a position of righteousness (and the polarising tribalism that is its accoutrement), and resisting the urge to grip tightly and brutally to ideological or epistemological dogma in order to salvage some certainty (and perhaps dignity) from the wreckage of neoliberal vacuity.

Still, our conversations revealed a struggle with this position, and we were aware that regularly we were dealing with a sense of anxiety or discomfort over our work. Am I good enough? What do I stand for? What would give my work meaning, relevance and legacy? We had concerns over never being enough, never being on time, not counting or mattering beyond a metric in the university systems of accounts, and feeling like a widget or cog in some giant machine. We are not alone in this respect – witness, for example, the various social media forums, blogs and stories that attest to similar feelings (see, for example, Anonymous 2014; Woolston 2018). We reflected on our struggles in dealing with a voluminous workload, which perpetuated a sense of dread and anxiety associated with always falling behind:

> **LW**   I don't think – is it exactly the same, like you were saying I always feel like I'm always behind, so that's one thing; but then there's this other thing I think, I don't know if they're the same.
>
> **DH**   Well –
>
> **LW**   Like this is a sense for me that I haven't really – I've got a radical uncertainty about whether I've developed the muscle [resilience needed for the job], whereas I think for you is that you're always behind, there's more to do but you have developed something, you know; so I think they're slightly different.
>
> **DH**   Feeling like I'm behind and experiencing the stress with that motivates me to keep doing the work because if I didn't feel stressed by it I just wouldn't bother.
>
> **LW**   Yeah, exactly.

DH   So that's important in that respect, but the difference is before the stress used to be distressing and now the stress is simply motivating.

LW   It's just there. Although you'd like it to stop, right?

DH   Well it'd be nice, to be comfortable.

LW   Is that the goal, like really shouldn't that [comfort] be the goal?

DH   I don't know.

LW   Maybe we've got the goals wrong, because if we want to develop antifragility [resilience] that means you never give up, you never get to the point where you're comfortable because then you're no longer developing antifragility.

DH   Antifragility. You're in a permanent state of discomfort of some kind . . . It's not meant to be easy or comfortable.

It is the work-induced discomfort and what to do with it that preoccupied much of our discussion. Recall the points made earlier from the literature on the neoliberal academy, particularly about the intensification of work and the acceleration of performance anxiety, among other problems. In the passage above, we are actually toying with an idea about antifragility and a stoic outlook as a dispositional attitude and practice to go beyond resilience, to 'build the muscle', as we put it, so as to cope with large workloads in a constantly shifting, changing and challenging context. Antifragility is a theory expounded by Nassim Taleb (2012) that contends that systems become progressively stronger through repeated exposure to stress and shock. In practice, this may appear as conscious efforts to embrace difficulty and intentionally subjecting oneself to a controlled range of stressful situations. From a stoic view, we were attempting to become more familiar and comfortable with the fact that although we may be able to exercise control over our impressions, we have little control over the context of our experience, some of which may be very difficult and indeed unpleasant (Pigliucci 2017). We were experimenting with these ideas in an attempt to transform our perceptions – and, to a lesser extent, the context of our work – so as to recover a sense of agency and autonomy.

It seems bizarre to us now that we were practising an approach to antifragility merely to build capacity for coping with the demands of academic work. However, on closer reflection, it is somehow related to de Beauvoir's point about freedom. Freedom in this sense is not just an abstract ideal, but something that exists through our actions in the world, and therefore, it involves a form of *practice*. de Beauvoir offers a more optimistic account of freedom than Sartre, proposing that it is a key task in the resolution of anxiety. In picking up this point, Slattery outlines an example that would be familiar to many educators:

It is always a struggle to become free because we want to fly away from it in anxiety; we tend to avoid wanting to make free choices since they may entail complexity and uncertainty. This is exemplified in the contradiction of students who desire freedom of expression in the classroom assignments while insisting that teachers provide detailed and unambiguous criteria for assessment. It is clear that the flight towards freedom is always in tension with the flight away from freedom.

1999: 27

The paradox is that freedom requires us to go *towards* the discomfort and to *embrace* the struggle that comes with uncertainty and difficulty. We consider that the pursuit of happiness and comfort in academia is an error because it is unattainable and inauthentic – it is actually the pursuit of meaning and freedom within the uncomfortable and difficult spaces of ambiguity that is key. This demands continuous work to transform ourselves, whilst at the same time seeking to critique and transform the oppressive power relations (Allen 2011) that constitute neoliberal academic subjectivities.

Resisting the neoliberal academic subjectivity

Our discussions revealed that we were each spending time trying to work out how to thrive and not just survive in academic work. These included a series of efforts, experiments and reflections on maintaining well-being, developing productivity hacks, practising different forms of resistance, and putting into practice reflexive adaptations and manoeuvres to the norms and moral economy of the workplace, which involved striving to maintain mental, emotional and intellectual well-being. But the contextual problem of the neoliberal university involves perpetual changes in norms and expectations, which invariably triggers a reflexive response, and one that forces a constant attempt to try and read and interpret the academic environment for clues and messages about how to work, how to be, what to pay attention to, what to watch out for and what the expectations are. This permanent state of reflexive self-awareness does account for surges in rumination and worry, which is where some counsel from the stoics can assist.

Marcus Aurelius famously wrote that 'external things are not the problem. It's your assessment of them. Which you can erase right now' (2003: 110). In other words, it is the reflection, interpretation and rumination that can be the source of stress, and not particularly the external event itself, although it may be. Still, the stoics are arguing for cognitive reappraisal and reframing of events, to more intentionally and rationally check perceptions for their biases and misinterpretations (Pigliucci 2017). Checking impressions is key to not taking some challenges of academic work too personally, especially when so much of it is deeply connected to one's sense of self, of value and of identity:

> **LW**   There is a real connection in my mind between the work that we do and identity-making activities, and so it is actually an intersection between the tasks if you like, and who you are as a person because so much of your intellectual work and your intellectual life is caught up with who you are as well, and I don't think it's easy to separate those things out, and so how you're treated does actually impact hugely on you. I'm not thinking academia is alone in this way, but it seems to me that it's very hard to do creative, innovative, thoughtfully intellectually engaged research or teaching, or all of those things that involve relationships, involve aspects of yourself in a way. And so if the environment is competitive and you know it's hard to walk that line between collaboration and competition . . . I think there are some things in the environment that make you vulnerable . . .

Neoliberalism alters the subject into an entrepreneurial, responsible self-maximising individual – responsible for their own needs, their successes and their failures (Siivonen and Brunila 2014). Neoliberalism ranks people in value hierarchies according to how productive they are and this drives cultures of overwork, competition and anxious worry. Neoliberalism involves cuts to publicly funded institutions, and it pushes the profit motive – it pushes people and systems to extract maximum value from available resources. Such environments can breed incivility, conflict, mental distress, asymmetrical relationships, tit-for-tat games and failures of recognition – all of which are conditions that are ultimately dehumanising. What then becomes of trust, virtue, relationship building and the development of relational goods (Donati and Archer 2015)? What does the neoliberal context do to create new normative frames (of non-cooperation, for example) and how might ethical subjects emerge from such a context? Speculating on these questions, we could identify our attempts towards finding some middle ground in the work. We conceptualised this middle ground as a form of *practice*:

> **DH**   It's about what you do as much as what you think, it is Aristotelian.

> **LW**   Yeah, it needs decisions.

> **DH**   You need the golden mean and you need to practise, you need to reflect on what you do in your life and try and keep it in the middle; that's how you thrive in an academic job.

It is a difficult and sometimes impossible task to achieve this state of the Aristotelian golden mean in a context that demands and expects so much, and which has little tolerance for failure. Undoubtedly, painful failure is inevitable, and it is doubly painful when we hold tightly to our cherished projects. Yet, failure is a condition of being, as de Beauvoir's states, 'without failure, no ethics' ([1947] 2018: 9). One cannot eliminate failure. To be authentic is to own up to one's failings and shortcomings. Our failings cannot be denied because these are part of what makes us human and they form the background of moral ambiguity. The problem is that the neoliberal university is risk averse – there is little to no room for admitting that the system and people in it are fallible. Consequently, this empties out from the university the very qualities within human relationships and academic work that make them satisfying and meaningful.

Stoics may have argued that we live our lives in relation to some fixed nature or order, but actually, problems appear when this nature, or context, or our work environment overwhelms us. Working in the neoliberal university can be overwhelming, which could be tolerable if only it held some transcendental meaning we could simply lift out of it. But it doesn't. It is difficult to suffer without some meaning, some wider project or higher purpose that makes the suffering worthwhile. The problem is the neoliberal university does not have a project, or perhaps it is better to say that we consider its project to be unsatisfactory. There does not appear to be an inherent meaning to it. Better put, the meaning seems arbitrary from a moral point of view. We have found these unsatisfactory as points of orientation towards work, but in our conversations we were very aware that the neoliberal imperative has filtered into our identities nonetheless. Fundamentally, we disagree with the neoliberal project in the academy because, ethically, we cannot *will* it for everyone as a matter of principle. It cuts into and undermines too much of what is valuable about academic work.

It seems to us, then, that the goal of academic life is to attempt to accept our own human frailties and limits in order to be free, and practise in a way that does not oppress the freedoms of others. Ethics means to *will* the freedoms of others into existence, and engage in struggle and in solidarity to creatively develop meaningful and meaning-filled projects, whilst at the same time as holding these projects lightly. In following de Beauvoir, academic ethics – and what it means to be – would emphasise relationships and their inherent goods: trust, reciprocity, collaboration, contemplation, mutuality, and the ability to creatively pursue an intellectual life in the pursuit of truth, justice and learning.

Critical reflections on social theory and methodology

The method of creating unstructured reflective dialogue was significant for this project because we wanted to build a 'space of reasons' (Laden 2012: 29) in which to consider our question. Laden suggests that reasoning 'is ... how we occupy a social space of reasons ... is something we inhabit, not merely invoke and deploy ... and that reasoning is just the ongoing activity of inhabiting that space' (2012: 29). This offered the opportunity for exploration of the key ideas and meanings each of us brought to the discussion as an ongoing activity between equals.

Inside this space of reasons, we engaged in 'a form of philosophical reflection on practices of governance that are experienced as oppressive in some way and are called into question by those subject to them' (Tully 2008: 16). We purposefully used our reflective dialogues as spaces to try and think differently and to open up a conversation about the impact of the neoliberal university on our felt experience, and what meaning we might derive or attribute to our work. Tully suggests that engaging in this kind of political philosophical reflection is achieved by problematising the various practices and language games that reside in the relations in question, and then try to free ourselves to think differently. This means to open up a critical dialogue so as 'to offer a disclosive sketch of the arbitrary and unnecessary limits to the ways they are constrained to think, deliberate and act, and of the possible ways of going beyond them in this context' (Tully 2008: 17).

Theoretically and methodologically what we were doing was exploring (and acting upon) the subject-producing nature of the neoliberal university context and its work on our sense of identity in the academy; to attempt to make visible the way that neoliberalism acts as a constitutive and interpolating force. Archer (2013) refers to this as a double morphogenesis, which is a relational process where we are attempting to transform our academic identities *and* the context and relations of power that are at the very same time constitutive of these same identities.

In terms of adopting critical realist social theory, we were primarily informed by Margaret Archer's (2000) work. Her work posits that the reflexivity of agents is the mediator of social change. Given our interrogation was aimed at understanding our struggles over the meaning and purposes of academic work within a neoliberal university environment, it made sense to choose methods that would activate our personal reflexive capabilities. Personal reflexivity is understood as 'the regular exercise of the mental ability, shared by all normal people, to consider themselves in relation to their (social) contexts and vice versa' (Archer 2007: 4). Indeed, Donati and Archer (2015: 95) suggest that the *'sense of self* is formed through our relations with the three orders of reality'. These orders of reality are *natural, practical* and *social*. In the case here, it means that we were considering neoliberal discourses and practices as they emerge within the university environments as productive because they have 'properties of [their] own which influence discursive relations' (Archer 2000: 173). Thus the method of reflective dialogue assisted us to consider not just the social order, but also our engagement in the practical/procedural aspects of academic work.

Finally, we took a lead from Korsgaard (1996) who makes the case that human reflection can be seen as a key source of normativity. For example, she says human consciousness:

> ... sets us a problem that no other animal has. It is the problem of the normative. For our capacity to turn our attention on to our own mental activities is also a capacity to distance ourselves from them, and to call them into question ... The reflective mind cannot settle for perception and desire ... it needs a reason.
>
> Korsgaard 1996: 93

In acknowledging this consciousness, we also have a responsibility. As Korsgaard suggests:

> when you come to see that your contingent practical identities are normative for you insofar as they are endorsable from the point of view of your human identity ... you come to see them as various realizations of *human possibility* and *human value*, and to see your own life that way: as one possible embodiment of the human.
>
> 2009: 212, emphasis added

In this respect, the choice of method and the engagement in reflection on the practices of governance in which we found ourselves made us acutely aware of our own agency within the interstices of the neoliberal practices and relations around us. It opened up new possibilities for engaging in ongoing deep dialogical reflective work somewhat in spite of the neoliberal practices around us.

References

Allen, A. (2011), 'Foucault and the politics of our selves', *History of the Human Sciences*, 24 (4): 43–59.

Alvesson, M. and Sköldberg, K. (2009), *Reflexive Methodology: New Vistas for Qualitative Research*, 2nd edition, London: Sage.

Anonymous (2014), *Depression & academia: There's no such thing as enough*. Retrieved from: http://nadinemuller.org/academia-and-mental-health/depression-and-academia/.

Archer, M.S. (2000), *Being Human: The Problem of Agency*, Cambridge: Cambridge University Press.

Archer, M.S. (2007), *Making Our Way through the World: Human Reflexivity and Social Mobility*. Cambridge: Cambridge University Press.

Archer, M.S. (2013), 'Morphogenic society: Self-government and self-organisation as misleading metaphors', in M.S. Archer (ed.), *Social Morphogenesis*, 145–164. Dordrecht: Springer.

Aurelius, M. (2003), *Meditations*, trans. M. Hammond, New York: Random House.

Beilharz, P. (2014), 'Critical theory and the new university: Reflections on time and technology', in M. Thornton (ed.), *Through a Glass Darkly: The Social Sciences Look at the Neoliberal University*, 37–47, Acton, ACT: ANU Press.

Berg, L.D., Huijbens, E.H. and Larsen, H.G. (2016), 'Producing anxiety in the neoliberal university', *Canadian Geographer / Le Géographe canadien*, 60 (2): 168–180.

Brunila, K. and Siivonen, P. (2014), 'Preoccupied with the self: Towards self-responsible, enterprising, flexible and self-centred subjectivity in education', *Discourse: Studies in the Cultural Politics of Education*, 37 (1): 56–69.

Davies, B. and Bansel, P. (2005), 'The time of their lives? Academic workers in neoliberal time(s)', *Health Sociology Review*, 14 (1): 47–58.

de Beauvoir, S. ([1947] 2018), *The Ethics of Ambiguity*, New York: Open Road Integrated Media.

Donati, P. and Archer, M.S. (2015), *The Relational Subject*, Cambridge: Cambridge University Press.

Freeman, J. (2018), 'The not-so-neoliberal university', *Renewal: A Journal of Labour Politics*, 26 (2): 88–95.

Gilmore, S. and Kenny, K. (2015), 'Work-worlds colliding: Self-reflexivity, power and emotion in organizational ethnography', *Human Relations*, 68 (1): 55–78.

Heath, M. and Burdon, P.D. (2013), 'Academic resistance to the neoliberal university', *Legal Education Review*, 23 (1/2): 379–401.

Hodgson, D. and Watts, L. (2016), 'What can moral and social intuitionism offer ethics education in social work? A reflective inquiry', *The British Journal of Social Work*, 47 (1): 181–197.

Korsgaard, C.M. (1996), *The Sources of Normativity*, Cambridge: Cambridge University Press.

Korsgaard, C.M. (2009), *Self-constitution: Agency, Identity, and Integrity*, Oxford: Oxford University Press.

Laden, A.S. (2012), *Reasoning: A Social Picture*, Oxford: Oxford University Press.

Maldonado, M. and Guenther, K. (2019), 'Introduction: Critical mobilities in the neoliberal university', *Feminist Formations*, 31 (1): vii–xxiii.

Pigliucci, M. (2017), *How To Be a Stoic: Ancient Wisdom for Modern Living*. London: Penguin Random House.

Rustin, M. (2016), 'The neoliberal university and its alternatives', *Soundings*, 63 (63): 147–170.

Saldaña, J. (2012), *The Coding Manual for Qualitative Researchers*, 2nd edition, London: Sage.

Schofield, T. (2005), 'Introduction: The impact of neoliberal policy on workplace health', *Health Sociology Review*, 14 (1): 5–7.

Siivonen, P. and Brunila, K. (2014), 'The making of entreprenurial subjectivity in adult education', *Studies in Continuing Education*, 36 (2): 160–172.

Sims, C. (2012), 'From hostility to hope: de Beavoir's joyful turn to Hegel in *The Ethics of Ambiguity*', *South African Journal of Philosophy*, 31 (4): 676–691.

Slattery, P. (1999), 'Simone de Beauvoir's ethics and postmodern ambiguity: The asssertion of freedom in the face of the absurd', *Educational Theory*, 49 (1): 21–36.

Slattery, P. (2008), 'Academic freedom: The ethical imperative', *Childhood Education*, 85 (1): 47–48.

Stahl, G. (2015), 'Performance anxiety: Audit culture and the neoliberal New Zealand university', *Culture Unbound: Journal of Current Cultural Research*, 7 (4): 618–626.

Taleb, N.N. (2012), *Antifragile: Things that Gain from Disorder*, New York: Random House.

Thornton, M. (2014), 'Introduction: The retreat from the critical', in M. Thornton (ed.), *Through a Glass Darkly: The Social Sciences Look at the Neoliberal University*, 1–15, Acton, ACT: ANU Press.

Tully, J. (2008), *Public Philosophy in a New Key*, vol. 1: *Democracy and Civic Freedom*, Cambridge: Cambridge University Press.

Watts, L. and Hodgson, D. (2019), *Social Justice Theory and Practice for Social Work: Critical and Philosophical Perspectives*, Singapore: Springer.

Woolston, C. (2018), 'Why mental health matters', *Nature*, 557 (May): 129–131.

Zabrodska, K., Linnell, S., Laws, C. and Davies, B. (2011), 'Bullying as intra-active process in neoliberal universities', *Qualitative Inquiry*, 17 (8): 709–719.

9

Gender and the University: Stories So Far and Spaces Between

Kate Carruthers Thomas

Introduction

Doreen Massey's social theory spans economic, urban, political, feminist and global subjects and questions. As a geographer, she attracts multiple labels but perhaps the most all-encompassing and appropriate is that of radical geographer 'embracing openness and multiplicity while resolutely confronting dominant forms of space and power' (Christophers et al. 2018: 30). Massey's understanding of space as plural, fluid and heterogeneous and her determination to 'leave openings for something new' (Massey 2005: 107) provide a powerful framework for my interest in researching the spaces between organisational rhetoric and lived experiences in the university and the academy.

Although Massey's social theory is now a compelling instrument with which I re-imagine higher education, theoretically and methodologically, I would call myself an accidental geographer. At secondary school, I dutifully learned about glaciation and oxbow lakes, but no lasting spark was lit then. Two decades later, I studied a Level 5 Human Geography module as part of an Open University Social Sciences degree programme. The module had been designed by Massey herself, then a Professor at the Open University. I enjoyed human geography more than glaciation but had no inkling how significant Massey's concepts of power geometry and uneven development would become for me as an academic researcher, two decades later.

This chapter discusses the application of Doreen Massey's socio-spatial concepts in my theorising of the university. It draws primarily on my research into the impact of gender and intersectional factors on experiences of the workplace and career in a post-1992 UK university (Carruthers Thomas 2019) in which Massey's theoretical concepts shape both the research questions and the development of a methodology 'sensitized to the social as inexorably also spatial' (Massey 1993: 80). The chapter also refers to an earlier application of Massey's social theory in a borderland analysis (Abes 2009, 2012), or hybrid theorising of student belonging in English higher education (Carruthers Thomas 2018). That borderland analysis, the principle of which is to 'to straddle multiple theories, using ideas from each to portray a more complete picture ... a new theoretical space' (Abes 2012: 190), brought Massey's theoretical constructs into dialogue with those of Pierre Bourdieu and Avtar Brah to re-imagine dominant narratives of student belonging in UK higher education.

The chapter first provides a brief outline of both projects, before summarising the key concepts of Massey's social theory. These are then brought together in a discussion of my use of Massey's concepts of space and power as an analytical framework to interrogate experiences of the university. In the case of *Gender(s) at Work*, the focus is on space, power and gender; in the case of *Dimensions of Belonging*, the focus is on student belonging. The chapter's penultimate section, 'Critical reflections on social theory and methodology', reflects on the ways in which Massey's theoretical constructs shaped my research methodology and instruments in both enquiries and the chapter concludes with a contemplation of Massey's influence on my work in the longer term.

Research contexts

Gender(s) at Work

The *Gender(s) at Work* project was conducted in and funded by the post-1992 university by which I am employed as a Senior Research Fellow specialising in interdisciplinary critical higher education studies and as the university lead for the Athena SWAN Charter, the UK's flagship accreditation system for advancing gender equality in higher education. This is an unusual dual role: working *in* gender as an organisational diversity worker and critically *on* gender as an academic researcher. The project emerged out of this dual role, initially seeking to gather qualitative data of gendered lived and living experiences of the university, to further the institution's Athena SWAN agenda. *Gender(s) at Work* is therefore institutional research in the sense that it aimed to increase corporate intelligence about gender equality and to contribute to the university's Athena SWAN agenda, but untypically, was underpinned by a theoretical framework, privileged qualitative methods and data, and reported its findings both internally and externally.

The project aimed to explore ways in which gender positions groups and individuals differentially in relation to power relationships within the university workplace and how gender, intersected with ethnicity, age and disability, positions groups and individuals in relation to the prevailing narrative of 'career' as a linear, upward, uninterrupted trajectory. It critiqued supposedly gender-neutral narratives 'aligned to male-defined constructions of work and career success ... which continue to dominate organisational research and practice' (Bilimoria et al. 2010: 727). Participants were recruited via an open call for staff participants of all genders, in academic and professional services roles and at all levels of seniority across the university hierarchy. Data collection via individual interview was conducted between November 2016 and May 2017. Of the 45 participants, 28 identified as female, 16 as male and one as gender non-binary. Thirty-one participants were in academic/academic management roles, and 14 in professional services/professional services management roles (IT, HR, Programme and Faculty Administration, Careers, Registry). Thirty-six of the participants identified as White, nine as Black Asian Minority Ethnic (BAME). Twenty-eight per cent of participants were aged 30–39 years; 28 per cent 40–49 years; 26 per cent 50–59 years; 13 per cent 18–29 years and one participant 60–69 years.

Dimensions of Belonging

This doctoral research project (2016), funded by the Higher Education Academy Mike Baker Doctoral Programme (2012–2015), challenges a powerful and ubiquitous phenomenon of student belonging in the context of an increasingly complex sector and a socio-economically, ethnically and educationally diverse student body. A multiple case study of four English universities, *Dimensions of Belonging* re-imagines dominant narratives of student belonging in higher education, in relation to mature, part-time undergraduates, a heterogeneous group with a very different set of characteristics, motivations and needs, as compared to their full-time counterparts. While the research focus differs from *Gender(s) at Work*, this project also foregrounds lived experiences of relationships of power in space. However, whereas Massey's social theory provides the sole analytical framework for the later project (*Gender(s) at Work*), in *Dimensions of Belonging*, Massey is part of a borderland analysis in dialogue with Pierre Bourdieu's field analysis (1988, 1990 *inter alia*) and Avtar Brah's conceptualisation of diaspora (1996).

All three theorists share 'an interest in articulating the interaction of individuals with their social environment in which power is unequally distributed' (Brah 1996: 39). Together, they emphasise belonging as shaped by space and power, inherently geographical. The inclusion of Massey in this borderland analysis enables not only a theoretical but a methodological re-imagining of the university as a site of power. This way of analysing a sense of belonging among a particular student constituency 'generates a multilayered analysis of a complex phenomenon – student belonging – compatible with the contemporary diversity of the student body' (Carruthers Thomas 2018: 42).

Doreen Massey: Social theorist

> Doreen Massey changed geography … she initiated new ways of seeing, understanding and indeed changing the world. She launched critiques, both in the relatively small world of economic geography and the much bigger worlds of social theory and progressive politics, that would prove to be truly transformative.
>
> Christophers et al. 2018: 1

Beginning her academic career in the field of spatial planning and industrial geography, Massey subsequently brought socialist and feminist sensibilities to economic, regional and human geography; applying her theoretical insights to regional development, globalisation, political economy and divisions of labour. While embracing post-modernism, she was nevertheless a respected critic of the masculinist gaze of fellow post-modernist geographers Harvey (1989) and Soja (1989) and towards the end of her life collaborated with Hall and Rustin on analyses of contemporary political and cultural issues (Hall et al. 2015). Massey spent 27 years as a teacher, researcher and professor at the Open University, 'to which she was strongly loyal because of its accessibility to all who wanted to learn' (Wainwright 2018: 367). There she pioneered innovative ways of teaching at a distance and was 'the key mover in an extended series of remarkably influential course texts' (2018: 5). In later life, she was actively engaged with political struggles in South Africa and Latin America.

Massey's radical approach defines space 'as social relations shaped by power and inherently temporal … a confluence and product of histories, relationships … the sphere in which distinct trajectories coexist' (Massey 2005: 9). She challenges 'the imagination of the spatial as petrification … a safe haven from the temporal … the notion of space as surface' (2005: 28). Space is fluid, always under construction, 'a particular moment in networks of social relations and understandings' (Massey 1994: 5). These propositions are the basis of Massey's engagement with feminist and gender debates. Though strongly influenced by Marxism, she critiqued 'a wider failure to account for who it was that filled the "empty spaces" of so many abstract Marxian categories . . .the unthinking recirculations of supposed universals which "are so often in fact quite particular; not universals at all but white, male, Western, heterosexual, what have you" formulations' (Christophers et al. 2018: 15). An analyst of gendered roles in changing industrial landscapes (McDowell and Massey 1984), uneven regional development (Massey 1988) and the meaning of 'home' (Massey 1992), Massey is a key figure in the diverse project of feminist geography which aims 'to investigate, make visible and challenge the relationships between gender divisions and spatial divisions, to uncover their mutual constitution to problematize their apparent naturalness' (McDowell 1999: 12). Later influenced by Harding and Haraway's thinking on feminist theory and situated epistemologies, Massey was nevertheless 'wary of currents within feminism that tended towards essentialism and narrow identity politics' (Christophers et al. 2018: 8).

Massey's contribution to social theory is characterised by a grounded engagement in the notion of places as trajectories and multiplicities. She criticises the way in which 'universalized arguments were so often decontextualized by jet-setter scholars who seemed to survey . . . the world from 30,000 feet, as if to project their own placelessness' (Christophers et al. 2018: 14). She observes 'much of life for many people . . . still consists of waiting in the bus-shelter with your shopping for a bus that never comes' (Massey 1992: 8). Massey's relational understanding of space and spatiality is central to every one of her engagements in complex debates and dialogues: on post-modernism, neoliberalism, globalisation and feminist theory among others. This is articulated through a set of interdependent concepts which form the building blocks for my own theorisation of the university: power geometry, a progressive sense of place and heterogeneity. I outline these below and then describe how they are encapsulated in, and put to work through, Massey's heuristic device of 'activity space'.

Power geometry

The concept of power underpins Massey's understanding of space. In power geometry she articulates the differential capacities groups and individuals have in relation to flows of capital, colonialism migration, social relationships and culture. 'Power geometry does not imply any specific form (any specific geometry). It is a concept through which to analyse the world . . . an instrument of potential critique' (Massey 2007: 321). Through power geometry, different social groups and different individuals are placed in very distinct ways in relation to flows and interconnections. Massey developed power geometry as an instrument of critique in response to Harvey's (1989) post-modernist argument of time-space compression (i.e. that the current period represents an accelerated phase of time-space compression caused by capitalism). Her argument is that time-space compression is not simply a geographical stretching-out of social relations, but that our experience of it is influenced by histories of colonialism, racism, social relations and relative wealth. If the pace and impact of physical, trade, financial and technological flows is socially differentiated, so is time-space compression. In fact, the way an individual is positioned in relation to those flows determines whether acceleration happens at all. 'Different social groups have distinct relationships to this differentiated mobility ... some initiate flows and movement, others don't; some are more on the receiving end of it than others; some are effectively imprisoned by it' (Massey 1993: 61).

Massey highlights the relationality of these socially differentiated groups. 'The socio-spatial processes that help shape and define places do not operate evenly, with different social groups and individuals relatively positioned as a consequence' (Kitchen 2016: 816). She examines the power geometry of time-space compression in the contexts of labour relations, industrial and regional development (McDowell and Massey 1984; Massey 1988) and diaspora where 'hitherto sharply differentiated cultures and people ... are forced to interact, often in profoundly asymmetrical ways in terms of their relative power' (Massey and Jess 1995: 193). Revisiting power geometry two decades later, following her visit to Venezuela where she had been invited to work with the new Chavez government to contribute to the building of a new power geometry, Massey emphasises its dynamic character, not only politically but across all spheres of society: 'an instrument through which to imagine and maybe to begin to build more equal societies' (Massey 2007: 321).

As a researcher, I am interested in how 'specific spaces ... are produced and stabilized by the dominant groups who occupy them' (Valentine 2008: 18) and apply Massey's concept of power geometry to frame the university and the wider higher education sector as sites of power and knowledge in which groups and individuals are differently and distinctly placed in relation to flows and interconnections. With its origins in the monastery and the early universities – specialised, male-dominated places of knowledge-production – the contemporary university is the product of social relations shaped by geographies of power socially coded masculine: patriarchy, tradition, academic and disciplinary discourses, as well as by exclusive spatiality. Groups and individuals, both staff and students, are differently positioned in relation to these social relations, these flows and connections, within the university and the higher education sector more widely. For example, female and minority ethnic staff are significantly under-represented in universities' senior academic and leadership roles (Advance HE 2019; Jarboe 2018) and mature students are clustered in post-1992 universities (Callender and Thompson 2018; Callender et al. 2010). In *Gender(s) at Work*, I apply Massey's power geometry to a consideration of how gender operates as a geography of power positioning female staff in relation to flows and connections within the activity space of the university and the sector more widely.

Progressive places

Massey challenges authoritative Western philosophical tendencies which 'turn space into time and geography into history ... the practice of thinking of space as a surface *over* which journeys are made' (Christophers et al. 2018: 23, original emphasis). She argues for a progressive sense of place in our 'global-local' times', that is, an understanding that what gives a place its specificity are not the boundaries which are drawn around it, nor a singular history, but 'particular constellations of relations, articulated together at a particular locus' (Massey 1994: 5). This acknowledgement of space and place as interconnected networks in flux also generates a sense of place as 'extraverted' – that is, 'where a large proportion of relations, experiences and understanding are actually constructed on a far larger scale than what we happen to define for that moment as the place itself' (1994: 153).

I apply this sense of place as progressive and extraverted to frame the university 'as a point of articulation of multiple social relations, each a node in the wider geography of the academy, pulling on identities and connections beyond their geographical boundaries' (Carruthers Thomas 2018: 40). In the hybrid theorising of *Dimensions of Belonging*, there is a synergy between a progressive sense of place and Brah's concept of 'diaspora space' (1996), both imagining a wider and more flexible territory in which connection and belonging are negotiated. This synergy enables the thesis to move beyond critique and towards a re-imagination of belonging.

Heterogeneity

Heterogeneity is fundamental to Massey's understanding of space as 'a confluence and product of histories, relationships ... the sphere in which distinct trajectories coexist' (Massey 2005: 9). Space is not static, but plural and relational. Expanding on this theme, Massey frequently references her neighbourhood, Kilburn, North London, emphasising its diverse population and everyday global interactions to challenge a sense of a coherent, singular identity. Space, she argues is 'a simultaneity of unfinished, ongoing, "trajectories" or "stories-so-far"' (1994: 5). I mobilise this proposition of heterogeneity in highlighting the diversity of staff and students' lived/living experiences juxtaposed with organisational narratives – that is, the stories universities tell about themselves through corporate literatures, branding and mission statements. This juxtaposition draws attention to spaces between organisational rhetorics of equality and diversity, of student belonging and individuals' lived/living experiences. This in turn unlocks a way of seeing research participants' experiences of the university as structured by geographies of power. The proposition of heterogeneity also influences my approach to the analysis of complex qualitative data. Instead of targeting thematic saturation in my data analysis, I map the university as 'a space of multiple centres experienced in multiple ways' (Carruthers Thomas 2018: 83). This will be addressed in more detail in the penultimate section of the chapter.

Activity space

Massey mobilises these key conceptual building blocks of her social theory – power geometry, a progressive sense of place and heterogeneity – through the heuristic device of 'activity space': 'the spatial network of links and activities, of spatial connections and of locations within which a particular agent operates ... within each activity space is a geography of power' (Massey 2005: 55). Activity space challenges the idea of place as stable and coherent and is a versatile, multi-scalar device, foregrounding relationships of power in space. It frames the university as a spatial network shaped by local geographies of power, but also as a node distinctly positioned in the wider activity space of the higher education sector, a knowledge-based labour market 'which gained (and continues to gain) at least a part of its prestige from the cachet and exclusivity of its spatiality' (Massey 2005: 75). Activity space complements the use of case study methodology, enabling analyses of cases as part of the higher education sector; as singular corporate entities and at the 'ground' level of spatial arrangements and campus geographies.

The multi-scalar character of activity space is demonstrated in Massey's (1996) study of dualistic thinking and the construction of gender in high-technology industry in Cambridge, UK. In the study, Massey conceptualises the science park as 'part of a global network of specialized places of knowledge production (elite; historically largely male)' (2005: 75) and 'a highly specialized envelope of space-time into which the intrusion of other activities and interests is unwanted and limited' (1996: 120). However, 'the home ... both temporally and spatially is porous and in particular it is invaded by the sphere of paid work' (ibid.). The study explores ways in which daily experiences of working in the activity space of the science park reflect a narrative of masculinity as constituting reason, logic and abstract thought and operate in complex territory between 'work' and 'home'. It provides a valuable foundation for a contemporary theorisation of gender, career and workplace experiences in the university in *Gender(s) at Work*.

Critical reflections on social theory and methodology

Spatial storytelling

In congruence with her grounded, activist approach, Massey urged others to 'think of spatiality in a highly active and politically enabling manner' (1993: 142). Applying Massey's spatial concepts to theorisations of the university has led me to develop a methodology I have called 'spatial storytelling', one 'sensitized to the social as inexorably also spatial' (Massey 1993: 80). Spatial storytelling combines two interdependent research instruments – narrative enquiry and visual mapping – in order to elicit participants' singular and particular stories of workplace and career within the social context of the university (Creswell 2007); to capture psychosocial dimensions of the interactions between individual and institution and to uncover and explore spaces between organisational rhetoric and lived/living experience.

Spatial storytelling starts with 'thinking spatially' about the university, building on Massey's concept of power geometry in which social and spatial boundaries define who belongs to and who is excluded from a place. How are spaces of higher education inhabited and by whom? Who is at the margins and what constitutes the spaces between? Thinking spatially about student belonging provides a methodological language with which to articulate dominant and marginal practices of belonging; the ways in which institution and individual interact in uneven territory. Thinking spatially in the context of staff experiences of the university as a workplace, 'emphasises not only the material and metaphorical power structures of the academy, but also a psychosocial sense of gender as a geography of power in terms of peripherality, constraints and power(lessness)' (Carruthers Thomas 2019: 202). Thinking spatially applies a spatial, qualitative lens to organisational structures and power relationships and frames a critique of organisational rhetoric.

My evolving practice of spatial storytelling involves the research instruments narrative enquiry and visual mapping. These are discussed separately but are interdependent in practice; the visual product inextricable from participants' words as they contemplate and complete the task. Massey's understanding of space as a 'simultaneity of stories so far ... places as collections of those stories' (Massey 2005: 130) supports the role of narrative in spatial storytelling. Participants are 'both living their stories in an ongoing experiential text and telling their stories in words as they reflect upon life and explain themselves to others' (Connelly and Clandinin 1990: 3). Narrative enquiry therefore foregrounds the way(s) participants create meaning of their lived experiences of the university, importantly allowing for complexities, ambiguities and silences (Bathmaker 2010). In practice, the *Gender(s) at Work* project used individual interviews of 45–60 minutes in which interviewees gave a 'potted history' of their employment to date, then responded to a common schedule of questions and prompts exploring their experiences of working at the university and in the sector more generally. They were then asked to reflect on their perceptions of the impact, or otherwise, of gender on those experiences. The measure of participant verification and the opportunity to remove or redact information was put in place to ensure anonymity.

Used in conjunction with narrative enquiry, visual mapping challenges the coherence of university spaces and the power of dominant narratives. Massey argues classical maps position 'the observer, themselves unobserved, outside and above the object of the gaze' (Massey 2005: 107). Mapping in its dominant form is problematic in that it gives authority to simplified, selective and bounded representations of space (Carruthers Thomas 2018: 2). But mapping as a research tool has the capacity to disrupt abstraction and neutrality; to unsettle what is taken-for-granted and to recognise the agency of the mapmaker. Rose argues: 'Participant-generated visual materials are particularly helpful in exploring the taken-for-granted things in their research participants' lives ... it gives them distance from what they are usually immersed in and allows them to articulate thoughts and feelings that usually remain implicit' (2014: 27). Both *Gender(s) at Work* and *Dimensions of Belonging* employ mapping as process and product to disrupt the taken-for-granted and make sense of co-existing stories within organisational space.

I first used a visual mapping task for data collection in *Dimensions of Belonging*. In a task entitled *Mapping Belonging*, student participants were provided with a campus map and two different coloured pens. They were invited to mark any places on campus where they felt they 'belonged' and any places where they did not. What emerged across all four case studies was a strikingly limited engagement with the campus beyond the classroom and the library, certainly not with the 'familiars' of contemporary student life: the Students' Union building, halls of residence, bars, the gym. Yet these are the sites in which the dominant narratives of 'student' life' are embedded: 'the student community is stitched together out of these places; it relies on this geography' (Crang 1998: 5). However, 'for many mature part-time undergraduates, empty corridors, distant satellite buildings and empty vending machines are more familiar experiences of institutional spaces' (Carruthers Thomas 2019: 73). Participants' enthusiasm and appreciation for higher level learning were overlaid with discomfort about their perceptions of difference from 'typical' undergraduates, experiencing a lack of 'fit' in communal areas such as libraries, computer stacks and social learning spaces. Instead, they occupied spaces between; those 'less visible to the strategic centre of the university but which ... offer multiple opportunities for connection and attachment' (2019: 76). The students' 'maps of belonging' reveal the university to be a multidimensional landscape of power and inequality within structured social spaces; territories and trajectories of privilege and disadvantage.

In *Gender(s) at Work*, I again use mapping as a research instrument, this time to elicit psychosocial dimensions of space, place and gender in relation to spatial hierarchies and norms of organisational engagement. During the individual interviews, participants were given a sheet of paper containing three shapes: a clear triangle with solid outline, a clear circle with dotted outline and a rectangle shaded blue with solid outline. They were invited to select the shape which best represented the university to them and with a pen, to position themselves in relation to it. Participants were allowed to modify and annotate their chosen shape, or to create their own. The activity was therefore both prescriptive – in using familiar shapes – and flexible. Those selecting the triangle commonly interpreted it as a representation of the university as a hierarchal organisation. The circle's dotted outline was variously interpreted as symbolising porosity, collaboration or escape. The shaded rectangle, the least frequently selected, represented for some the experience of claustrophobia or constraint in their professional roles. Where the participants placed themselves in relation to their chosen shape triggered discussions of peripherality, centrality, career aspirations and power. These discussions formed part of their recorded narrative.

As a research methodology, spatial storytelling results in multiple mappings of the university reflecting Massey's plural and fluid understanding of space. Reading participant narratives and maps through the lens of heterogeneity articulates 'the multidimensionality of gendered and intersectional lived experiences within the contested space of the university' (Carruthers Thomas 2019: 202). The intertwining of narrative and map uncovers spaces between corporate rhetoric and lived experience; for example, the space between a corporate flexible working policy and a female senior manager's negative experience of making use of it in a male-dominated environment. Another example would be multiple instances of sexist language, attitude and practices in a workplace regulated by equality and diversity legislation. An additional example would be mature part-time students' sense of exclusion from large swathes of 'their' university campus labelled 'inclusive'. Spatial storytelling loosens the hold of the binary and uncovers the periphery, the hidden and the contradictory. Viewing the university through the lens of power geometry reveals stories of student persistence under the organisational radar despite organisational othering; of negotiated belonging in peripheral, diasporic spaces, of the continued disadvantage of women in the workplace despite equality and diversity legislation.

The challenges of mapping

There are practical and analytical challenges in the use of mapping as a research tool. As a participant activity it needs careful management. It can be time-consuming and lead to questions of relevance and validity from participants. A large minority of participants across both of my studies assumed that there was a 'right' way to complete the task and/or felt insecure about its visual nature; it certainly took some academic participants out of a verbal/textual comfort zone. Once the mapping data are collected, the challenge shifts to interpretation. I make no claims to be an expert in semantics or visual culture. The visual map is, as I have stated, a constituent element of a spatial storytelling by the participant; it should not be viewed in isolation but alongside and in relation to the participant's commentary. These elements can be contradictory – for example, in *Gender(s) at Work*, a senior manager placed themselves on the periphery of the chosen shape because of a perceived lack of 'fit' with the university's management culture, and a successful mid-career academic placed themselves outside the shape, expressing a sense of powerlessness to change anything about the university. As Massey states: 'loose ends and ongoing stories are real challenges to cartography' (2005: 107).

Concluding remarks

I have applied Massey's socio-spatial concepts, her clear articulation of the relationality of space and power and inherent temporality of space to theorise gender as a geography of power within the university and as part of a hybrid theorising of student belonging. Massey's social theory gives me a syntax with which to interrogate dominant narratives of the academy, to problematise the 'naturalness' of university space, to examine lived experiences and uneven representations of different groups within that space. As this chapter has shown, this has led to the development of a methodology 'sensitized to the social as inexorably also spatial' (Massey 1993: 80), of thinking spatially and spatial storytelling. These have generated new theoretical and methodological spaces between geographical, sociological and psychosocial ways of seeing the university.

I continue to apply Massey's theoretical constructs in new research and practice. *Being Between Binary* (Carruthers Thomas, forthcoming) is a visual critical auto-ethnography, i.e. 'not only a contemplation of the self but also an examination of systems, cultures, discourses and institutions that privilege some and marginalise others' (Lipton and Crimmins 2019: 229). The piece is a form of spatial storytelling, a textual and visual experiment combining map and memoir in the form of a collaged scrapbook. *Being Between Binary* continues the themes of my earlier research into the university: experiences of binaries and geographies; of othering, inequality and opposition but in the context of sexuality and gender. It places Massey's (1993) concept of power geometry into dialogue with the personal and is structured by a creative cartography of Global North and Global South in which individuals and groups are differently positioned in relation to flows of wealth, resources, sexual and gender politics.

Academic audiences are not always inclined to think outside their disciplinary boxes and applying and presenting the work of a theorist closely identified with one discipline to topics and audiences of another can present challenges. Fortunately, the field of critical higher education studies and educational researchers in general, demonstrate a generous attitude to such boundary-crossing. There is also a growing interdisciplinary literature in geographies of education (Gulson and Symes 2017) which addresses a multitude of spatial concerns about higher education, ranging from international student mobility (Brooks 2018), student housing and accommodation (Holton 2016), to remote and rural disparities in higher education options and provision (Steel and Fahy 2011). Massey's own work ranged widely across the sub-disciplines of geography and social science more generally. She framed the concept of power geometry and heuristic device of activity space as critical instruments for all spheres of society, always stressing the importance of leaving openings for something new.

References

Abes, E.S. (2009), 'Theoretical borderlands: Using multiple theoretical perspectives to challenge inequitable power structures in student development theory', *Journal of College Student Development*, 50 (2): 141–156.

Abes, E.S. (2012), 'Constructivist and intersectional interpretations of a lesbian college student's multiple social identities', *Journal of Higher Education*, 83 (2): 186–216.

Advance HE (2019), *Equality in higher education: Statistical report 2018*. Available online: https://www.ecu.ac.uk/publications/equality-higher-education-statistical-report-2018/ (accessed 10 December 2019).

Bathmaker, A.-M. (2010), 'Introduction', in A.-M. Bathmaker and P. Hartnett (eds.), *Exploring Learning, Identity and Power through Life History and Narrative Research*, 1–10, London: Routledge.

Bilimoria, D., O'Neil, D.A., Hopkins, M.M. and Murphy, V. (2010), 'Gender in the management education classroom: A collaborative learning journey', *Journal of Management Education*, 34 (6): 848–873.

Bourdieu, P. (1988), *Homo Academicus*, trans. P. Collier, Cambridge: Polity Press.

Bourdieu, P. (1990), *The Logic of Practice*, trans. R. Nice, Cambridge: Polity Press.

Brah, A. (1996), *Cartographies of Diaspora: Contesting Identities*, London: Routledge.

Brooks, R. (2018), 'Higher education mobilities: A cross-national European comparison', *Geoforum*, 93: 87–96.

Callender, C. and Thompson, J. (2018), *The Lost Part-timers: The Decline of Part-time Undergraduate Higher Education in England*, London: Sutton Trust.

Callender, C., Hopkin, R. and Wilkinson, D. (2010), *Futuretrack: Part-time Students Career Decision-making and Career Development of Part-time Higher Education Students*, Manchester: HECSU.

Carruthers Thomas, K. (2018), *Rethinking Student Belonging in Higher Education: From Bourdieu to Borderlands*, London: Routledge.

Carruthers Thomas, K. (2019), 'Genders at work: Gender as a geography of power', in G. Crimmins (ed.), *Strategies for Resisting Sexism in the Academy: Higher Education, Gender and Intersectionality*, 187–206, London: Palgrave Macmillan.

Christophers, B., Lave, R., Peck, J. and Werner, M. (2018), *Doreen Massey: A Reader*, Newcastle upon Tyne: Agenda Publishing.

Connelly, M. and Clandinin, D.J. (1990), 'Stories of experience and narrative inquiry', *Educational Researcher*, 19 (5): 2–14.

Crang, M. (1998), *Cultural Geography*, London: Routledge.

Creswell, J.W. (2007), *Qualitative Inquiry and Research Design: Choosing among Five Approaches*, Thousand Oaks, CA: Sage.

Gulson, K. and Symes, C. (2017), 'Making moves: Theorizations of education and mobility', *Critical Studies in Education*, 58 (2): 125–130.

Hall, S., Massey, D. and Rustin, M. (eds.) (2015), *After Neoliberalism? The Kilburn Manifesto*, London: Lawrence & Wishart.

Harvey, D. (1989), *The Condition of Postmodernity: An Enquiry into the Origins of Cultural Change*, Oxford. Blackwell.

Holton, M. (2016), 'The geographies of UK university halls of residence: Examining students' embodiment of social capital', *Children's Geographies*, 14 (1): 63–76.

Jarboe, N. (2018), *Women Count: Leaders in Higher Education 2018*, London: WomenCount.

Lipton, B. and Crimmins, G. (2019), 'Recipes on arts-based research practice as a form of feminist resistance', in G. Crimmins (ed.), *Strategies for Resisting Sexism in the Academy: Higher Education, Gender and Intersectionality*, 187–206, London: Palgrave Macmillan.

Massey, D. (1988), 'Uneven development: Social change and spatial divisions of labour', in D. Massey and J. Allen (eds.), *Uneven Development: Cities and Regions in Transition*, 250–276, London: Hodder & Stoughton.

Massey, D. (1992), 'A place called home?', *New Formations*, 17: 3–15.

Massey, D. (1993), 'Power-geometry and a progressive sense of place', in J. Bird, B. Curtis, T. Putnam, G. Robertson and L. Tuckner (eds.), *Mapping the Futures: Local Cultures, Global Chance*, 59–69, Abingdon: Routledge.

Massey, D. (1994), *Space, Place and Gender*, Cambridge: Polity Press.

Massey, D. (1996), 'Masculinity, dualisms and high technology', in N. Duncan (ed.), *BodySpace: Destabilizing Geographies of Gender and Sexuality*, 109–126, London: Routledge.

Massey, D. (2005), *For Space*, London: Sage.

Massey, D. (2007), *World City*, Cambridge: Polity Press.

Massey, D. and Jess, P. (1995), *A Place in the World? Places, Cultures and Globalisation*, Oxford: Oxford University Press.

McDowell, L. (1999), *Gender, Identity and Place: Understanding Feminist Geographies*, Cambridge: Polity Press.

McDowell, L. and Massey, D. (1984), 'A woman's place', in D. Massey and J. Allen (eds.), *Geography Matters! A Reader*, 128–147, Cambridge: Cambridge University Press.

Rose, G. (2014), 'On the relation between "visual research methods" and contemporary visual culture', *The Sociological Review*, 62 (1): 24–46.

Soja, E. (1989), *Postmodern Geographies: The Reassertion of Space in Critical Social Theory*, London: Verso.

Steel, N. and Fahy. P.J. (2011), 'Attracting, preparing, and retaining under-represented populations in rural and remote Alberta-North communities', *International Review of Research in Open and Distance Learning*, 12 (4): 35–53.

Valentine, G. (2008), 'Living with difference: Reflections on geographies of encounter', *Progress in Human Geography*, 32 (3): 323–337.

Wainwright, H. (2018), 'Epilogue: "How we will miss that chuckle": my friend, Doreen Massey', in M. Werner, R. Lave, J. Peck and B. Christophers (eds.), *Doreen Massey: Critical Dialogues*, Newcastle upon Tyne: Agenda Publishing.

10

On Epistemonormativity: From Epistemic Injustices to Feminist Academic Caringzenship[1,2]

Luísa Winter Pereira[3]

Introduction, or critical reflections on social theory and methodology

Since 1985[4] Gayatry Chakravorty Spivak has been asking if it is possible for the subaltern to speak. A lot has been debated about this text that is fundamental in post-colonial reflection. The most recent translation into Portuguese, by Antonio Sousa Ribeiro (Spivak, forthcoming), innovates both by understanding the subaltern as a woman and by deepening the meaning of the word *speak* as the possibility of taking the floor.

The subaltern is necessarily defined by her position as a colonised subjectivity and as a woman: '[i]f, in the context of colonial production, the subaltern has no history and cannot speak, the subaltern as female is even more deeply in shadow' (Spivak 1988: 287–288). The position occupied by the subaltern in hegemonic power relations is such that her silencing occurs from her non-existence in conditions of enunciation to be listened to. Hence, the term *speak* – understood simply as 'to say words, to use the voice, or to have a conversation with someone'[5] – is insufficient. Because the subaltern speaks. The problem lies in the fact that the subaltern's *speak-speech* is heard by the hegemonic discourse through its tools. To be heard in this sense, without being understood, is equivalent to silence. And this is what generates the silencing of the subaltern. Therefore, Spivak's speak-speech goes beyond simple speaking-speeching: it is *taking the floor*, in the sense of demanding recognition of the voice and experience of the subaltern, so that she can intervene in the scene of communication and be attentively listened to and comprehended.

Thus, Spivak claims a *room of one's own* in the universe of discourse. In a dialogue with Virginia Woolf and her famous text (1929), Spivak, in the essay *Collectivities* (2003), discusses which voices are contemplated in the figure of *we* and which are excluded from it. The Indian author understands that Woolf, at first, tries to construct her text through the collectivity, but then formulates it through the *self*, because the only possible voice would be that in the very first person singular. And 'by speaking in her own person, Woolf solicits the risk of being read' (Spivak 2003: 42).

While Woolf risks being read, Spivak's subaltern risks being listened to. And she does so with her own body, because the only experience the subaltern can have is the one of the body itself. To be able to speak of and from the body, it is first necessary to *situate* it. And the subaltern's body, situated and *speechable*, can be wounded.[6]

This chapter is dedicated to critical reflections in the 'knowledge-production factory' (Spivak 2010) that is the Westernised academy. Therefore, I bring Spivak's much-debated question to this sphere: *can the subaltern produce knowledge?* The normativity that exists in the construction and production of knowledge (what I call *epistemonormativity*) offers the space of speak-speech to the subaltern only through testimony, which will be heard through the tools of hegemonic discourse so that it can formulate knowledge and the subaltern can thus speak. If her speech is silenced, she can only testify of her own experience. She cannot produce knowledge; she can only testify. As a subaltern, I offer my testimony, that is, my metatheory presented in the hidden form of testimony. I situate myself through language.

On testimony. My grandmother's tongue is German, and my mother tongue is Portuguese. I am a Latin American woman living in Europe. I am white in Brazil, racialised in the Iberian Peninsula. I am a Brazilian who speaks German at home, who studies in English, who has written a master's dissertation in Spanish and is writing a PhD thesis in Brazilian-Portuguese, in Portugal. But I continue to be *una otra*, *uma extrangeira*, even if my message is the same in the Rio Uruguai or in the Rio Tejo. And as a foreigner who speaks a non-mother tongue, *uma língua sem infância*, as Emine Sevgi Özdamar[7] would tell us, to what extent is the way I say what I say taken seriously? Here we have two possible Luísas speaking in one other tongue. It remains for us to ask for the person who exercises the interlocution. If these two Luísas say X, how is X received by a person from London or São Paulo? What is the social imaginary that will be activated in the person who receives the message when it actually reaches the brain?

What I have just raised could become a mere anecdote when asking for an address or a cake in the bakery. It is not that simple. We can think of a judicial process. Imagine that I am accused of a crime punishable by several years in prison. Suppose I am not Brazilian speaking 'inglés con un "accent"'(Anzaldúa 2007: 75–76), but Iranian who speaks English with a Persian accent. What social imaginary will be produced in the head of the judge? This question will automatically be answered with a *justice is impartial*. And yes, this is what the majority of Western constitutions state. But if the so-called legal realism taught us something (Ross 1958), it is that in formal terms justice is impartial because legal norms are assumed to be neutral, but the interpretation and application of the norms are loaded with emotions, history, ideology, to name only three elements that interfere in that impartiality. Even how the coffee of the morning suits the judge also determines the outcome of the sentence. Clearly, *aesthetics* in law does matter. And accent and tongue are also aesthetic components, such as skin colour. Just think about what happened in the novel *To Kill a Mockingbird* by Harper Lee (1960).

Where do I want to go with these stories of voices, testimonies, tongues and accents? In the same sense of Spivak (1985, 1988, 1999, 2010, forthcoming), this text is an attempt to expose the mechanisms of silencing the subaltern and suggest some strategies of resistance so that the subaltern can effectively take the floor. Higher education policies, like general public policies, have equity as their ultimate objective. What is necessary to combat is: the inequality of material means of life and the discrimination produced by the very institution. For this reason, it is necessary to analyse higher education itself in order to identify what *epistemic injustices* it causes, thus knowing from where it is possible to think of solutions.

This chapter is concerned with critical reflections on social theory and methodology and as such it has to be taken as a kind of methodology on epistemology, as a metatheory. By metatheory I mean a theory about theory, that is, to think about the material conditions of construction of my academic subjectivity, as ontological conditions of Luísa's academic subalternity. Because I can only speak from my situatedness. It is from this position that I perform the introspection in the Westernised academic institution. With this inward-looking, towards the umbilicus of this university, I seek a way to perceive the inequalities and discriminations that exist in its structure.

That is why this chapter is focused on several ideas that constitute my hybrid reading cabinet: epistemic injustice, *epistemonormativity*, situated knowledge, performativity and vulnerability, and *academic caringzenship*.[8] I say hybrid reading cabinet because it presents my material conditions for writing: limited, precarious and inspired by several reflections. That is why it is not a museum in which all the pieces of knowledge can be exhibited to form a *status quaestionis*, as I have been trained by the academy. As Maria do Mar Pereira (2017: 16) points out, a conventional bibliographic review implies demonstrating oneself as 'the well-read researcher who has considered relevant texts and identified a gap in the literature and/or significant problems in others' analyses, and so sets out to correct them or fill the gaps through their own project'. Therefore, it is not about doing a technical exercise of compilation and gloss that promotes individuality, hierarchy and competitiveness in the production of knowledge, but a political exercise of ordination and situation of my reading tools in an attempt to share from and to where I speak. This hybrid reading cabinet leads us to understand the material inequalities and institutional discriminations that are experienced in and produced by academia.

From the hybrid reading cabinet I propose a toolbox of research instruments with which to read the problems of the academy. A way to make a diagnosis based on concepts: the path I call *academic caringzenship* – a community, some bonds, a friendship– that avoids the violence of the academy itself, its epistemonormativity and its epistemic injustices.

Epistemic injustice

Miranda Fricker (2007) has theorised the first of the concepts that will serve as my guide in this journey. *Epistemic injustice* occurs when the subject's ability to transmit knowledge is nullified.

In her book, Fricker analyses two types of injustice in knowledge from socially situated contexts: (1) testimonial injustice and (2) hermeneutical injustice. The first injustice 'occurs when prejudice causes a hearer to give a deflated level of credibility to a speaker's word' (Fricker 2007: 1). The second injustice, the hermeneutical one, operates at a prior stage: 'when a gap in collective interpretive resources puts someone at an unfair disadvantage when it comes to making sense of their social experiences' (2007: 1). Two examples are given: when the police do not believe a person's testimony because it is a black person (testimonial injustice) and when a person is a victim of sexual harassment in a context where that category does not (yet) exist (hermeneutical injustice).

Fricker departs from a concept of power as identity power to analyse testimonial injustice. By this type of power she understands as 'a form of social power which is directly dependent upon shared social-imaginative conceptions of the social identities of those implicated in the particular operation of power'

(2007: 4). This kind of social power requires both practical social coordination and the social coordination of the imagination. Gender, as an example, is a type of identity power in that a set of stereotypes will be activated in the discursive exchange to give greater (excess) or less (deficit) credibility to the message. Obviously, only the credibility deficit can be embedded in the injustice.

In testimonial injustice as a credibility deficit, this power is nourished by *identity prejudices*, by which 'the injustice that a speaker suffers in receiving deflated credibility from the hearer owing to identity prejudice on the hearer's part' (Fricker 2007: 4). But this prejudice must be persistent and systemic. Consider the example of the police officer with the black person or of a language spoken with an accent other than that hegemonic one in a certain place. What causes this identity prejudice is an *identity prejudicial credibility deficit*: damage to one's own condition as a subject of knowledge, to human dignity (2007: 44).

Others are derived from this primary epistemic wrong. In the example of the black person whose testimony is not believed by the authorities, this attack on their dignity is a subject of knowledge but also results in a fine, years of imprisonment or death by a gun that is fired before uttering a word. Alongside this practical wrong, we also find another secondary wrong of an epistemic nature:

> the recipient of a one-off testimonial injustice may lose confidence in his belief, or in his justification for it, so that he ceases to satisfy the conditions for knowledge; or, alternatively, someone with a background experience of persistent testimonial injustice may lose confidence in her general intellectual abilities to such an extent that she is genuinely hindered in her educational or other intellectual development.
>
> Fricker 2007: 47–48

For this reason, epistemic injustice acquires the proportions of oppression when we encounter 'a culture in which some groups are separated off from that aspect of personhood by the experience of repeated exclusions from the spread of knowledge' (Fricker 2007: 58–59).

In the hermeneutical injustice there is a gap in the shared pool of social interpretation, that is, 'a gap in collective hermeneutical resources ... where it is no accident that the cognitive disadvantage created by this gap impinges unequally on different social groups' (Fricker 2007: 6). This lacuna implies that in the hermeneutical injustice there is no direct implication of an agent but of the collective hermeneutical resources. It is unlike what occurs in the testimonial injustice in which there is a direct action of the subject, and, therefore, the damage is produced from individual to individual (which provokes the analysis of the culpability or not of the subject with whom the interlocution is carried out).

In the example of harassment, precisely because of this conceptual gap, the person harassed (in a context where this concept does not exist) would not be able to understand their own experience, '[h]er hermeneutical disadvantage renders her unable to make sense of her ongoing mistreatment, and this in turn prevents her from protesting it, let alone securing effective measures to stop it' (Fricker 2007: 151). The unequal participation in the 'practices through which social meanings are generated' (2007: 6) provokes *hermeneutical marginalisation*. And the harm that is produced from it is a *situated hermeneutical inequality* (2007: 7). The primary harm 'concerns exclusion from the pooling of knowledge owing to identity prejudice on the part of the hearer' (2007: 162), which can lead not only to a disadvantage, but also to an identity construction contrary to their own interests.

Considering this framework of epistemic injustice, in the context of research in feminist lenses, it would be necessary to analyse what role identity prejudices play and the gaps in the collective hermeneutical resources with respect to women as subjects of knowledge. Although it is true that after the Second World War and the Declaration of Human Rights of 1948, legal systems incorporate (gradually) precepts related to formal equality between men and women, which, in some measure, could alleviate or reduce the hermeneutical injustice in the production of knowledge by women, testimonial injustice has worsened since women have been able to access the university not only as learners but also as lecturers.

The rupture with the androcentric monopoly of the production of knowledge has incorporated into the academy the prejudices that have been constructed about women, in such a way that their testimony has a credibility deficit. Although this monopoly has been broken (and this must be taken with caution), there are still spaces where both types of injustice – testimonial and hermeneutical – go hand in hand.

Epistemonormativity

The question here is why epistemic injustices remain. Which brings me to the second of the concepts. Judith Butler's reflections on sex-gender can help in this regard. The term *heterosexual matrix* was raised as a 'grid of culture intelligibility through which bodies, genders, and desires are naturalized' (Butler 1990: 292). What this means is that there is a hegemonic normative model of gender intelligibility that demands coherence in the bodies by means of the stability of a single sex expressed in a single stable gender (masculine = man; feminine = woman), 'that is oppositionally and hierarchically defined through the compulsory practice of heterosexuality' (Butler 1990: 282). Anatomical sex, gender, desire and sexual practices must be united in a coherent and stable way.

It is a question of constructing an acceptable identitarian bodily unit, intelligible, through constant control in the name of a hypothetical common good. Those who escape from the heterosexual matrix are those in which there is no coherence and stability. Therefore, the idea of normative code is important here. The heterosexual matrix is a regulatory discourse that organises the human being around sex, gender, desire and sexual practices. The code naturalises the subject who complies with its norms. And just as with legal codes, the heterosexual matrix also has a preventive function and a sanctioning function to construct (perform) bodily reality as a universal and natural reality, despite being an artificial imposition. The heterosexual matrix works in such a way that it implies that it reproduces a reality external to it with which it would correspond (naturalness; truth as correspondence), although it actually produces that reality (it corresponds to itself).

The academy works in the same way. Epistemic injustice, in this case, would refer to a matrix of intelligibility within the university. A normative set, a hegemonic discursive/epistemic model of intelligibility of knowledge, a grid – to paraphrase Butler – of academic intelligibility through which the production of knowledge is naturalised. Just as there is a heteronormativity or a heterosexual matrix as a normative code that prescribes coherence between sex, gender, desire and practices, in the university we find what I like to refer to as the neologism *epistemonormativity* or *matrix of academic intelligibility* as a normative code that prescribes coherence in the production of knowledge. A regulatory framework of academic identity that separates legality and illegality in the production of knowledge. Those who do not adjust to the patterns of academic production are situated in illegality and the sanctions of the epistemonormative code fall on them.[9]

Situated knowledge

The idea of 'situated knowledges' belongs to Donna Haraway (1988). Before discussing it, I shall briefly consider Sandra Harding's introduction to *Feminism and Methodology*, entitled 'Is there a feminist method?' (1987). The first thing this text raises is the distinction between method as a technique for gathering information, methodology as theories and analysis of research procedures, and epistemology as questions related to the theory of knowledge or to strategies for justifying knowledge (Harding 1987: 2). It is the latter on which I am interested in reflecting in this chapter: 'who can be a "knower" (can women?); what tests beliefs must pass in order to be legitimated as knowledge (only tests against men's experiences and observations?); what kind of things can be known (can "subjective truths" count as knowledge?)' (Harding 1987: 3). In short, epistemologies have become strategies to justify certain beliefs, from divine to masculine authority. Therefore, it is precisely these beliefs that must be put forward in order to construct a different epistemology in which epistemic injustices disappear. It is useless *to add* women as object of study if there are not changes in the structures of knowledge and its production (Harding 1987: 3–5). Concerning the method and the methodology in the writing process of this chapter: my own experience as testimony is information by means of which I construct one theory or another, one which I pair with other theories that, paraphrasing Michel Foucault (1980: 53–54), I use, I deform, I make them groan and protest, I take them to the limit.

One of the first tasks in building a knowledge that escapes epistemonormativity and epistemic injustices is to get rid of the idea of neutrality. Sciences are not neutral, because they have historically been translated into masculine experience: '[i]t has unconsciously followed a "logic of discovery" which we could formulate in the following way: [a]sk only those questions about nature and social life which (white, Western, bourgeois) men want answered' (Harding 1987: 6). Hence, given this supposed neutrality or objectivity, this research bets on subjectivity, on the personal experience told through testimony in which my condition of subaltern intersects issues of gender, race and class.

Haraway will reproach Harding's *feminist standpoint* for its essentialism and dualism. First, because Harding seems to understand that there is only *one experience of women*, a certain closed conception. Moreover, Harding also opposes this experience of women to the experience of men, also as if it were a monolithic essence (Haraway 1988, 1990). Haraway argues that 'feminist objectivity means quite simply *situated knowledge*' (1988: 581). It is not only a question of recognising the historical and social character of knowledge, but also of answering the question of why or how some conceptions are accepted for the development of research as legitimately objective. Hence, the place from which one departs, from one's own subjectivity, becomes relevant. It is an openly political and ethical positioning with respect to epistemology, to how and from where we observe. It is not possible to look from anywhere (what would be the scientific utopia). That is why Haraway claims 'only partial perspective promises objective vision ... Feminist objectivity is about limited location and situated knowledge, not about transcendence and splitting of subject and object. It allows us to become answerable for what we learn how to see' (Haraway 1988: 583).

That partial perspective starts from the occupation of a place: '[p]ositioning is, therefore, the key practice in grounding knowledge organized around the imagery of vision, and much Western scientific and philosophic discourse is organized in this way. Positioning implies responsibility for our enabling practices' (Haraway 1988: 587). That is why feminist responsibility requires a knowledge linked

> to resonance, not to dichotomy. Gender is a field of structured and structuring difference, in which the tones of extreme localization, of the intimately personal and individualized body, vibrate in the same field with global high-tension emissions. Feminist embodiment, then, is not about fixed location in a reified body, female or otherwise, but about nodes in fields, inflections in orientations, and responsibility for difference in material-semiotic fields of meaning.
>
> Haraway 1988: 588

Haraway's own partial perspective of situated knowledge allows for unexpected connections and openings. Only by being in a particular place can one have a wider vision. From the situated knowledge, the subjects that are studied are not understood as objects, but as agents in the production of knowledge (Haraway 1988: 592).

Therefore, partial perspective on such situated knowledge positions me on how to approach this research. If I began this chapter stating that I am a Brazilian who speaks English with an accent, I did it to position my situated knowledge on the *border*. And it is on the border where the author of this chapter stands. This is my standpoint, my situated knowledge, my 'consciousness of the Borderlands' (Anzaldúa 2007: 99).

Performativity and vulnerability

Although from her first writings Butler has been exploring the concept of performativity in relation to the construction of gender and sex, it is in her book *Excitable Speech: A Politics of the Performative* where she elaborates the idea. This is where she highlights how acts of speech hurt. Our vulnerability also occurs in language (Butler 1997a). Words hurt because we need language to constitute ourselves.

Butler maintains the thesis that speech is always *excitable*, meaning, 'speech is always in some ways out of our control' (Butler 1997a: 15). Performativity refers to the ability of words to produce changes in material reality. Hence, performative emissions are not susceptible to truth or falsity, but are characterised by their effectiveness. This is the illocutionary force: when it is named, it is instituted (Butler 1997b).

But this force is also manifested in or by the body, which means that it has a bodily dimension. It should not be overlooked that the body is the vehicle of speech, the space of verbalisation. So much so that the act of speech of the body has a double action: that of the utterance itself and the action of the body. And speaking in itself is a bodily act. As Butler (1997a) stresses, hate speech not only produces a wound in the identity of the person but also in their body.

From the relationship between interlocutors, we move on to what constitutes us as living beings: our vulnerability. Butler (2004: 20) points out that 'each of us is constituted politically in part by virtue of the social vulnerability of our bodies'. What does *vulnerability* mean? She addresses it in *Frames of War* (2009) and in *Precarious Life* (2004). She suggests thinking about a new body ontology through the resignification of precariousness or vulnerability, given that '[t]he "being" of the body to which this ontology refers is one that is always given over to others, to norms, to social and political organizations that have developed historically in order to maximize precariousness for some and minimize precariousness for others' (Butler 2009: 2–3). The university as an institution does not escape from this logic of maximisation or minimisation of precariousness.

Butler proposes two terms: *precariousness* and *precarity*. The first moves within the framework of existence as a shared condition of human life. Precariousness is what places us in relation, dependent to survive, because it 'implies living socially, that is, the fact that one's life is always in some sense in the hands of the other' (Butler 2009: 14). Hence, precariousness coincides with the moment of birth. This, the birth, is our first precarious fact inasmuch as the survival of the newborn person depends on a 'social network of hands' (2009: 14). In short, precariousness is a generalised condition in which it is necessary to build living conditions that make us live a liveable life and also make us live a grievable life.

The second of the terms, precarity, moves in the field of politics. Butler defines it as 'that politically induced condition in which certain populations suffer from failing social and economic networks of support and become differentially exposed to injury, violence, and death' (2009: 25). Precarity is distributed differently. The paradox of precarity is that those who are affected by violence are forced to turn to the same state (or any other institution, such as the university) against those who need protection (2009: 26).

To sum up, if precariousness is a shared condition that calls into question the ontology of individualism (Butler 2009), precarity is the politically induced condition that produces an unequal exposure according to the distribution of the material conditions of life. Nevertheless, Butler notes that '[t]he recognition of shared precariousness introduces strong normative commitments of equality and invites a more robust universalizing of rights that seeks to address basic human needs for food, shelter, and other conditions for persisting and flourishing' (2009: 28–29). The question is, therefore, why certain lives endure more precarity. The solution lies in 'alliance focused on opposition to state violence and its capacity to produce, exploit, and distribute precarity for the purposes of profit and territorial defense' (2009: 32). It is necessary to remember that there are no invulnerable bodies.

Moving into public space. In her book *Notes Toward a Performative Theory of Assembly* (2015), Butler proposes the struggle that bodies in alliance can carry out. Specifically, she refers to the movements that have taken place since the Arab springs, passing through 15M in Spain and Occupy Wall Street in the United States. In the unexpectedly appearing assemblies, the bodies meet and talk, putting political signifiers into play (Butler 2015). In these spaces there is a performativity embodied in the fact of appearing in public, thus resignifying the category of *people* that is traditionally restricted to certain bodies in certain spaces. Hence, the joint action of the bodies that occupy the public space supposes a political questioning from the shared precariousness: 'the bodies assembled *say* we are not disposable, even if they stand silently. This expressive possibility is part of a plural and embodied performativity that we have to understand as marked by dependency and resistance' (Butler 2015: 18).

What Butler thus proposes is that bodies gather in assembly around shared vulnerabilities through performative practices. Performativity can produce wounds or it can lead to a resignification of the political field. The epistemic injustice of which I have already spoken produces a wound in its double aspect of producing damage in the identity as in the body. But performativity may also lead us to resignify the political field of academia from where epistemic injustice occurs: with the development of a model in which bodies gather around *caringzenship*.

Academic caringzenship

Would it be possible, therefore, to seek other routes that escape epistemonormativity and epistemic injustices in the university context? I imagine a path that is not hegemonic, perhaps stony, but always cosy, which is the model of care and caring. Maybe what happens within academic safe zones – paraphrasing Mary Louise Pratt (1991) – is a way of becoming university citizens from what I call *academic caringzenship*[10], thus opening fissures in the neoliberal academic system.

A path close to the one I am pursuing here is what the Great Lakes Feminist Geography Collective has called *Slow Scholarship* (Mountz et al. 2015). Both they and I started from a common ground with Sarah Ahmed's (2014) 'selfcare as warfare'. We distance ourselves on how to walk it, because here it will be performed with Butler's (2009) ideas of precariousness and precarity. Precariousness is shared by all the people who intend to make an academic career. In a way, the first academic act is the doctoral thesis, the moment in which we are formally *made* and *born* as academics. Precarity is not shared. There is an unequal distribution, a political induction of precarity, that is, of a situation of greater precariousness.

To elaborate on this point, I bring here an anecdote by Rosalind Gill on the situation of neoliberal academia in the UK in the 2000s:

> [o]ne female lecturer told me: 'I was at breaking point. I went to see my mentor to complain about my workload. I mean, I'm really, really conscientious – you know that – and my mentor just said: "welcome to modern academia. We're all working these crazy hours. I'm sorry to be blunt, but you know what you have to do: if it's too hot, get out the kitchen"'.
>
> Gill 2009: 233

If it's too hot, get out the kitchen, as simple as the title of a bad comedy from the 1980s. The academy's kitchen seems too hot for all the academics, especially women. The promoters of the *Slow Scholarship* manifesto denounced that 'the effects of the neoliberal university are written in the body' (Mountz et al. 2015: 1245). Just think of the symptoms: stress, exhaustion, overloads, insomnia, anxiety, irritability, obesity, shame, pain, guilt, impotence, fatigue, uncertainty, insecurity, frustration, burn-out, feeling out of place, fear of exposure, life/work imbalance (Gill 2009; Cielemcka and Revelles-Benavente 2017; Rogowska-Stangret 2017). All of these *affective embodied experiences* (Gill 2009) are common to academics. Although ordinary, everyday and common, they remain hidden in the neoliberal academy.

These symptoms, which profoundly affect and impact our lives, are not often spoken of in academy. If they are not verbalised, they *do not exist*. Or, when they exist – that is, when they are named – they are treated as individual experiences and not as structural characteristics of the contemporary university. Not being taken as a common problem, but merely individual, what happens is that the experiences of the academics 'are often overlooked or deemed insignificant' (Mountz et al. 2015: 1239). As in the anecdote Gill tells us, the *taken for granted backdrop* (2009: 229) is the institutional context necessary for the production of neoliberal academic knowledge.

The somatisation we observe in the academic bodies cannot be seen as side effects, as the neoliberal university tries to convince us. Anxiety, frustration or fatigue when it comes to carrying out the tasks of the university are not collateral damage that, by bad luck, a specific individual suffers, as opposed to others who, fortunately, escape from suffering them. It is not an individual fact, but a pretension of the university to pass for individual what is a structural element, one more facet of the institutional violence that leads to epistemic injustice. Epistemonormativity not only establishes what and how much work must be done in order to accomplish a legitimate investigation, but also what body one must have in order to resist damages or effects. In Gill's words:

> [t]he 'kitchen' of academia is, it would seem, too hot for almost everyone, but this has not resulted in collective action to turn down the heat, but instead to an overheated competitive atmosphere in which acts of kindness, generosity and solidarity often seem to continue only in spite of, rather than because of, the governance of universities ... This is a collective, structural problem that is a direct result of workloads which leave many people with no 'slack' to take on anything beyond that which is directly required of them.
>
> 2009: 236

Here we are dealing with emotions that the academy relegates to the realm of the merely individual. In order to confront this idea, Butler stated (2009) that the solution resides in weaving alliances that focus on opposition to the epistemic injustice of the university as an institution and its capacity to produce, exploit and distribute from the top down precarity for its own benefit. These alliances lead us to the idea of communities of care and caring. One of the possibilities that has become real in recent decades of the neoliberal university are the spaces built as safe zones[11] that make possible a *friendship* among academics.

In this chapter, I have tried to raise the need to build a community of care from a feminist perspective that protects us and empowers us in the face of the epistemic injustices we suffer in academy. If what characterises us as living bodies is our vulnerability and the need of the others to survive, care must be placed as the central axis. Through 'sharing concerns and vulnerabilities' (Rogowska-Stangret 2017), it is possible to deal collectively with the embodied experiences from the acceptance, understanding, respect for bodily needs and care can become a practice of resistance. Going from individual isolation and shame to feminist academic praxis (Cielemcka and Revelles-Benavente 2017), through self-care and care of others, to build bridges and narrow bonds in order to create communities of care and caring.

Concluding remarks: From academic citizenship to academic caringzenship

The daily practice of the neoliberal university consists of positioning ourselves as individual and competitive beings in order to achieve a 'full academic citizenship' (Gill 2009: 241). But not everybody can effectively become academic citizens. The model of academic citizenship is a violently exclusionary model that forces us to reproduce epistemonormativity or to deny subjectivity in case of epistemic injustice. Therefore, it is necessary to sow and cultivate another model. The performative seeds that I have proposed using are seeds of care and caring: moving from academic citizenship to *academic caringzenship*. More than a simple change in some letters, the expression implies situating the axis not in the solitary path, but in shared vulnerability that leads to a collective performative act.

The epistemic justice that Fricker tries to construct is based on the diagnosis of epistemic injustice, which in turn produces epistemic injustices. And denouncing Fricker for reproducing epistemic injustices also means exposing myself to a position to be criticised: in the end, I have also reproduced epistemic injustices by producing a North-North dialogue in this chapter. My hybrid reading cabinet, as explained above, is limited, but also adapted, so that the system of knowledge production located in the global north can accept me as just another academic. In this sense, my voice can be heard, even if it is through hegemonic tools. Obviously, as a subject of the epistemic south, there are epistemologies of the south that question me and place me better than those of the north. But those are reflections for discussions in future writings.

What I have done in this chapter is to raise a *meta epistemic justice*. It would be justice over epistemic justice, as well as justice over the epistemology that tries to do epistemic justice. As an initiatory part of implementing that meta epistemic justice, I inform you that the opening question of the chapter is tricky. Because if we ask ourselves if the subaltern can produce knowledge, we ask ourselves if the subaltern can be(come) epistemonormative. The model of meta epistemic justice does not seek to substitute one epistemonormativity for another, but to recognise the epistemic structures of power and overcome them. There is no intention of reproducing epistemonormativity. The question would then be whether the subaltern can produce another way of understanding epistemology, another way of understanding academy, in order to create another academic space, where it is possible for us to (co-)inhabit, with care at the centre. Therefore: *can the subaltern produce another knowledge, different from that of the hegemonic academy, and be recognised as a subject to dialogue and intervene in the scene of communication?*

Notes

1   A first version of this text was presented as part of my master's dissertation conducted between the Universities of Granada (Spain) and Łódź (Poland).
2   I would like to thank Daniel J. García López for the ongoing conversation we had throughout the various stages of the writing of this work. This chapter was shaped by seminars and conversations with colleagues at the Centre for Social Studies of the University of Coimbra and at the Institute of Women's and Gender Studies of the University of Granada. I greatly appreciate the suggestions made by Antonio Sousa Ribeiro and hope to do justice to the comments received.
3   Doctoral student in Gender Studies at the University of Granada (Spain) and in Post-colonial Studies at the University of Coimbra (Portugal). As a geoepistemic migrant, I am writing my PhD thesis amid precarious work and terrific academic enthusiasm. luisa.w.pereira@gmail.com.
4   Spivak 1985; Spivak 1988; Spivak 1999; Spivak 2010.
5   Cambridge Dictionary definition.
6   The tragic case of Bhubaneswari Bhaduri's suicide as 'the figure who wrote with her own body' (Spivak, forthcoming) is quite illustrative.
7   'In the foreign language, words have no childhood' (Özdamar 1994: 54).
8   Both approachs – *epistemonormativity* and *academic caringzenship* – will be developed throughout the chapter.
9   An illustrative historical example: the epistemonormativity points out that women are biologically inferior to men so they cannot have access to the university. If a woman tried to get into university, she would automatically be excluded because that administrative rule would reproduce what biology imposes. Such is the intelligibility matrix. However, what is really happening is that first, there is the administrative

rule that prohibits women from entering universities that produces (does not reproduce) the biological norm according to which women are inferior.

10 In Spanish, *cuidadanía* is a term derived from the untranslatable game of words involving ciudadanía (citizenship) and c*uidadanía* (caringzenship, a mix of cuidar – to care – and ciudadanía). It comes from an experience that was lived in Madrid by the feminist group *Precarias a la Deriva* (2004). They were a community that resignified the concept of care as the starting point for a different logic of government, in which the relationship with the other was fundamental.

11 I think of university institutes and departments of feminist and gender studies, for example, and of the activities carried out by the Centre for Social Studies of the University of Coimbra – as a space in which new epistemologies are practised – as is the case of the Popular University of Social Movements.

References

Ahmed, S. (2014), 'Selfcare as Warfare', *Feministkilljoys*, 24 August. Available online: https://feministkilljoys.com/2014/08/25/selfcare-as-warfare/ (accessed 30 December 2019).

Anzaldúa, G. (2007), *Borderlands/La Frontera*, San Francisco, CA: Aunt Lute Books.

Butler, J. (1990), *Gender Trouble. Feminism and the Subversion of Identity*, New York: Routledge.

Butler, J. (1997a), *Excitable Speech: A Politics of the Performative*, New York: Routledge.

Butler, J. (1997b), *The Psychic Life of Power. Theories in Subjection*, Stanford, CA: Stanford University Press.

Butler, J. (2004), *Precarious Life: The Powers of Mourning and Violence*, New York: Verso.

Butler, J. (2009), *Frames of War: When is Life Grievable?*, New York: Verso.

Butler, J. (2015), *Notes Toward a Performative Theory of Assembly*, Cambridge, MA: Harvard University Press.

Cielemcka, O. and Revelles-Benavente, B. (2017), 'Knowmadic Knowledge Production in Times of Crisis', in B. Revelles-Benavente and A.M. González Ramos (eds.), *Teaching Gender: Feminist Pedagogy and Responsibility in Times of Political Crisis*, 25–41, London: Routledge.

Foucault, M. (1980), 'Prison Talk', in C. Gordon (ed.), *Power-Knowledge: Selected Interviews and Other Writings, 1972–1977*, 37–54, Brighton: Harvester Press.

Fricker, M. (2007), *Epistemic Injustice. Power and the Ethics of Knowing*, Oxford: Oxford University Press.

Gill, R. (2009), 'Breaking the Silence: The Hidden Injuries of the Neo-liberal Academia', in R. Gill and R. Ryan-Flood (eds.), *Secrecy and Silence in the Research Process: Feminist Reflections*, 228–244, London: Routledge.

Haraway, D. (1988), 'Situated Knowledges: The Science Question in Feminism and the Privilege of Partial Perspective', *Feminist Studies*, 14 (3): 575–599.

Haraway, D. (1990), 'Reading Buchi Emecheta: Contests for Women's Experience in Women's Studies', *Women: A Cultural Review*, 1 (3): 240–255.

Harding, S. (1987), 'Introduction: Is there a Feminist Method?', in *Feminism and Methodology*, 1–14, Indianapolis, IN: Indiana University Press.

Lee, H. (1960), *To Kill a Mockingbird*, London: William Heinemann.

Mountz, A., Bonds, A., Mansfield, B., Loyd, J., Hyndman, J., Walton-Roberts, M., Basu, R., Whitson, R., Hawkins, R., Hamilton, T. and Curran, W. (2015), 'For Slow Scholarship: A Feminist Politic of Resistance through Collective Action in the Neoliberal University', *ACME: An International E-Journal for Critical Geographies*, 14 (4): 1235–1259.

Özdamar, E.S. (1994), *Mother Tongue*, trans. C. Thomas, Toronto: Coach House Press.

Pereira, M.M. (2017), *Power, Knowledge and Feminist Scholarship*, London: Routledge.

Pratt, M.L. (1991), 'Arts of the Contact Zone', in *Profession*, 33–40, New York: Modern Language Association.

Precarias a la deriva (2004), *A la deriva por los circuitos de la precariedad femenina*, Madrid: Traficantes de Sueños.

Rogowska-Stangret, M. (2017), 'Sharing Vulnerabilities: Searching for "Unruly Edges" in Times of the Neoliberal Academy', in B. Revelles-Benavente and A.M. González Ramos (eds.), *Teaching Gender: Feminist Pedagogy and Responsibility in Times of Political Crisis*, 11–24, London: Routledge.

Ross, A. (1958), *On Law and Justice*, Berkeley, CA: University of California Press.

Spivak, G.C. (1985), 'Can the Subaltern Speak? Speculations on Widow Sacrifice', *Wedge*, 7/8: 120–130.

Spivak, G.C. (1988), 'Can the Subaltern Speak?', in C. Nelson and L. Grossberg (eds.), *Marxism and the Interpretation of Culture*, 271–313, Urbana, IL: University of Illinois Press.

Spivak, G.C. (1999), *A Critique of Postcolonial Reason: Toward a History of the Vanishing Present*, Cambridge, MA: Harvard University Press.

Spivak, G.C. (2003), 'Collectivities', in *Death of a Discipline*, 24–70, New York: Columbia University Press.

Spivak, G.C. (2010), '"Can the Subaltern Speak?" Revised Edition, from the "History" Chapter of *Critique of Postcolonial Reason*, in R.C. Morris (ed.), *Can the Subaltern Speak? Reflections on the History of an Idea*, 21–78, New York: Columbia University Press.

Spivak, G.C. (forthcoming), *Pode a subalterna tomar a palavra?*, trans. and preface A.S. Ribeiro, Lisboa: Orfeu Negro.

Woolf, V. (1929), *A Room of One's Own*, London: Hogarth Press.

11

Governing the 'Good' Casual Academic: Institutionalised 'Othering' Practices

Alexandra Jones, Jess Harris, Nerida Spina and Jennifer M. Azordegan

Introduction

Precarity of work in universities has increased as a result of university and research funding, the marketisation of higher education, and worldwide trends towards workforce casualisation (Broadbent and Strachan 2016; Brown et al. 2010; Courtois and O'Keefe 2015). Increasing precarity has re-shaped how higher education institutions position and constitute subjectivities of the 'good' casual academic, and how these subjectivities align with the requirements for ongoing academic roles.

Centred around advanced liberal discourses of productivity, responsibility and the individualisation of the subject, the management of casual academics is focused on self-regulatory and self-disciplining technologies (Apple 2005). Contributing to research on casual academic identities in higher education, this chapter highlights the ways that 'othering' practices emergent from dominant discourses in the changing higher education space shape exclusionary practices, which can prevent casual academics' inclusion in key institutional processes, meetings and networks. These practices hold the potential to perpetuate inequities that suppress and interfere with casual academics' sense of agency and work against what many universities define as 'quality' research (Kimber 2003; Ryan et al. 2017). The data that informs this chapter was generated through in-depth interviews with twenty-seven casual academics, working in Australian universities. Interviews were designed to explore personal experiences and perceptions of their roles as casual research academics and the ways in which they position themselves and are positioned by others within higher education institutional contexts. To understand the construction of the participants' identities, the authors draw from Foucault's notion of 'governmentality' (Foucault 2003) and concept of 'technologies of power' (Foucault 1982).

Governmentality is understood as the ways in which dominant knowledge systems and their associated discourses shape and position individuals. We draw on the concept of governmentality to show how casual research academics are 'othered' and positioned through normalised understandings of their work, and spatial practices within the university. A Foucauldian-inspired analysis is valuable, as it maps the subjectification of casual research academics, and the ways in which they are disciplined and governed in ways that place them on the periphery both spatially and intellectually. This analysis also brings to light the often unproblematised ethical dimensions of casual academic work within higher education institutions. We argue that interrupting normalised understandings of the casual academic is an important step in creating a space for counter-discourses that work against inequitable, unethical and institutionalised exclusionary practices.

Governing the subject

Career path? [Laughter] I don't believe I've ever had one of those ... I did have someone I was working with one time saying 'Oh, you need to think about your career, and your career path' and I just thought, 'I've got too much to do to think about my career!'

Audrey

Audrey is in her mid-thirties and has worked as a research academic on casual and short-term contracts at numerous universities, hospitals and institutes for most of her working life. Audrey's comment (above) was in response to questions about her academic 'career'. Her interview was conducted as part of a project that sought to understand the experiences of research academics who are employed on fixed-term and casual contracts. Despite having worked full time as a researcher for more than a decade, Audrey retained a sense that she didn't really have an academic 'career'. The focus of this chapter is on how a blend of theoretical approaches, drawing on Foucauldian discourse analysis and the feminist sociology developed by Dorothy Smith can be used to understand and problematise the view of what constitutes an academic and what constitutes a 'good' casual academic. Audrey's statement provides a glimpse into the standpoint of the insecurely employed academic: a group whose perspectives have typically been excluded from writings about academia. We have chosen to use such descriptions of the everyday experiences of this group as the *point d'appui* (point of entry) (Smith 2005: 10). Smith's theoretical approach provides an opportunity to start with everyday experiences and offers a point of reference for understanding the 'bifurcated consciousness' (1987: 82) of researchers, like Audrey, who are conditioned to accept and adapt to the views and expectations of the traditionally dominant group in academia (tenured academics). Our method of inquiry affords an opportunity to bring to light issues that privileged groups (in this case, tenured academics and managers) – whose perspectives are embedded within dominant discourses and institutional practices – may otherwise be oblivious to.

The analysis presented in this chapter incorporates the work of Foucault to examine how relations of privilege are operationalised in universities through 'dividing practices' (Foucault 1972). This analytic approach allowed us to examine discursive practices that demarcate insecurely employed academics from their tenured colleagues. When viewed through this theoretical lens, Audrey's statement (above) illustrates that there are taken-for-granted 'truths' about what counts as an academic career and who is considered an academic. Our chapter proceeds in three steps. First, we provide a discussion of the blend of social theories that we have employed in analysing the everyday lives of non-tenured academics, focusing on how dominant discourses about the 'precariat' (Standing 2011) can be examined. Drawing on a larger project, in which we interviewed twenty-nine insecurely-employed research academics, we present an analysis to demonstrate how these theoretical approaches can be used to highlight dividing practices that reproduce inequities via neoliberal governmentalities. Our discussion focuses on the discursive construction of the academic, which is used to 'other' and dominate non-tenured workers. Finally, we consider the impact of this form of analysis and how applying this theoretical lens can inform or disrupt the regime of truth that obfuscates the subjugation of a large and growing group of professionals within higher education – precariously employed research academics.

Discourse, dividing practices and 'othering' in academic employment

Foucault's work sets out 'to show that "discourses" in the form in which they can be heard or read, are not, as one might expect, a mere intersection of things and words' (1972: 49). Rather, the analysis of discourse can reveal 'the emergence of a group of rules proper to discursive practice. These rules define not the dumb existence of a reality, nor the canonical use of a vocabulary, but the ordering of objects' (ibid.). These 'rules of formation' (Foucault 1972) explain how statements and discursive formations work to create classifications through 'dividing practices' that make comparisons with something or someone else. Discursive rules underpin our systems of thought, determining who has the authority to speak, what can be known (and by whom), and whose interests and views are prioritised. In analysing precariously employed academics' accounts, we have drawn on Foucault's notion of regimes of truth:

> Each society has its regime of truth, its 'general politics' of truth; that is, the types of discourse which it accepts and makes function as true; the mechanisms and instances which enable one to distinguish true and false statements, the means by which each is sanctioned; the techniques and procedures accorded value in the acquisition of truth; the status of those who are charged with saying what counts as true.
>
> Foucault 1980: 131

Discourse is thus capable of carrying an authoritative voice that renders certain perspectives relevant, while creating discursive prohibitions around other points of view. These discursive formations are historicised – united in given places and periods of time. That means truth is only ever a partialised and localised version of knowledge. Taken-for-granted truths about what it means to be a 'good' casual academic (or a 'good academic' for that matter) are evident in institutional processes, and in the ways that people within institutions view themselves and act. These truths legitimise particular ways of being and delineate between the normal ('us') and the abnormal (or other – 'them'). By examining the truths that people take for granted in their everyday lives, Foucauldian analysis provides a lens to understand how dominant discourses, through processes such as normalisation, support the replication of power relations and practices.

In analysing 'othering' practices, we also found Smith's (1987) insights into how institutions exert power through text-based practices instructive. As Smith (1987) explains, institutional texts can 'unleash' chains of action that organise the everyday lives of people within institutions. For example, industrial texts that govern employment contracts – and even the *naming* of workers as 'academics' – can be seen as a dividing practice to divide and classify workers. In Australia, 'academic' contracts range from Level A (Tutor/Associate Lecturer) through to Level E (Professor). In contrast, researchers on casual and short-term contracts are often employed on a 'professional' salary scale for 'Higher Education Workers (HEW)', which as we will show later in the chapter, can restrict access to institutional systems and structures. Casually employed teaching staff (lecturers and tutors) are paid according to yet another classification system, often referred to as 'sessional' staff. These institutional texts discursively view 'real' academic staff as those employed on 'academic' contracts, thus positioning those who are conducting what is ostensibly very similar work (teaching and research), albeit on a short-term basis, as the 'other'. As Foucault indicates, within a system of surveillance, people are engaged with documentation and a network of writing in ways that 'capture and fix them' ([1975] 1995: 198). Describing how she extended on Foucault's perspective, Smith said that, 'in preserving the active presence of subjects, I have displaced the central place given by Foucault to the textual, bringing into view the social relations in which texts are embedded and which they organize' (1990: 163).

The utility of Foucauldian-inspired analysis in neoliberal institutions

Foucault's notion of governmentality is particularly useful in understanding the experiences of casual academics because it affords the opportunity to examine the range of techniques and procedures through which academic conduct is governed. Garland explains: 'This kind of power does not seize hold of the individual's body ... Instead, it holds out technologies of the self, to be adopted by willing individuals who take an active part in their own "subjectification"' (1997: 175). In this chapter, we argue that insecurely employed academics are active subjects, who are both subjugated and participants in their own subjugation. That is, individual researchers who are precariously employed may have the freedom to leave academia, yet many do not; they have the freedom to go against 'the norm' but do not. Governmentality is thus not a means of controlling behaviours, but the ways in which people come to understand their lives and roles within society (Foucault 2003).

Neoliberalism as a form of governmentality is used to organise behaviours, attitudes and understandings through specific institutional and societal practices. This form of post-welfarism has hollowed out the role of the state, instead outsourcing responsibility onto individuals within the population who are expected to look after themselves. As Larner states, 'neoliberalism is both a political discourse about the nature of rule and a set of practices that facilitate the governing of individuals from a distance' (2000: 6). These technologies, evidenced in dominant discourses, authorise particular actions, shape subjectivities and produce normative understandings of how one should behave within the context of an institution (Weberman 1995). Neoliberal practices constitute subjectivity by 'extending and disseminating market values to all institutions and social action' (Brown 2003: 40), that is, neoliberal practices position all institutions and actions through an economic lens. It is within this market-driven rationality that precariously employed academics are situated – where relations are organised through acts of 'free choice'. Neoliberalism in higher education institutions offers the idea of 'freedom' through the capacities of one's right to choose and be responsible for your own success. Success, in this sense, is reduced to one of celebrating the possibilities of self-realisation, freedom and the resources to invest in opportunities to position oneself as valuable human capital (Brown 2003; Lolich 2011). Subjectivity from this post-structural understanding (and within a neoliberal discursive field) is thus constituted through a relation of neoliberal technologies, discourses and institutional practices. Foucault and Smith have both acknowledged that modern forms of power are not 'held' by institutions or individuals, but rather work both on and through people: 'Let us ask ... how things work at the level of on-going subjugation, at the level of those continuous and uninterrupted processes which subject our bodies, govern our gestures, dictate our behaviours, etc....' (Foucault 1980: 97). Power is thus viewed as movement in the form of strategies, techniques and technologies within the institution and society. It is for this reason that Ball suggests subjectivity is a 'key site of political struggle' (2015: 1129). Drawing on the everyday experiences of precariously employed academics, and examining their changed subjectivities is therefore an important starting point for explicating and contesting the current regime of truth around academic employment.

Critical reflections on social theory and methodology

The Foucauldian-inspired discourse analysis presented in this chapter is understood as a way to provide insight into the way that 'sense is being made' and 'the ways in which the real is constructed' in interviews with casual research academics (Davies 2004: 4–5). In designing data collection, we drew on Smith's approach that requires researchers to start by inquiring into the actualities of the subject, examining participants' everyday practices before moving to explicate how 'what people are doing and experiencing in a given local site is hooked into textually-coordinated sequences of action implicating and coordinating multiple local sites where others are active' (Smith 1999: 7). As such, our research commenced with extended interviews with researchers on short-term and casual contracts from around Australia and Australian researchers working internationally. The interviews were conducted face-to-face and via video-conferencing. Our theoretical framework informed the design of interview schedules, which involved detailed questions about the everyday activities of academics in precarious employment, how they would define a 'good' contract researcher, and how they were discursively constructed and positioned within higher education institutions. Generally lasting 60–90 minutes, these interviews explored researchers' experiences of working on casual and short-term contracts, and the ways in which the precarity of their employment shaped their work and lives. A unique contribution from Smith (2003) is the emphasis on acknowledging all forms of work, not just the forms of work that are observable using dominant discursive parameters. As Smith writes, it is important to see work in all forms to turn it 'from its extraordinary invisibility into visibility' (2003: 63). We adopted this generous definition of work, including 'anything done by people that takes time and effort, that they mean to do' (Smith 2005: 151–152) to ensure that we included all work undertaken by our participants. They reported much of their time was spent on tasks that extend beyond traditional boundaries of academic work, allowing us to explicate the everyday realities of people who spend significant time filling in timesheets, emailing supervisors about contracts, undertaking unpaid work so as to appear more 'efficient' and so on. We invited participants to talk about texts that were activated as part of their work, which led to conversations about documents, including employment contracts, timesheets and emails. We draw on Smith's (2001) lens to collect these documents as evidence of textually mediated relations of ruling that connect everyday actualities and work of people with the matrix of social and institutional relations that extend beyond the local and sustain power relations in the higher education space. Smith's theorisation of ruling relations draws on Foucault's notions of discourse and discursive events to analyse discourses that are located 'externally to subjectivities as an order that imposes and coerces them' (Smith 1987: 17).

By adopting a Foucauldian-inspired post-structural understanding of the subject, we were able to draw insights from these interviews about the subjectivities of participants. Our use of Smith's work further enabled the analysis of textually mediated relations of ruling that have been embedded in the institution. Rather than being viewed as a fixed product or identity, our approach views subjectivity as a process whereby people are constituted in discourse, through the relation between knowledge and power. In applying these approaches to the context of academic employment, knowledge could include the expertise that is developed by the professoriate that serves to characterise people in very particular ways (such as an adjunct teacher, sessional tutor and so forth). In turn, these discourses not only govern conduct but also create the conditions where outside forces change how we come to know and govern ourselves as subjects. Thus, our analysis is grounded in an understanding of subjectivity and described in terms of processes and practices that are linked to subjectification, as precariously employed academics form understandings of self, and seek to act upon themselves as subjects.

Each of the extended interviews with academics in precarious employment were transcribed and coded according to a framework that was developed with reference to the key theoretical approaches of Foucault and Smith. This process drew on Smith's notion of a 'bifurcated consciousness' (1987: 82) through the identification of instances where interviewees described their understanding of the constituent features of 'being a "good" contract researcher' and the characteristics that they related to the role of 'academics in ongoing employment'. We looked for instances of discourses where forms of consciousness were 'properties of organisation and relations rather than individuals' (Smith 1987: 220). In analysing our interviews, we examined how relations were coordinated and systems of knowledge were formed in and through discourse and text.

Coding was, therefore, undertaken to examine explicit descriptions of 'boundary work' (e.g. Gieryn 1983; O'Mahony 2013), governmentality and textually mediated practices (Smith 2005) that are central to the ruling apparatus and distribution of power within the higher education context. Our coding process facilitated deeper analyses of issues of power relations within the experiences of these academics that uncovered the discursive construction of the 'precariat' (Standing 2011) as 'other' within higher education institutions.

Discursive constructions of the 'good' academic

Following preliminary coding, data were interrogated to identify how interviewees discursively constructed each of the areas under examination. In talking about identity formation in academia, for example, interview participants discursively framed academics (both tenured and non-tenured) as 'giving' workers who demonstrated loyalty and commitment to their work through working extensive hours for the 'greedy institution' (Bone et al. 2018). The work of academia was frequently described as overshadowing all other aspects of life. For example, this is what Bailey had to say:

> At the end of the day, it was too many people that I see that I've seen for years in there who just looked sick every time I see them. They look run-ragged, or they put on heaps of weight. And you know that it's like that. It's a bubble you live in of stress and sitting at your desk. You can't get up and go for a walk for 10 minutes ...

Through the analysis of data related to constituent characteristics of academics in ongoing employment, we identified an emergent view of academics as being consumed by their work. This discursive construction resonates with the frame described by Pitt and Mewburn as the rise of the academic 'superhero' who 'is a multi-talented, always ready and available worker' (2016: 12). However, our analysis identified that our participants excluded themselves from this dominant discourse of the academic 'superhero'. They suggested that, for the precariat, dedication and working long hours do not necessarily lead to more secure employment, a career, nor this construction of 'success'. As Carolyn stated:

> I do want a successful academic career, and it's still challenging now to even get any ... kind of permanent position. You need to be a superstar. And so you have to build yourself up to be that in order to even get considered for roles, even at a low Level B role.

Foucault's (1980) notion of regimes of truth, and Smith's (1987) notion of the disjuncture between ruling and experiential ways of knowing uncovered the discourse of needing to be a 'superstar' to build a career is in many interviews. This finding reflected a dominant, taken-for-granted truth that securing 'a career' or 'permanent position' are typical goals for researchers, but are only accessible to the elite. This 'regime of truth' (Foucault 1980) shapes what is known and understood by contract academics regarding successful careers and their relationship with success in academia, as evident in Noah's interview. Despite working in academia for well over a decade, Noah reported, 'I felt like a bit of a failure though because I never really got into a career as such'. Foucault and Smith's contributions allowed space for an examination of such experiences, which shape subjectivities, yet sit outside of dominant orders of discourse. What can be said and known about academic careers is discursively determined in ways that conceal the everyday experiences of non-tenured researchers like Noah.

In exploring issues of power relations within our interviews, we identified the development of divisive classifications of tenured and non-tenured academics that included discursive constructions of institutionalised powerlessness for those in insecure employment. Sasha, for example, explained that a high turnover of casual researchers on a project was directly related to power relations. She reported that casual researchers resigned largely because 'they're powerless' and the only way to avoid unfair working conditions was to leave the project. Audrey's description of her employment further illuminated this discourse of powerlessness:

> Some of these [tenured academics], you can't reason with them, and you just can get put in a position where you're having to do these really dysfunctional or pointless tasks, because they're directing you to do them.

The analysis of power relations within the descriptions of the everyday work of precariously employed academics demonstrated a need for them to navigate relations of power with tenured academics in order to sustain employment. Interviewees explained that their lack of power in the workplace left them with little choice but to take up the expectations and conditions imposed by institutionally dominant groups.

Othering and boundary work

Dominant discourses and institutional processes meant divisive practices were used to exclude the precariat from the classification of an 'academic superhero' with individual power. Feminist sociological approaches, such as that of Smith, have explicated how the world is 'put together' (Smith 1987) through institutional practices that support the construction of a dominant worldview, resonating with Foucault's notion of the 'other', or those who do not fit within dominant ideologies of normalcy. These approaches allowed us to explore how socially constructed grids of specification allow dominant groups to define what it means to be an academic, and build hierarchical structures that exclude non-tenured staff in subtle (and not-so-subtle) ways. To better understand 'othering' practices, we looked for discursive practices and texts that provided instances of these socially construction categories, and through which subjectivities were shaped (and re-shaped). We used these instances to examine how dominant discourses changed how both the tenured and non-tenured learned to 'be' within the academy. As Kitzinger and Wilkinson (1996: 9) state, 'other is a construction of a set of discourses through which the dominant group defines itself' – in other words, the 'other' sits outside of the 'normal' discourse.

Understanding how precariously employed researchers discursively positioned themselves, and how they were positioned by dominant discourses and text was crucial in our analysis. Accounts of what constitutes normalcy in academic employment was analytically important as we worked to understand how 'othering' works to create boundaries, exclude and shape subjectivities. Analysis of our interviews enabled us to identify these taken-for-granted truths within higher education institutions. For example, an instance of dividing practices was identified in Sasha's statement that:

> [You are] utterly shut out of institutional networks, mentoring, whether that's mentoring in terms of content, like your actual area of research or whether it's mentoring in terms of just management, higher level leadership. There's no modelling in terms of how to do that.

This sense that precarious academics were 'utterly shut out' was reflected throughout the interviews. The application of Smith's lens highlighted that power was often exerted through textually mediated practices of 'the ruling apparatus' (Smith 1990: 161) which served to construct boundaries that excluded those without tenure. As Sasha said:

> So professional development is one of the things that I feel, I just can't get. Because projects are always externally funded or even if it comes from within the organisation, every aspect of that funding is very carefully allocated, and because you're never considered core business to the institution, even if you've been there nine years.

Sasha's experience highlights the significance of 'othering' practices that are exerted through policies that only provide professional development for those with ongoing appointments. However, her sense of being 'shut out' of conversations about career development are also part of wider grids of specification in which only tenured academics are invited into meetings, mentoring conversations about career development, or access to other institutional information. Despite almost a decade of work at one university, Sasha (like Audrey and others) was positioned as the 'other', who was not able to access many of the opportunities offered to tenured academics.

These analytic techniques allowed us to uncover many instances where institutionalised discourses and textually mediated power relations had a deeply personal impact. Bailey described how:

> . . . [the academic who employed me] turned round to me before Christmas and said, 'I'm away now and I'm taking time off, so I'm not going to need you till the

end of next February', and I was going, 'Well, that's just fantastic, three months of no pay . . '. You know? And then this is — you see, there's probably nobody nicer than her to work with. She's just gorgeous, you know? It's indicative of the way they think of you. You're just superfluous.

As Bailey's experience shows, these struggles are private, with individuals left to manage complex situations such as suddenly being thrown into periods of unemployment. Smith's analytic work of exploring the disjuncture between objectified and embodied ways of knowing was also important in analysing these experiences. Bailey's account made it clear that the supportive and considerate academic she worked for was very likely unaware of the effect of her vacation on Bailey (and her family). Yet, for those employed insecurely, the threat of not having work meant holidays and vacations were out of reach.

Our analysis further revealed how exclusionary practices are deeply entrenched in institutional systems and discourses. As Sasha said:

> . . . it's everything from HR and finance systems through to how decisions are made, through to professional development, through to all these things that are considered, only given to staff that are full-time really. Except that you *work* full time but you're *not considered* full-time staff.

Despite the participants' working hours amounting to a full-time staff member, they were not *perceived* as such by themselves, other staff or the institution. The perceptions of not being part of the dominant class within the institution illuminated the impact that this boundary work had on the subjectivities of precarious workers and the systemic exclusion to institutional systems that both aided and advanced one's career.

The burden of several years of precarious work re-shaped the subjectivities of precarious academics, summoning a sense of disposability and questioning of their professional value or worth. Sasha, for instance, indicated that her employment experiences left her feeling that she did not feel of value to the organisation, and this peripheral positioning was taking a deeply emotional toll:

> No, and I think, I was trying to summarise it in my head and I think that it's, you're always treated as periphery. You're never actually considered as core business. Or of having worth . . . You are *totally* excluded.

For Sasha, and others, this toll was both very personal and long-term. Through tears, Sasha commented, 'It's been ten years of my life'. The experience of feeling othered through boundary work and exclusionary practices commonly led to this feeling of disposability. The impact of these everyday micro-practices of power, and the ongoing uncertainty around future employment had a significant impact on how individuals saw and managed themselves. The tenured academic as a mode of subjectivity was something precariously employed academics strived towards, and sought evidence of within themselves.

The emotional toll on participants ultimately left many grappling with how a tenured academic is constituted, and whether or not they were 'good enough' or met the 'superstar' criteria to join this classification. As the majority of our participants had worked full time in insecure academic positions for over a decade, this may seem curious. However, as Audrey and others described, there was a taken-for-granted 'truth' that only tenured academics were truly constituted as academics at all. Again, the effects of these power relations were deeply personal. Andrew, for instance, demonstrated/described how he at times falls prey to the idea that his precarious employment status must be linked to his quality as a researcher:

> I think I get caught up in this idea that because I don't have a permanent position I must not be good enough, which is such bullshit, and it's, well I tell people that's bullshit, and I tell students that it's bullshit, but that's not what reality is . . .

While one part of him understands that permanency of a role is not indicative of being 'good enough', Andrew admitted that he bought into this construction of how a successful academic is discursively constructed. The 'ontological insecurity' (Giddens 1991) of our participants was entwined with the view of themselves in comparison to these perceptions of success, and to the textually mediated and discursive boundaries that worked to position them as other. Numerous researchers we talked with made comments such as 'what's wrong with me?'

For Giddens (1991), while the ontologically insecure may grapple with significant psychological tolls, the ontologically secure are likely to be oblivious to these kinds of existential questions. One might wonder why those who have earned postgraduate degrees would continue to seek precarious work, given the impact of 'othering' practices described above and the lingering cloud of uncertainty that created an atmosphere of despair and, at times, panic. In Dale's estimation, the answer lay in the desire to be constituted as an academic – to 'do' academic work:

> Well [people continue to take on insecure work] not because they still feel hopeful – although they do – there is that. No. It is because they *want* to do it. It takes a couple of years for the pain to get really painful. So, they, it's not that they think they're going to get a job. If they are sensible, they will already have worked

that out. It's that they *want* to keep writing. They *want* to keep doing the research that they are doing. They have a *vocation* ...

The paradox of insecure employment is that while it is often positioned as a pipeline into academia, there is clear evidence that securing tenure is now the exception (Ivancheva 2015). Yet for Dale and many others we talked with, years were spent employing technologies of the self as they struggled to secure and maintain employment.

Technologies of the self and the precarious academic

In their quest to sustain employment, precariously employed researchers are shaped by changed subjectivities that change desires, and the operation of power through technologies of the self. Foucault defines technologies of the self as those technologies that 'permit individuals to effect by their own means a certain number of operations on their own bodies and souls, thoughts, conduct and way of being' (1994: 225). We drew on these understandings to discern the frequent descriptions by researchers of managing their own conduct, and the ways they imposed constraints upon themselves with regards to being seen as successful. Exploring our data using this theoretical understanding allowed us to understand how researchers came to feel inferior through discursive and textual practices, and how they worked on themselves in order to meet or exceed standards they imagined were needed to be a 'good' academic.

The term governmentality foregrounds how mentalities, or rationalities, are entwined with modes of governance. In examining the discourses and practices that lie behind technologies of the self, we can begin to account for the ways in which the university apparatus has made precarious employment thinkable and governable. Foucault's understanding of governmentality was useful in illuminating how the mundane and often invisible practices within the university institution are related to the broader rationalities of neoliberalism and co-construct technologies of the 'self'. Neoliberal governmentality is underpinned by a deep faith in free market mechanisms as a means of organising conduct (Rose 1999). It is within this free market academic labour environment that individual, precariously employed academics are located. Drawing on Foucault's notion of governmentality in analysing our interviews, we became attuned to the ways institutional practices place casual academics in a position where they have no choice but to sustain dominant discourses if they want to continue research work. Decision-making practices in regard to these events were governed by neoliberal rationalities, overridden by the prospect of future job offerings and the casual academic's need or desire to work in the university institution. We became aware of how these practices, which positioned them as 'powerless' and 'irrelevant', were a part of the relational assemblage in which casual academics constructed understandings of themselves and the ways in which they were entangled in their desire to attain ongoing academic employment.

Further reflection on the interplay of social theory and methodology

This chapter employed a Foucauldian-inspired analysis, framed by Dorothy Smith's feminist sociological approach to examining how institutional practices and texts can contribute to the formation of discourses. Starting with the everyday experiences of contract research academics, this blend of theoretical approaches has allowed us to build an understanding of the discourses and dividing practices in ways that position non-tenured researchers in ways that contribute to their subjugation within the academy. Our analysis of interview data with casual researchers has demonstrated that neoliberal discourses that are dominant within higher education work not only to position casual academics as the 'other' but also to individualise their notions of success and/or failure in relation to securing ongoing employment in the academy. Researchers interviewed for this project described a shared view that success is an individual endeavour, a result of being a 'superstar' researcher, who can produce publications, secure grant funding and maintain teaching while continuing to engage in flexible work for others as a 'good' casual researcher. The dominant discourse that they describe conversely has serious ramifications for researchers who are unable to secure ongoing employment in academia. While researchers are aware that the number of ongoing academic positions has reduced and the number of PhD graduates has increased over the last few decades, this individualised discourse promotes the view that each researcher is solely responsible for their own success or failure.

Our methodological approach was grounded in Smith's sociology that begins by close examination of the everyday (and night) doings of people, based on the assumption that they are experts in their own lives. This method of data collection enabled us to reveal how non-tenured academic work is textually coordinated, and discursively positioned within the academy. Smith helped us relocate the participants' understandings of themselves as casual academics from being something inherent in their being or direct experiences to something that is a function of a set of textual practices. Smith allowed us to highlight how 'the disjuncture between the experienced actualities of those caught up in such a process and what is recognized in the form of words that represent them [casual academics] institutionally is an important dimension of institutional power' (2005: 194). In other words, the examples addressed in this chapter begin from the starting point of the casual academic, but through mapping the texts entangled in such practices, illustrate the problematic of 'othering' practices that mark them as a casual academic.

Our approach to analysis illuminated dividing practices that cast non-tenured academics as 'other' in higher education institutions. Frequently excluded from professional development, internal funding opportunities and the perks of academic work that are offered to those within tenured positions, the subjugation of researchers on short-term and casual contracts is constructed through textually mediated practices of the 'ruling apparatus' (Smith 1987). Institutional texts, including employment contracts, established boundaries between those in the 'tenured core' and those on the 'tenuous periphery' (Kimber 2003). The data collected using this method of inquiry revealed how institutional structures can inhibit casual academics from meeting criteria required to secure ongoing employment and thus pose an institutional barrier to individuals reaching success as defined by the dominant neoliberal discourse. This approach to data collection allowed us to examine the multitude of work that goes into being a non-tenured academic, and to explore how grids of specification between precariously employed and tenured academics are created and sustained.

The purpose of adopting this lens was to uncover how the dominant discourse establishes and reinforces relations of privilege in the university workplace. Our analysis exposed ways that both the traditionally dominant group in academia (tenured academics) and those who are subjugated (the precariat) have come to view these inequitable power relations as normal. In bringing these power relations to light, this analysis has the potential to disrupt the dominant discourse associated with casual researchers in universities. As researchers ourselves, this analysis has directed our attention to the role of textually mediated institutional practices in maintaining dominant discourses that function to position casual academics as 'other'. As such, this analysis has highlighted the need for research into the ethical responsibilities of the higher education institution in remediating this positioning of those in precarious positions, who now form a large proportion of the academic workforce. The untold stories of researchers we talked with, and analysed using a bricolage of Smith and Foucault's theoretical contributions, demonstrate how this approach can explicate relations of ruling, so that they can ultimately be challenged and disrupted.

References

Apple, M.W. (2005), 'Education, markets, and an audit culture', *Critical Quarterly*, 47 (1/2): 11–29.

Ball, S.J. (2015), 'Subjectivity as a site of struggle: Refusing neoliberalism?', *British Journal of Sociology of Education*, 37 (8): 1129–1146.

Bone, K., Jack G. and Mayson, S. (2018), 'Negotiating the greedy institution: A typology of the lived experiences of young, precarious academic workers', *Labour and Industry: A Journal of the Social and Economic Relations of Work*, 28 (4): 225–243.

Broadbent, K. and Strachan, G. (2016), 'It's difficult to forecast your longer term career milestone': Career development and insecure employment for research academics in Australian universities, *Labour and Industry: A Journal of the Social and Economic Relations of Work*, 26 (4): 251–265.

Brown, T., Goodman, J. and Yasukawa, K. (2010), 'Academic casualization in Australia: Class divisions in the university', *Journal of Industrial Relations*, 52 (2): 169–182.

Brown, W. (2003), 'Neo-liberalism and the end of liberal democracy', *Theory and Event*, 7 (1). Available online: https://muse.jhu.edu/article/48659.

Courtois, A.D.M. and O'Keefe, T. (2015), 'Precarity in the ivory cage: Neoliberalism and casualisation of work in the Irish higher education sector', *Journal for Critical Education Policy Studies*, 13 (1). Available online: http://www.jceps.com/archives/2458.

Davies, B. (2004), 'Introduction: Poststructuralist lines of flight in Australia', *International Journal of Qualitative Studies in Education*, 17 (1): 1–9.

Foucault, M. (1972), *The Archaeology of Knowledge*, trans. A. Sheridan, New York: Routledge.

Foucault, M. ([1975] 1995), *Discipline and Punish: The Birth of the Prison*, trans. A. Sheridan, New York: Vintage Books.

Foucault, M. (1980), *Power/Knowledge: Selected Interviews and Other Writings, 1972–1977*, New York: Vintage Books.

Foucault, M. (1982), 'The subject and power', *Critical Inquiry*, 8 (4): 777–795.

Foucault, M. (1994), *Ethics, Subjectivity and Truth*, vol. 1, trans. R. Hurley, ed. P. Rabinow, New York: St. Martin's Press.

Foucault, M. (2003), *The Essential Foucault: Selections from Essential Works of Foucault, 1954–1984*, ed. P. Rabinow and N. Rose, New York: The New Press.

Garland, D. (1997), '"Governmentality" and the problem of crime: Foucault, criminology, sociology', *Theoretical Criminology*, 1 (2): 173–214.

Giddens, A. (1991), *Modernity and Self-Identity: Self and Society in the Late Modern Age*, Cambridge: Polity Press.

Gieryn, L.F. (1983), 'Boundary work and the demarcation of science from non-science', *American Sociological Review*, 48 (6): 781–795.

Ivancheva, M.P. (2015), 'The age of precarity and the new challenges to the academic profession', *Studia Europaea*, 60 (1): 39–47.

Kimber, M. (2003), 'The tenured "core" and the tenuous "periphery": The casualisation of academic work in Australian universities', *Journal of Higher Education Policy and Management*, 25 (1): 41–50.

Kitzinger, C. and Wilkinson, S. (1996), 'Theorizing representing the other', in S. Wilkinson and C. Kitzinger (eds.), *Representing the Other: A Feminism and Psychology Reader*, 1–32, London: Sage.

Larner, W. (2000), 'Neo-liberalism: Policy, ideology, governmentality', *Studies in Political Economy*, 63 (1): 5–25.

Lolich, L. (2011), '. . . and the market created the student to its image and likening. Neo-liberal governmentality and its effects on higher education in Ireland', *Irish Educational Studies*, 30 (2): 271–284.

O'Mahony, S. (2013), 'Boundary work', in V. Smith (ed.), *Sociology of Work: An encyclopedia*, vol. 1, 34–35, Thousand Oaks, CA: Sage.

Pitt, R. and Mewburn, I. (2016), 'Academic superheroes? A critical analysis of academic job descriptions', *Journal of Higher Education Policy and Management*, 38 (1): 1–14.

Rose, N. (1999), *Powers of Freedom: Reframing Political Thought*. Cambridge: Cambridge University Press.

Ryan, S., Connell, J. and Burgess, J. (2017), 'Casual academics: A new public management paradox', *Labour and Industry: A Journal of the Social and Economic Relations of Work*, 27 (1): 56–72.

Smith, D.E. (1987), *The Everyday World as Problematic: A Feminist Sociology*, Boston, MA: Northeastern University Press.

Smith, D.E. (1990), *The Conceptual Practices of Power: A Feminist Sociology of Knowledge*, Toronto, ON: University of Toronto Press.

Smith, D.E. (1999), *Writing the Social: Critique, Theory, and Investigations*, Toronto, ON: University of Toronto Press.

Smith, D.E. (2001), 'Texts and the ontology of organizations and institutions', *Studies in Cultures, Organizations and Societies*, 7 (2): 159–198.

Smith, D.E. (2003), 'Making sense of what people do: A sociological perspective', *Journal of Occupational Science*, 10 (1): 61–64.

Smith, D.E. (2005), *Institutional Ethnography: A Sociology for People*, Oxford: Rowman Altamira.

Standing, G. (2011), *The Precariat: The New Dangerous Class*, London: Bloomsbury.

Weberman, D. (1995), 'Foucault's reconception of power', *Philosophical Forum*, 26 (3): 189–217.

Part Three

Social Theory and the Politics
of Student Experience

12

Student Politics: Resistance, Refusal and Representation

Rille Raaper and Ciaran Burke

Neoliberalism is a ubiquitous term that has been used to define mainstream economic and political systems in the global north for over 40 years. This includes the UK where, despite shifts in the colour of the ruling party, the government has been driven by neoliberalism and a similar observation can be made of other countries, including the United States. As with any ubiquitous term, it has enjoyed extended application beyond perhaps its original intention and begins to lose the sharp edge of its definition. As such, we begin this section with a definition of neoliberalism from David Harvey:

> Neoliberalism is in the first instance a theory of political economic practices that proposes that human well-being can best be advanced by liberating individual entrepreneurial freedoms and skills within an institutional framework characterised by strong private property rights, free markets, and free trade.
>
> Harvey 2005: 2

From Harvey's definition, neoliberalism advocates rugged individualism, limited government / oversight and market forces. The principles of managerialism and private business principles now organise public institutions such as the health system and the judiciary. As a result of managerialism, employees are required to account for their actions and justify their contribution through various metrics.

Traditionally, higher education has been seen as an autonomous institution, only loosely connected to macro institutions such as the economy and politics. However, higher education has not escaped from the emergence and firm development of neoliberalism throughout the global north (McCaig 2018; Naidoo and Williams 2015; Saunders 2010; Tavares and Cardosa 2013). Naidoo and Williams (2015) see the introduction of tuition fees in higher education systems as the origin of a neoliberal higher education system and the development of students as consumers – this, they argue, is what occurred in the US in the 1970s, Australia in the late 1980s and in the UK in the late 1990s. Until recently, they continue, most Western European countries have had state-supported higher education systems. However, the change in funding structures for higher education institutions (HEIs) from state-funded to primarily based on tuition fees requires these institutions to be marketable and attract students to remain solvent. As Burke (2016) outlines, the introduction of tuition fees in the UK and the subsequent increase in those fees, was rationalised based on personal benefit over the public good. This relationship between funding structures and a neoliberal higher education system is linked to the emergence and development of the knowledge economy (Tholen and Brown 2018). Higher education has been increasingly associated with the development of potential for employability and life chances, echoing the narrative that individual drive brings 'success'. As a result, higher education provides the workforce required by the economy and is required to provide increasingly regulated skills and attributes to support that economy (Case 2014) and by extension the neoliberal system. Such a position is supported by an increasing student rationale that taking up higher education is related to employment prospects (Burke 2016; Purcell et al., 2012; Saunders 2010).

A neoliberal higher education system operates under the principles of managerialism and performativity, observed and evaluated through assumed objective metrics. In the UK context, Naidoo and Williams (2015) argue that there is a market *within* higher education, which is supported by a range of now taken-for-granted elements of higher education that include Key Information Sets and various student surveys reviewing both courses and university services – culminating in the National Student Survey (NSS). However, beyond how universities are organised and additional benefits and opportunities for students, the curriculum is also driven and directed by market demands diluting the intellectual element of higher education in order to satisfy metrics (Naidoo and Williams 2015; Saunders 2010).

The impact of neoliberal policies and practices on higher education staff has been well documented (Mahony and Weiner 2019; Maisuria and Helmes 2019). As a result of performative expectations, staff autonomy has been drastically reduced and replaced with strict metric-driven tasks organised and observed through bureaucratic processes. Owing to the pressures in an increasingly unstable sector, higher education staff gradually become compliant in meeting these neoliberal requirements (Slaughter and Rhoades 2004), at times maintained through bullying (Mahony and Weiner 2019; Maisuria and Helmes 2019).

Turning to the impact of neoliberalism on students, Naidoo and Williams (2015) reflect on previous research by Shumar in the US. Shumar suggests that via an expansion in market practices in higher education, a consumer persona replaces that of the scholar and meeting expectations supersedes intellectual development. Through this process, students become disconnected and passive towards larger debates within the university through a focus on their individual experience and the benefits they accrue through their attendance (Cardosa 2012; Tavares and Cardosa 2013). Higher education students in the UK adopt a consumer identity within the higher education system owing to an early introduction to comparative information on courses based on metrics such as the NSS and employment prospects. As such, students drive and push academic staff to meet neoliberal metrics as they are the main source of information concerning the current student experience and potential student information. Students are now what Naidoo and Williams term 'a competitive economic actor' (2015: 213) – in other words, students determine the priorities of a once autonomous institution.

Students' political engagement in marketised universities

There is evidence to suggest that the neoliberalisation of higher education and consumer culture has led to the fragmentation of group loyalties and belonging, which, in turn, has had an impact on students' political engagement. When discussing contemporary student politics, comparisons are often made with the mid-twentieth century. Barker (2008) argues that the students of the 1960s and 1970s not only protested against various institutional regulations and traditions, but also involved themselves in a variety of social movements, including the civil rights and anti-Vietnam War movements. This also made the student movement of the time more than a simple campus demonstration or representation of students' rights (Raaper 2020a). The most recent worldwide student demonstrations of 2009–13 were largely aimed at the increasing costs of higher education (Klemenčič 2014). For example, the UK student protests in 2010–2011 were a reaction to the government's plans to treble the tuition fees from £3000 to £9000 per year, and took the form of national demonstrations and campus occupations (Hensby 2017). Similar protests were seen across the globe. Luescher-Mamashela (2013) and Altbach and Klemenčič (2014) suggest that these more recent demonstrations provide an example of how marketisation of education may have become the main mobilising force for contemporary student activism. However, we recognise that at the time of writing, there are a number of protests taking place involving students that relate to matters beyond the university and student fees, including privatisation and rising inequalities in Chile, the Anti-Extradition Law Amendment Bill in Hong Kong, as well as protests against global climate change. Each of these examples deserves scholarly attention.

It is also argued that changes in student demographics (e.g. diversity in social and ethnic background) can further affect the nature of student politics; this is especially so because a more diverse student population makes it more difficult for a collective student identity to emerge – and that includes political activism (Klemenčič 2014). Klemenčič (2015) suggests that not only has the understanding of politics changed but the concept of studentship has become more varied among students from different backgrounds. It may be that we have entered an era of more personalised politics where lifestyle choices and identity formation have become the key focus (Wright and Raaper 2019). While it is difficult to encapsulate what counts as student politics in contemporary society and on university campuses, where the number of identity-based groups and associations has increased significantly, there is evidence to suggest that the role of students' unions is in the process of change. Some would argue that their primary role is to safeguard the interests of students-as-consumers (Luescher-Mamashela 2013). Students' unions have also become important stakeholders at both national and institutional policy levels, advising governments and universities on how to improve the student experience (Wright and Raaper 2019). Research has shown that there is now a closer relationship between students' unions and senior university management, and there is a tendency for students' unions to employ increasing numbers of professionals and advisers (Brooks et al. 2015, 2016). This approach to students' unions as key stakeholders in higher education governance allows universities and the sector more broadly to demonstrate that student voice and satisfaction are being taken seriously and acted upon (Brooks et al. 2015). However, this also means that the role of student collectives in mobilising students for wider political causes has been weakened, and their practices are now more closely aligned with the interests of university management (Nissen and Hayward 2017). It is also clear that students from minority backgrounds, students not living on-campus or who work part-time are less likely to take up activities provided by students' unions (NUS 2012, 2013). This raises questions about the representativeness of students' unions and whose interest they protect. It is also the case that the priorities of students' union sabbatical officers tend to differ from those of the wider student population, and that when they sit on university governance bodies (e.g. University Senate or Council in the UK), they do not have a mandate to negotiate on behalf of an increasingly diverse and complex student body (Wright and Raaper 2019).

While there is evidence to suggest that there has been a shift from a collective student movement to more professional and individualised practices (Raaper 2020b), it is difficult to encapsulate how exactly students develop their political identity and practices in marketised higher education settings. It is clear that students are worried about the negative impact of high tuition fees and student debt on their well-being and capacity to participate in university life and political/student communities (Nissen 2019). Furthermore, recent research has shown (e.g. Nissen 2019; Raaper 2020a, 2020b) that many students in England and New Zealand have become more professional in their approaches to political engagement, such as lobbying politicians and accessing professional advice from students' unions, and are adopting less controversial practices to make their views heard.

Power and resistance: The role of social theory

A thread running through contemporary social theory is its concern with power and the conditions required for emancipation and resistance to the reproduction of the dominant privileged group, however that group is understood to be comprised. In reflecting on power and resistance, we began with Steven Lukes' (1974) essay *Power: A Radical View*, where he argues that power has many faces or layers with the most potent face of power being when it is seen to be natural, acceptable and beneficial to both the powerful and the powerless. When power is both ubiquitous and invisible, it begs the question how such conditions can be resisted. As with other taken-for-granted or 'natural' conditions of social space, social theory provides us with the language or the gaze to critically and reflectively examine power relations and opportunities for resistance. In this spirit, we provide some short reflections on the theoretical contributions from leading theorists on power and resistance. This is by no means an exhaustive list – indeed, we could have chosen a completely different set of theorists, but we feel that those chosen complement the following chapters and approach power from both a macro and micro perspective and similarly resistance on a personal and collective level.

From an Arendtian perspective, student politics (*as resistance to neoliberalisation of higher education*) could be viewed through a somewhat normative lens whereby 'acting in concert' equates to power (Arendt 1958: 245).

For Arendt, power is therefore a manifestation of freedom. In her book *The Human Condition* (1958), Arendt distinguished three core human activities – labour, work and action – of which the latter is the main means through which we disclose ourselves to others. Political action (*as resistance*), therefore, is a superior human capacity but also very difficult, requiring certain conditions, such as a willingness to take the initiative and begin something new and unpredictable (Arendt 1958). Action also takes place in relationship with others (Arendt 1968), and is irreversible, therefore requiring significant courage and risk-taking (Arendt 1970). Throughout her career, Arendt emphasised the importance of collectiveness and interaction in the operation of power and resistance; she argued that power 'is simply non-existent unless it can rely on others' (Arendt 1963: 230). In neoliberal higher education contexts where university studies are costly and increasingly individualised, competitive and employment-oriented, it is uncertain to what extent students are able to take risks and mediate unpredictability associated with action. Therefore, an Arendtian theorisation might help us to explore the claims around depoliticisation of contemporary students and the potential lack of collective student resistance.

At the centre of Bourdieu's theoretical project sits power, the extent to which it is reproduced, the avenues which we pursue to demonstrate distinction and legitimacy, and the complicity of those without power in the reproduction of their conditions and circumstance. For Bourdieu, power is both covert and overt, knitted together by a mix of micro-processes of tastes, cultures, attitudes, accents, etc., bestowing power on those who demonstrate 'fit' and authority. Fundamental to power are the processes which allow it to be taken for granted or seen as 'how things are', in the face of blatant reproduction and inequality. Bourdieu describes neoliberalism as 'a programme of methodical destruction of collectives' (1998: 95–96). Neoliberalism, he continues, is the active pursuit of an economic and political ideology – it is a 'strong discourse' (1998: 95) and one which is reinforced and armed by those who benefit from deregulation and individualism: the powerful and the privileged. In addition to the support of those it makes secure, neoliberalism also relies on the complicity of those it abuses. This paradoxical process comes about, Bourdieu suggests, as the consequence of an increasingly deregulated and destabilised labour market where adherence to the system is required to survive. We would argue that alongside passive permission, neoliberalism is reinforced via the misrecognition of doxic relations within a field or fields. As such, power is maintained through a combination of symbolic violence of the individual/group and the threat of abandonment by the system, which is at once punitive but also deemed necessary. Reflecting on Arendt's position that resistance is irreversible, without a suitable and viable alternative, resistance will be limited and judged on a range of factors beyond any reaction to injustice and inequality.

Resistance to such neoliberal practices within higher education and beyond is diluted through the act of resistance being interpreted as old-fashioned and self-serving, directed by an unwillingness to accept change and progress (Bourdieu 1998). As such, neoliberalism becomes a norm and an influential environment in constructing and reinforcing the habitus. As a consequence, resistance is dealt a further blow as dissent from the collective habitus is not only mistrusted but actively fought against for the greater good of the collective and interests of the individual (Bourdieu 1966). However, this does not mean that resistance is futile but does require a concerted effort, for as Bourdieu argues, 'habitus is not eternal' (Bourdieu and Wacquant 1992: 130). The habitus is both constructed and maintained through a range of factors including environment; for a habitus to shift perspective, a new environment is therefore required (Bourdieu and Wacquant 1992). Here Bourdieu maintains the need for 'subversion orientated towards conservation or restoration' (1998: 104), an endeavour which will be realised through collective engagement and collective action.

The final theorist we wish to discuss concerning collective resistance is Habermas. A primary concern for Habermas' work was to provide an understanding of power relations and processes within an increasingly complex social space and reaffirm the reflexive and democratic principles of the enlightenment. Habermas argues that contemporary social space operates simultaneously between the two layers of the system and the lifeworld (1979, 1984, 1989), although this is a fractious coupling where the social and cultural values of the lifeworld can often be contradictory to the system imperatives, resulting in conflict and the system exerting power over the lifeworld. As a result, the advanced capitalist and neoliberal system imperatives blur into and colonise the lifeworld, remaking culture and agency in the individualistic and atomic image of the economic and political system. Echoing Bourdieu, Habermas attributes the reproduction of power and inequality through the slow inculcation of advanced modern ideologies such as neoliberalism to individuals' distraction and preoccupation with cultural consumption and superficial causes. In this context, power is reproduced through collective inertia and acceptance of the status quo through what Marcuse (1964) would describe as a 'one-dimensional' society.

For Habermas (1992), a central institution for the protection and advancement of democracy and critical engagement with the reproduction of power is the public sphere. Directed by the principles of an 'ideal speech situation', the public sphere is a site of reflection and debate that provides an opportunity to reinforce lifeworld values and push back the instruments and mechanisms of the system. The public sphere provides a means of resistance by creating an epistemological break with a taken-for-granted system, 'in the salons the mind was no longer in the service of a patron; "opinion" became emancipated from the bond of economic dependence' (Habermas 1992: 33). Here Habermas provides us with the blueprints to consider the institutional support required to reinforce the lifeworld and resist encroaching neoliberal policies. For Habermas, as is true for Arendt and Bourdieu, resistance comes from collective debate and collective action.

An alternative view of power and resistance comes through Foucauldian social theory. Power for Foucault is always present, and it exists 'in the whole network of the social' ([1982] 2002: 345). This also means that from a Foucauldian perspective, all human relationships – both social and private relations – are part of relationships of power (Foucault [1983] 2002), and therefore always political (Franek 2014). Furthermore, power can be 'at once visible and invisible, present and hidden, ubiquitous' (Foucault and Deleuze 1977: 213). It is not necessarily negative, but power can be productive even if sometimes risky or dangerous. It could therefore be argued that a Foucauldian perspective of power might offer a helpful alternative to explore more subtle and identity-related forms of resistance and political action compared to the collective form discussed previously. From a Foucauldian perspective, any action/resistance needs to be viewed in relation to the discursive production of certain types of (political) subjects. It is a political subjectivity that becomes a precondition for agency (Allen 2002; Raaper 2020b). We would therefore suggest that as market discourses dominate most Western higher education sectors, it can also be assumed that resistance will take place within and in response to such discourses. From a Foucauldian perspective, it would also be important to question the role of the technologies of the self (Foucault [1984] 2000), and the importance of resisting oneself and who one has become to defend political and societal change. In other words, Foucault could potentially help us to understand the role of micro-level resistance in contemporary student politics.

References

Allen, A. (2002), 'Power, Subjectivity, and Agency: Between Arendt and Foucault', *International Journal of Philosophical Studies*, 10 (2): 131–149.

Altbach, P. and Klemenčič, M. (2014), 'Student Activism Remains a Potent Force Worldwide', *International Higher Education*, 76: 2–3.

Arendt, H. (1958), *The Human Condition*, Chicago, IL: University of Chicago Press.

Arendt, H. (1963), *On Revolution*, London: Faber & Faber.

Arendt, H. (1968), *Between Past and Future*, New York: Penguin.

Arendt, H. (1970), *On Violence*, New York: Harcourt.

Barker, C. (2008), 'Some Reflections on Student Movements of the 1960s and Early 1970s', *Revista Crítica de Ciências Sociais*, 81: 43–91.

Bourdieu, P. (1966), 'The School as a Conservative Force: Scholastic and Cultural Inequalities', in J. Eggleston (ed.), *Knowledge and Control: New Directions for the Sociology Education*, 189–209, London: Collier Macmillan.

Bourdieu, P. (1998), *Acts of Resistance*, Cambridge: Polity Press.

Bourdieu, P. and Wacquant, L. (1992), *An Invitation to Reflexive Sociology*, Cambridge: Polity Press.

Brooks, R., Byford, K. and Sela, K. (2015), 'The Changing Role of Students' Unions Within Contemporary Higher Education', *Journal of Education Policy*, 30 (2): 165–181.

Brooks, R., Byford, K. and Sela, K. (2016), 'The Spaces of UK Students' Unions: Extending the Critical Geographies of the University Campus', *Social and Cultural Geography*, 17 (4): 471–490.

Burke, C. (2016), *Culture, Capitals and Graduate Futures: Degrees of Class*, London: Routledge.

Cardosa, S. (2012), 'Students' Perceptions of Quality Assessment – Is There an Option Besides Treating Them as Consumers?', in B. Stensaker, J. Valimaa and C.S. Sarrico (eds.), *Managing Reforms in Universities: The Dynamics of Culture, Identity and Organisational Change*, 135–155. Basingstoke: Palgrave Macmillan.

Case, J. (2014), *Researching Student Learning in Higher Education: A Social Realist Approach*, London: Routledge.

Foucault, M. ([1982] 2002), 'The Subject and Power', in J.D. Faubion (ed.), *Power: Essential Works of Foucault 1954–1984*, 326–348, London: Penguin.

Foucault, M. ([1983] 2002), 'The Risks of Security', in J.D. Faubion (ed.), *Power: Essential Works of Foucault 1954–1984*, 365–381, London: Penguin.

Foucault, M. ([1984] 2000), 'The Ethics of the Concern for Self as a Practice of Freedom', in P. Rabinow (ed.), *Ethics: Essential Works of Foucault 1954–1984*, 281–301, London: Penguin.

Foucault, M. and Deleuze, G. (1977), 'Intellectuals and Power', in D.F. Bouchard (ed.), *Language, Counter-Memory, Practice: Selected Essays and Interviews*, 205–217, Ithaca, NY: Cornell University Press.

Franek, J. (2014), 'Arendt and Foucault on Power, Resistance, and Critique', *Acta Politologica*, 6 (3): 294–309.

Habermas, J. (1979), *Communication and the Evolution of Society*, London: Heinemann.

Habermas, J. (1984, 1989), *The Theory of Communicative Action*, 2 vols., Cambridge: Polity Press.

Habermas, J. (1992), *The Structural Transformations of the Public Sphere*, Cambridge: Polity Press.

Harvey, D. (2005), *A Brief History of Neo-Liberalism*, Oxford: Oxford University Press.

Hensby, A. (2017), 'Campaigning for a Movement: Collective Identity and Student Solidarity in the 2010/11 UK Protests Against Fees and Cuts', in R. Brooks (ed.), *Student Politics and Protest: International Perspectives*, 13–29, Abingdon: Routledge.

Klemenčič, M. (2014), 'Student Power in a Global Perspective and Contemporary Trends in Student Organising', *Studies in Higher Education*, 39 (3): 396–411.

Klemenčič, M. (2015), 'What is Student Agency? An Ontological Exploration in the Context of Research on Student Engagement', in M. Klemenčič, S. Bergand and R. Primožič (eds.), *Student Engagement in Europe: Society, Higher Education and Student Governance*, 11–29, Strasbourg: Council of Europe Publishing.

Luescher-Mamashela, T. (2013), 'Student Representation in University Decision-Making: Good Reasons, A New Lens?', *Studies in Higher Education*, 38 (10): 1442–1456.

Lukes, S. (1974), *Power: A Radical View*, Basingstoke: Palgrave Macmillan.

Mahony, P. and Weiner, G. (2019), 'Neo-liberalism and the State of Higher Education in the UK', *Journal of Further and Higher Education*, 43 (4): 560–572.

Maisuria, A. and Helmes, S. (2019), *Life for the Academic in the Neoliberal University*, London: Routledge.

Marcuse, H. (1964), *One-Dimensional Man*, Boston, MA: Beacon Press.

McCaig, C. (2018), *The Marketisation of English Higher Education*, Bingley: Emerald.

Naidoo, R. and Williams, J. (2015), 'The Neoliberal Regime in English Higher Education: Charters, Consumers and the Erosion of the Public Good', *Critical Studies in Education*, 56 (2): 208–223.

Nissen, S. (2019), *Student Debt and Political Participation*, Christchurch: Palgrave.

Nissen, S. and Hayward, B. (2017), 'Students' Associations: The New Zealand Experience', in R. Brooks (ed.), *Student Politics and Protest: International Perspectives*, 147–160, Abingdon: Routledge.

National Union of Students (NUS) (2012), *First Report of the Union Development Zone Committee: Moving from Passive Participation to Deep Participation*, London: NUS.

National Union of Students (NUS) (2013), *Mapping Participation: The Journey of Students' Union Participation in Higher Education*, London: NUS.

Purcell, K., Elias, P., Atfield, G., Behle, H., Ellison, R., Luchinskaya, D., Snape, J., Conaghan, L. and Tzanakou, C. (2012). *Futuretrack Stage 4: Transitions into Employment, Further Study and Other Outcomes*, Warwick: Institute for Employment Research, University of Warwick.

Raaper, R. (2020a), 'Students' Unions and Consumerist Policy Discourses in English Higher Education', *Critical Studies in Education*, 61 (2): 245–261.

Raaper, R. (2020b), 'Constructing Political Subjectivity: The Perspectives of Sabbatical Officers from English Students' Unions', *Higher Education*, 79 (1): 141–157.

Saunders, D.B. (2010), 'Neoliberal Ideology and Public Higher Education in the United States', *Journal for Critical Education Policy Studies*, 8 (1): 42–77.

Slaughter, S. and Rhoades, G. (2004), *Academic Capitalism and the New Economy: Markets, State and HE*, Baltimore, MD: Johns Hopkins University Press.

Tavares, O. and Cardosa, S. (2013), 'Enrolment Choices in Portuguese HE: Do Students Behave as Rational Consumers?', *Higher Education*, 66 (3): 297–309.

Tholen, G. and Brown, P. (2018), 'Higher Education and the Myths of Graduate Employability', in R. Waller, N. Ingram and M.R.M. Ward (eds.), *Higher Education and Social Inequalities: University Admissions, Experiences and Outcomes*, 153–167, London: Routledge.

Wright, A. and Raaper, R. (2019), 'Contesting Student Identities: Making Sense of Students' Positioning in Higher Education Policy', in A. Bagshaw and D. McVitty (eds.), *Influencing Higher Education Policy: A Professional Guide to Making an Impact*, 65–77, Abingdon: Routledge.

13

Habermas and Foucault: Understanding Hostility to Higher Education and Graduate Debt[1]

Cedomir Vuckovic

Introduction

This chapter uses Habermas and Foucault in dialogue as a critical lens through which to understand contemporary English higher education, tuition fees, and graduate responses to student debt. It reports on a series of focus groups conducted with recent graduates, amongst the first to experience £9000 tuition fees, whom were asked to create desirable alternative models of tuition fees. These methods were also informed by Habermas and Foucault, and were designed to facilitate communicative action, while simultaneously testing the limits of discourse by gauging the degree to which participants could remove themselves from neoliberal conceptualisations of the university. Three key findings from research are revealed. First, that graduate criticisms of higher education are derived from the tensions introduced by instrumental rationality to higher education. Second, I show that these graduates are engaged in an 'everyday' resistance at the level of culture, such as cathartic humour that critiques contemporary higher education. The third finding reveals that in constructing alternative fee models, participants desire homogeneity in higher education. Throughout, I show that Habermas and Foucault are able to illuminate both participants' hostilities to higher education and graduate debt, and strategies of everyday resistance which mitigate some of the consequences of that debt.

I first introduce literature on neoliberalism and higher education to contextualise the contemporary sector. I present Habermas's colonisation thesis, and indicate how recent changes to higher education are symptomatic of colonisation. I then discuss Foucault's work on power and resistance, which informs discussion on how subjectivities are formed within the institution. A review of methods, and a critical reflection on theory and methodology follows, identifying the benefits and some difficulties in the use of 'creative' methods imbued with sociological theory.

Research findings are presented and, as outlined above, they allow me to argue that humour is a micro-resistance that defends the participants' lifeworld from tensions introduced to higher education by the system. For this 'resistance' to function, participants invoke collective cultural frames, and speak to a shared opposition to commodification of higher education, in part through imagining alternative universities that tackle some of the issues they identified. I conclude by demonstrating how participants' attitudes to higher education, strategies of everyday resistance, and imagined futures of the university are made visible and intelligible through a dialogue between Habermas and Foucault.

Neoliberalism and English higher education

The Browne Review (2010), part of the 2011 Education Act's advisory framework, facilitated the rise in the variable rate of tuition fees from £3000 to £9000. Changes were introduced despite research conducted on behalf of the review, unpublished in its final version, which found 'the highest reasonable amount' students were prepared to pay was £6000 (Morgan 2011). Tuition fee changes came into effect in 2012, and English students were hardest hit, being made to pay £9000 regardless of which British university they studied in. In comparison, Scottish students received free tuition, Northern Irish students experienced fees of £3500, while Welsh students received a subsidy for fees above £3465.

Alongside fee increases, these reforms intensified neoliberal discourses positioning students as consumers of higher education, framing undergraduates as having an obligation to pay for the private benefits gained from a degree (Johnston 2013). Browne, and indeed the broader marketisation of higher education (such as fee increases to £3000 in 2004–2005), witnessed more immediate repercussions too, most notably the student occupations and demonstrations of 2010–2011 (Solomon and Palmieri 2011).

While there has always been 'competition' amongst British universities (Foskett 2010), recent policy changes have driven higher education towards a more intense marketisation, and there is now a prevailing use of consumer language, with frequent attempts being made to restructure educational practices based on business models. Recent reforms to higher education have encouraged competition between universities for prospective students based on evaluative 'performance indicators', such as teaching quality and research outputs (Olssen and Peters 2005: 127). Meanwhile, students are increasingly positioned as consumers, with discourses such as 'value for money' framing relationships between undergraduates and institutions (Tomlinson 2017). Central to this style of competition, and the 'student-consumer', is positioning the university as a 'service' provider (Visagie 2005). Consequently, Molesworth et al. (2009: 278) insist, 'students seek to "have a degree" rather than "be learners"', with many expecting guarantees of value for money in line with individual investments (Tomlinson 2017). The relative pervasiveness of neoliberal discourse within higher education is perhaps best epitomised by employability narratives and practices (see Boden and Nedeva 2010; Brancaleone and O'Brien 2011), which, alongside metrics such as the Teaching Excellence Framework, serve to justify increased *individual* financing of degrees (O'Leary and Cui 2020).

To understand these changes, a contributor to the relative normalisation of debt amongst students and graduates (see Horton 2015), Habermas's colonisation thesis offers a lens with which to approach higher education's refiguring, and indeed the changing nature of institutional relationships for students and professionals. In addition, Habermas and Foucault in dialogue can be shown to provide an effective way to uncover and conceptualise the everyday forms of resistance people engage in as a response of higher education colonisation.

The colonisation of the lifeworld by the system

Habermas (1987) understands the social world to hold two spheres of interaction, each operating according to competing forms of rationality. With the development of capitalism, initial separations between 'lifeworld' (everyday life) and 'system' (state and economy) spheres become increasingly blurred, and the system encroaches upon, or colonises, the lifeworld.

The 'lifeworld' – or sphere of everyday life – is constituted by 'culture, society, and personality' (Habermas 1987: 222). These constitutive elements are drawn upon in the process of, and are simultaneously reproduced through, communicative action. Habermas (1984: 84–87) understands communicative action to represent a genuine dialogue geared towards establishing mutual consensus, and insists that this guides our interactions and our capacity to understand the world (see also Dews 1986: 12–17; Outhwaite 1996: 160–169). Communicative action is thus integral to the successful operation of speech acts – the everyday means by which subjects understand themselves (and others) in the world, and the way in which people can *mutually* recognise the world around them to be true.

By contrast, the 'system' denotes interactions guided by instrumental rationality, geared towards maximising money, power and profit, and exerting coercive control (Habermas 1984: 84–87; see also Dews 1986: 12–17; Outhwaite 1996: 160–169). Constituted largely by state and politico-economic institutions, prior to the emergence of advanced forms of capitalism, the system remained removed from lifeworld institutions such as the family. However, with the development of capitalism, the system (along with capitalism) began to encroach upon daily life. Consequently, the system and its corresponding instrumental rationality impinges upon the lifeworld, and interactions in everyday life previously driven by communicative action start to operate according to instrumental rationality. Communicative action and its capacity to reproduce the lifeworld becomes obfuscated by instrumental rationality – a process that Habermas (1987: 332–373) terms 'the colonization of the lifeworld by the system'.

The changes above are also indicative of colonisation processes in higher education. Jütten (2013), for instance, insists that the commodification of higher education has altered the social role of university, arguing it is now perceived as a private, rather than public good. Similarly, Geppert and Hollinshead (2017) argue that colonisation in higher education has increased the precariousness of academic work, and that the impingement of the system into academic lifeworlds has taken an immeasurable psychological toll on professionals.

Habermas does, however, retain a degree of optimism despite colonisation. In response to the encroachment of the system, he identifies new social movements (NSMs) that *resist* colonisation through their concern with ways of living, or as Habermas puts it, 'the grammar of forms of life' (1981: 33). Committed to resolving conflicts 'at the seam between the system and life-world' (Habermas 1981: 36), these movements step away from traditional Marxist class-based politics, and concern themselves with 'new' politics of identity and culture (see Edwards 2014). Such groups *defend* the lifeworld and its structural components from encroachment by the state and politico-economic system, and seek to maintain its necessary communicative infrastructure (Dews 1986). The question regarding higher education is thus whether, in response to colonisation and respective changes to the university, students, graduates and staff are engaged in forms of resistance that defend the lifeworld from the system?

While Habermas's concept of colonisation captures the marketisation of higher education and the negative consequences here for communicative forms of interaction, it also opens up some questions about what people might be doing in response to those changes. A dialogue with Foucault is useful here, as it furthers our understanding of the impact of colonised higher education, and complements Habermas in a way that allows us to effectively grasp the nature of student and graduate resistance.

Foucault, power and higher education

Foucault (1977) refigures 'power', arguing that it should be understood as a force (enmeshed in discourse and knowledge) that '... produces reality; it produces domains of objects and rituals of truth. The individual and the knowledge that may be gained of him belong to this production' (1977: 44). According to Foucault, power produces subjectivities; our sensibilities, capacities for judgement, and the means by which we identify ourselves, perceive the world around us, and how our identities are recognised by others (Foucault 1977, 1978, 1982). Subjectivities are the consequence of various forms of power and knowledge, produced and reinforced through practices and structures which seek to know, organise and anticipate the actions of those subjects, as Foucault (1978) identifies within his dissection of disciplinary regimes and confessional apparatuses, for example.

Power and knowledge 'imply one another' (Foucault 1977: 27), and knowledge in the context of universities relies on metrics – specifically, metrics that measure universities, such as institutional rankings. The production of such knowledge about universities and the way this knowledge is used within universities (to facilitate the increasing neoliberalisation of institutions, and in particular the student experience, mentioned earlier) are two forces which shape the colonisation of higher education.

Thus, in the context of higher education, we can understand competitiveness, financialisation and individualisation, and all the metrics and ranking systems which go alongside them, as being indicators of the shifting set of power-knowledge relations occurring through the colonisation of the sector. Through the disciplinary mechanisms present throughout education, and perhaps in particular within higher education institutions (HEIs), a specific array of subjectivities may thus be produced, which Morrissey (2013) suggests operate in part through the more traditional modes of measuring academic achievement that function as regulatory metrics of success and encourage a specific form of studenthood.

Integral to understanding power for Foucault, however, is the inability to be 'free' from it (Foucault 1977, 1978). Freedom, argues Foucault (1978), would imply an 'authentic' human 'truth' which subjects could revert to. This would be incompatible with the contention that who one is and how one comes to recognise oneself, is contingent on the socio-historic specificity of power and discourse. Thus Foucault stresses the inability to exist outside of the power-relations which seek to produce, maintain and regulate subjectivities. However, 'power relations' imply a potential reversal of those 'relations' (Foucault 1982). As Foucault insists, in relations of power 'resistance is the main word, *the key word*, in this dynamic' (1997: 167, original emphasis).

Habermas, Foucault and resistance in higher education

Habermas and Foucault both allow us to understand how actions outside of traditional protest can constitute 'resistance' to forms of power. Foucault, on the one hand, offers scope for a focus on 'everyday' action and interaction, and how these may be performed by individuals (in action or on the body), intentionally or not (Edwards 2014), as resistances oriented towards specific sites of power. Habermas (1987), on the other hand, opens up possibilities for considering the ways in which shared cultures and identities and the reassertion of communicative interactions may be considered forms of resistance. Both, therefore, afford a focus on discourse and the role of language and interaction as a form of resistance. This is important when considering the ways in which students construct understandings of tuition fees, how they challenge these, and – importantly – on what grounds (Habermas 1981).

Jasper (1997) complements such 'everyday' analyses, as he borrows from Habermas in order to understand how culture and identity may be resources for protest (see also Edwards 2008), but also how culture and identity may be at the core of manifestations of protest, resistance and subversion. Jasper (1997) stresses that despite some political action appearing individual, such 'everyday' behaviours must always operate as repertoires which are bound up with collective culture, social networks and common moral values, something which reminds us of Habermas's (1987) constitutive features of the lifeworld (society, personality and culture).

There are explicit similarities here to Foucault's (1982) resistance, whereby subjectivity is continuously in the midst of competing power-relations. Power is everywhere, operating through culture and identity to the same degree as through institutions. As power is pervasive, Foucault (1982, 1997) locates resistance at the level of culture and everyday practice – what is done in everyday action, how culture is embodied or reconstructed as new, and how we transgress limits of our identities, are all forms of resistance in much the same way as they are forms of power.

This everyday relationship between Habermas's and Foucault's contentions on resistance is a theme drawn out throughout this chapter, and the findings presented shortly will explore this dialogue in the context of humour. However, I first explore some critical reflections on theory and methodology.

Critical reflections on theory and methodology

Research with recent university graduates was conducted in 2018–2019 using mixed methods informed by Habermas and Foucault, and included a survey, focus groups and a participatory design task. Such mixed and creative methods generated varied data, affording new ways to operationalise social theory, and in this particular context, allow researchers to explore how the tensions and relations of Habermas's and Foucault's theories can be used to interpret data.

Seventeen participants were involved across five focus groups. The sample was composed of nine male and eight female home graduates from English universities. Twelve of the sample attended Russell Group institutions, while five studied at post-1992 ('new universities') or formerly 1994 Group institutions (a research-intensive body of HEIs established in response to the 'Russell Group'). Focus groups explored participants' responses to colonised higher education, and in particular concerns surrounding student debt. This was done by asking graduates to discuss general attitudes towards higher education, the social role of higher education, and the ways they felt higher education could be improved through changes to tuition fees.

The aim of the focus groups was in part to operationalise communicative action, and with the additional participatory design component, these creative methods opened up avenues to explore the degree to which 'mutual consensus' could be achieved through such communicative interactions (Habermas 1984). Moreover, borrowing from Foucault, the sessions were designed to 'test' the limits of discourse, and the extent to which graduates were able to imagine an alternative model of higher education funding that detached the contemporary university from the neoliberal discourses currently describing the sector.

At the start of each focus group, participants were given an article (see Coughlan 2017) showing figures on English higher education and graduate debt, and were asked to discuss surprising features. This eased graduates into discussion, and provided them with information about what their debt looked like on a national scale. This was done to mitigate concerns identified in the literature about disproportionately negative views towards fees and debt due to unfamiliarity with the student loan system (Harrison et al. 2015; Jones 2016). Following this, participants looked through their group's survey results, and I asked what they thought about the data. Many found the data amusing, and participants seemed reassured by a common lack of knowledge. In order to further engage with questions derived from Habermas's and Foucault's theories, participants were required to 'do' something, either through creative participatory design, or the focus group's *collective* communicative interactions. As such, interviews alone were seen as an inadequate method, and the final research component involved asking participants to design 'ideal' alternative models of tuition fees, based on the focus group's accumulated knowledge and shared experience. Interestingly perhaps, the *lack* in their knowledge identified earlier partly framed their discussions of alternatives, and three groups took up transparency as a key theme for the future.

Asking graduates to consider and interrogate alternative models of tuition fees gave insight into their subjective conceptualisations of their lived world (Guba and Lincoln 1994). Articulated through communicative forms of interaction, orientated ultimately to a form of 'mutual consensus', research explored participants shared views, cultural references and personal experiences relating to higher education. By asking participants to 'create' a model, I was able to interrogate subjective perceptions of existing social phenomena in a way that was oriented to the future (Lupton 2017), while also having the ability to explore the interaction and discursive encounter of the research itself (Mason and Davies 2011).

Informed in part by action research, focusing on collaborative expression (Lichtman 2014), the design element of the research aligns itself to the emancipatory potential Habermas (1966) saw in social research. Crucially, it was also an opportunity to operationalise and 'sociologically test' (Habermas 1987: 167) communicative action and mutual consensus, by encouraging participants to orient their communicative interactions towards a mutually agreed alternative model.

Certain difficulties emerge when using creative methodology, however. First, Heath and Walker note that using 'creative' methods may encourage participants to be 'less guarded about their personal lives than they might be in the context of more formal research encounters' (2012: 11). While this was not the case in this research, some participants began to discuss mental health, a possibly difficult feature of daily life that participants may not have initially wanted to speak about.

Specific issues also emerge when such creative methodology is imbued with theory, particularly what is often understood as the diverging understandings of Habermas and Foucault. The 'sociological testing' of communicative action, for instance, became problematic when participants struggled to work with a 'blank sheet' when designing alternative fee models for higher education, and they would struggle to put pen to paper working from the ground up. In one group, for instance, little was written and most of the session was spent debating where to start. Participants not being able to agree where to start indicates the difficulty people may experience in removing themselves from the captivating neoliberal discourses of what higher education *should* be like. While this made achieving 'mutual consensus' challenging, it was not impossible, and several groups managed to design at least some elements of an alternative model that was *mutually agreed*. In the future, researchers using participatory design may wish to provide participants with some loose structure or framework that they could apply during 'design' components.

Identifying contentions towards higher education and graduate debt

In all five focus groups, participants used consumerist language such as 'value for money' to frame their critiques of higher education. This allowed them to highlight issues such as 'quality' as key things that should be reflected in the increased price they paid. For instance:

> Well, if you keep paying it, you should get your . . . there should be more value for money. You know when you had to start paying 5p for plastic bags, all the supermarkets improved the quality of their plastic bags? Have you noticed this? It should be similar you know . . . if you've gotta pay, you've gotta up the value for money somewhat.
>
> Hugh, 1994 Group, Group 1

Given the language immediately available to participants when talking about the university, they are thus able to illuminate contradictions in the university system.

For instance, the notion of value helped frame critiques around institutions spending 'their' (participants') money on something future students would benefit from. Two groups discussed their institutions' willingness to spend on 'vanity projects', and I asked one group whether they knew what the money was spent on:

> Yeah on the expansion of [my university]. Which seemed like a vanity project more than anything else I think. It wasn't being spent on our education. Like long-term profits for the university is how I see it.
>
>   Issy, Russell Group, Group 3

Hugh and Paul agreed:

> **Hugh**   I had a bit of a chip on my shoulder at my uni. Cos we had like a lot of building works going on that were taking place while I was there, but I was never gonna see the finished result. So I felt like . . . in three or four years this uni's gonna be a lot better than it is now. And I'm paying the increased price and not seeing any of that? (1994 Group, Group 1)
>
> **Paul**   Do you think the tuition fees went towards building new structures? (1994 Group, Group 1)
>
> **Hugh**   I mean you'd like to think so yeah.
>
> **Paul**   So it's like we're charging you 9 grand, and 'x' amount of that is going towards something you won't experience . . .
>
> **Hugh**   . . . and in five years, all those students are gonna be having a great old time with these new facilities.

Despite these critiques being rooted in neoliberal, consumer-oriented language such as 'value for money' (Tomlinson 2017), their concerns were not those of 'customers'. Most participants emphasised that paying £9000 in principle was not *the* issue, so long as institutions catered for student needs, rather than the needs of university-as-business. In this way, participants' criticisms certainly emerged from the tensions introduced to higher education through colonisation and instrumental forms of rationality (Habermas 1987; Jütten 2013) – that is to say, students' (lifeworld) needs being sacrificed for the (instrumental) needs of the university system-institution. These critiques thus emphasise the need for institutions to provide for the student-lifeworld, in a way that engages with the needs of students as determined by those students beyond arbitrarily quantifiable metrics of 'satisfaction' and limited imagining of what a 'lifeworld' might contain.

Most focus groups identified transparency as a key issue, and some participants were confused by the continuously changing terms of their debt, alongside opaque institutional spending arrangements. Zain was concerned with the changing interest rate, and was unable to fully understand the implications of having loans transferred to another company:

> So for me it's a case of I don't understand what it actually transpires to 'cos . . . this could be an incredibly privileged thing of me to say, and it almost definitely is, but I still . . . the implication is kind of unclear. 'Cos we heard that we transferred all of our debt to a company, thus increasing the interest rate because we were told there was no interest or very minimal interest and that's a totally illegal thing, because if you did that with a bank or a loan company then it's totally illegal . . . but obviously the government do it 'cos . . . fuck me . . . it's not the first time the government's done anything horrible.
>
> Zain, 1994 Group, Group 4

Liz similarly abhorred the lack of transparency, but like Zain, she epitomises how these grievances are rooted in discourses that seem to defend the lifeworld inasmuch as they identify and critique the contradictions introduced to higher education by colonisation.

> A lot of the institutions generally feel quite, like cash starved at the moment. I feel like there's a lot of narratives around at the moment about how there's not enough money in education, and it's like, where's all the bloody money we're being charged going?
>
> Liz, Russell Group, Group 4

Given the nature of the contentions expressed by participants, there was certainly a sense of hopelessness towards graduate debt and the future of higher education. However, despite this, participants found a way to challenge the perceived absurdity of higher education and graduate debt. Through humour, a feature shared across all five groups, participants were able to subvert current discourses around higher education, resist colonisation, while simultaneously establishing common cultures bound by shared norms and values.

Humour and cultures of resistance

Humour emerged during all focus groups as a form of 'everyday' resistance. However, understanding humour-as-resistance must be done so contextually – nothing is intrinsically resistance as action happens in contexts that subvert forms of control. In other instances, displays of humour may act as a form of self-preservation (see 't Hart 2007). In the context of these focus groups, humour pushes back at attempts to encourage the internalisation of the obedience demanded by neoliberal higher education discourses.

These displays of humour invoked common cultural references such as shared attitudes towards institutions, and this marked out certain higher education discourses as absurd. Humour as a strategy of resistance or subversion thus epitomises resistances located at both the level of shared culture and individual everyday practice (see Barreca 1988; Yoels and Clair 1995). In the instances of humour presented here, a dialogue between Habermas's and Foucault's contentions on resistance opened up, as participants simultaneously identified and challenged dominant discourses concerning higher education, while defending lifeworld interests in response to higher education's colonisation.

Participants' displays of humour were wide-ranging. Lucy, for instance, stressed she would rather remain 'blissfully ignorant' of the state of her debt:

Lucy   What's the point in knowing? Like I don't think it's gonna change the fact that I need to pay it back. (Russell Group, Group 2)

Researcher   It just doesn't bother you?

Lucy   No it's not that it doesn't bother me, I just don't think that knowing it is gonna change that it has to be paid back.

[...]

Lucy   Rather not know and be ignorant . . . like blissfully ignorant of it. [laughing]

Another common form of humour was sarcasm, ridiculing its target by demonstrating the absurdity of loans for higher education, undermining the authority of institutions (Sombatpoonsiri 2015). For instance, a discussion on mental health led to a conversation about the lack of institutional support, to which Shaun responded with sarcasm:

Liz   Mental health services at my institution were decimated at the time I was there . . . (Russel Group, Group 4)

Zain   . . . absolutely. . . (1994 Group, Group 4)

Liz   . . . and it was . . .

Zain   . . . It's a national crisis! It's a joke! [exasperated]

Liz   Yeah and it was . . . it was just . . . the fall in provision was shocking. And like the university . . . the institution still feels quite rich and it's like, literally what are you doing? There was no transparency in our institution over funding at all, and then I don't wanna put the fall on all institutions for not being transparent enough.

Shaun   Bet they've probably given themselves a nice new building. (Russell Group, Group 4)

Liz   I mean they have ...

[All laugh]

Below, Hugh makes a joke about undergraduates receiving the 'full package', and shows how his wealthier peers had become the victim of a peculiar manufactured inequality between students.

> ...as someone that got ...like I got the full package if you like. So I got the grant and I had like whatever the maximum amount was. And I thought it was unfair at the time that like my supposedly richer peers didn't get any of that. And they, a lot of the time, were a lot worse off. Like I was completely ... I didn't go to uni in London so my costs were pretty low but ... I had a great old time, and so did the other people that had the maximum amount. Like, they were walking around with Gucci belts on. Yet my rich friends had ... like some of them didn't have enough money to cover their rent.
>
> Hugh, 1994 Group, Group 2

The displays of humour shown here served two key roles. First, through making jokes about the sheer size of student loans, unrealistic chances of clearing debt, and the lack of institutional investment despite tripling fees, graduates were able to identify the shared perception of the absurdity of student loans. Their jokes provided a direct challenge to dominant discourses of higher education, and their collective laughter represented an undermining of the legitimacy of debt through ridicule, by refusing to recognise the knowledge and power that underpins those discourses as legitimate (Barreca 1988; Vitis and Gilmour 2016).

Second, participants implicitly shared their perceptions of the socio-cultural world (or lifeworld) when invoking collective cultural and social references to make jokes (Habermas 1987; Jasper 1997). Through this communicative relationship, graduates were able to reproduce networks, common politico-cultural frames, and the shared meanings through which jokes (and critique) can operate (Vitis and Gilmour 2016), and arguably reproduce alongside this the very lifeworld itself (Edwards 2008). Humour might thus be one of the ways in which students or graduates maintain the lifeworld, as a kind of micro-resistance to the encroachment of the system into their lives and experiences.

For the participants, culture acts as a 'resource' for protest; it allows this humour to make sense in the shared lifeworld of participants, and culture also allows it to operate as a strategy of subversion (Jasper 1997; Sombatpoonsiri 2015). Culture is a means through which people *do* humour-as-subversion (it is recognised as culturally legitimate and appropriate) (Jasper 1997). Humour's potential to identify common grievances amongst participants helps highlight where dominant forms of 'knowledge and power coalesce as discourse' (Yoels and Clair 1995: 54), and participants' humour identified the current tensions in higher education that are in part due to colonisation. Their jokes, sarcasm and wit pointed towards the possibility that things can, and should, be otherwise. In this respect, their shared humour is an alternative strategy of power within current discourses at work in this particular nexus of power-relations (Foucault 1982, 1997). Hugh's quote exemplifies this, as his story not only identifies the absurdity of manufactured hardship in higher education, but it implies that things *should* be different.

It is not simply actions that can be resisted, but also the internalisation of certain discourses and ways of being in circumstances where that internalisation (becoming the obedient graduate) would be the 'natural' thing to do. By laughing, participants subvert this internalisation – marking out the absurdity of particular features of higher education is what resists the internalising of those discourses. The methods, and theoretical frame used here, allow us to interpret this data as resistance, and Habermas and Foucault, in dialogue, allow us to understand the interactional moments of these focus groups as puncturing the logic of colonised higher education.

Homogenised higher education

Participants mostly failed to develop totally finished alternative models, but future-oriented discussions revealed strong criticisms of accessibility and inequalities within higher education. Most agreed that future models should strive for parity between traditional university-goers and non-traditional learners. As shown earlier, participants did not mind paying £9000, provided access was broadened, and money was invested to ensure equality in higher education:

> **Hugh**   I think if people knew that . . . a lot of money was going towards like apprentices and that kinda thing, maybe they'd be . . . it should be like a more holistic thing . . . so they know yeah, we're paying money for uni, but we're paying money for people to do a lot of other stuff as well. (Group 2, 1994 Group)

Lucy   … goes to everyone. (Group 2, Russell Group)

Hugh   Goes to everyone, like not just the more privileged kids that went to uni, but people that don't as well.

Liz and Zain, however, went a step further

Liz   I've always fantasied about having universities for people when they retire. (Group 4, Russel Group)

Zain   That would be really good. (Group 4, 1994 Group)

[…]

Liz   and I've done a lot of adult learning stuff since I left uni and really appreciate the spaces for adults to learn, and how different that feels to university. Like … like [Adult Learning Programme] is in that kind of stuff, and I've always thought it's a shame those things didn't have that feel on campus because it feels so like … held for a particular age group and a particular lifestyle.

Group 1, in an attempt to mitigate the inequalities identified in higher education, proposed a body that ensured fair distribution of students' tuition fees. The group named this the 'Council for Students and Higher Education', and insisted that any future model, regardless of tuition cost, would ensure students at lower-ranked institutions were afforded the same privileges and opportunities to those at more 'elite' institutions, by proportionately distributing collectivised tuition. This 'all in it together' attitude emerged during all focus groups, and below, Jamal and Ben from Group 1 insist students' collective fees are fairly distributed

Jamal   I think that distribution could be an issue though, cos one university could think that they're worth more than the money that's being contributed to that university. Like let's say for example the university that I was going to was getting £20,000 per year, but people who were going to [a Russell Group] were getting £700,000 per year I'd be … I'd feel like I was out of pocket do you know what I mean. (Group 1, Post-1992)

Ben   Yeah, yeah I was gonna say it's kinda similar to like how local authorities work in the sense that there are some local authorities that are much more nice. It's already a nice area, they don't need a whole lot more investment, so like naturally the money would go to the places that do need more. So like Oxbridge say are probably much more self-sufficient. (Group 1, Russell Group)

[…]

Cos to me I feel like further education should be a collective effort amongst everyone. Just cos I went to [a Russell Group university] and you went to [a Post-1992 university] doesn't mean that we don't have the same intentions sort of thing. So I shouldn't be worried about making sure that my uni's better than yours, because we both are getting an education to contribute back. So I should make sure that you're doing alright as well.

Both Habermas and Foucault can offer us a way to understand the positions of these graduates. What has been shown is that participants provided a different schema with which to *value* the university. This invoked in part personal moral values, but spoke also to shared frames, conceptualisations and hopes for the university (Jasper 1997) that made sense in the context of the research encounter through communicative interactions (Habermas 1987). Participants' hostilities and alternative futures emphasised what has become de-emphasised in current discourses around higher education; they performed a different politics of education, through discourse, which directly challenged those dominant forms today, and this was itself a political act (see Foucault 1977, 1982). For Habermas, these discourses may respond to colonisation; a challenge to the pervasiveness of the instrumental, or 'private good' principle of higher education, reinstating instead a collective, arguably lifeworld-driven 'public good'. For Foucault (1978, 1997), these graduate discourses, like those in displays of humour, may invoke a different way of viewing, knowing and doing the university; it is the deployment of a different form of power-knowledge that challenges dominant forms in operation today.

Conclusion: Habermas and Foucault

Participants' humour-as-resistance and their alternative visions for higher education can both be understood in an explicit dialogue between Habermas and Foucault. Humour and alternative futures both represent an engagement with daily life in a different way, and through cultural frames that are misaligned with dominant discourses and forms of culture, and this challenges certain ways of *doing* university and understanding the institution's role (Foucault 1997; Habermas 1981). In part, participants' alternatives, alongside their resistances and critiques, responded to colonisation by seeking to re-imagine a university that would incorporate non-traditional learners, and that would benefit students at less financially capable institutions. This desire for homogenisation and parity in higher education is arguably a defence of the lifeworld, reminiscent of NSMs, as it responds to the increasing competitiveness, individualisation and instrumentalisation of social relations within higher education symptomatic of colonisation. In this study, graduates defended the lifeworld by striving to incorporate students into the university who may not otherwise have the same opportunities to engage. For participants, this would diversify academic and cultural interactions as well as make sure institutions are properly funded, and as a result would prevent institutional relations existing on a purely instrumental basis.

Within this defence, however, participants fundamentally rejected dominant discourses of individualism, competitiveness and consumerism. In this sense, their alternative models of tuition fees and HEIs existed as a simultaneously 'Foucauldian' resistance at the level of discourse, as it stands in opposition to the dominant discourses concerning universities and their purpose. Participants were able to distance themselves from individualising neoliberal discourses, resisting their internalisation, and were instead able to frame alternative models of higher education in homogenised and collective ways which challenged issues of access and participation. Both humour and withdrawal speak to the personal identities of participants too, as they highlighted their subjective attitudes towards fees and debt. Crucially, the resistances on display in this study were shared and mutually understood, and this demonstrates that despite being 'individual' acts, these everyday strategies are firmly rooted in collective frames, cultures and attitudes (Manning 2015). Understanding humour as resistance in this specific context helps understand how it is that graduates preserve ideas which are misaligned with instrumental logics, and thus continue to resist, partially and not consistently, the encroachment of the system.

Note

1   This project was funded by the ESRC, North West Social Science Doctoral Training Partnership (NWSSDTP).

References

Barreca, R. (1988), 'Introduction', in R. Barreca (ed.), *Last Laughs: Perspectives on Women and Comedy*, 3–22, New York: Gordon & Breach.

Boden, R. and Nedeva, M. (2010), 'Employing discourse: Universities and graduate "employability"', *Journal of Education Policy*, 25 (1): 37–54.

Brancaleone, D. and O'Brien, S. (2011), 'Educational commodification and the (economic) sign value of learning outcomes', *British Journal of Sociology of Education*, 32 (4): 501–519.

Browne, J. (2010), *Securing a sustainable future for higher education: An independent review of higher education funding and student finance* (Browne Report), London: Department for Business Innovation and Skills. Available online: https://www.gov.uk/government/publications/the-browne-report-higher-education-funding-and-student-finance (accessed 19 June 2019).

Coughlan, S. (2017), '10 charts that show the effect of tuition fees', *BBC News*. Available online: https://www.bbc.co.uk/news/education-40511184 (accessed 1 June 2019).

Dews, P. (1986), *Habermas: Autonomy and Solidarity*, London: Verso.

Edwards, G. (2008), 'The "lifeworld" as a resource for social movement participation and the consequences of its colonisation', *Sociology*, 42 (2): 299–316.

Edwards, G. (2014), *Social Movements and Protest*, Cambridge: Cambridge University Press.

Foskett, N. (2010), 'Markets, government, funding and the marketization of UK higher education', in M. Molesowrth, R. Scullion and E. Nixon (eds.), *The Marketisation of Higher Education and the Student as Consumer*, 25–38, London: Routledge.

Foucault, M. (1977), *Discipline and Punish*, London: Penguin.

Foucault, M. (1978), *The History of Sexuality*, New York: Random House.

Foucault, M. (1982), 'The subject and power', *Critical Inquiry*, 8 (4): 777–795.

Foucault, M. (1997), 'Sex, power, and the politics of identity', in P. Rabinow (ed.), *Ethics: Subjectivity and Truth. Essential Works of Michel Foucault*, 163–173, New York: The New Press.

Geppert, M. and Hollinshead, G. (2017), 'Signs of dystopia and demoralization in global academia: Reflections on the precarious and destructive effects of the colonization of the Lebenswelt', *Critical Perspectives on International Business*, 13 (2): 136–150.

Guba, E.G. and Lincoln, Y.S. (1994), 'Competing paradigms in qualitative research', in N.K. Denzin and Y.S. Lincoln (eds.), *Handbook of Qualitative Research*, 105–117, Thousand Oaks, CA: Sage.

Habermas, J. (1966), 'Knowledge and interest', *Inquiry*, 9 (1–4): 285–300.

Habermas, J. (1981), 'New social movements', *Telos*, 49: 33–37.

Habermas, J. (1984), *Theory of Communicative Action*, vol. 1, Boston, MA: Beacon Press.

Habermas, J. (1987), *Theory of Communicative Action*, vol. 2, Boston, MA: Beacon Press.

Harrison, N., Agnew, S. and Serido, J. (2015), 'Attitudes to debt among indebted undergraduates: A cross-national exploratory factor analysis', *Journal of Economic Psychology*, 46: 62–73.

Heath, S. and Walker, C. (2012), *Innovations in Youth Research*, Basingstoke: Palgrave Macmillan.

Horton, J. (2015), 'Young people and debt: Getting on with austerities', *Area*, 49 (3): 280–287.

Jasper, J.M. (1997), *The Art of Moral Protest*, Chicago, IL: University of Chicago Press.

Johnston, R. (2013), 'England's new scheme for funding higher education through student fees: "Fair and progressive"?', *The Political Quarterly*, 84 (2): 200–210.

Jones, S. (2016), 'Expressions of student debt aversion and tolerance among young academically able young people in low-participation English schools', *British Educational Research Journal*, 42 (2): 277–293.

Jütten, T. (2013), 'Habermas and markets', *Constellations*, 290 (4): 587–603.

Lichtman, M. (2014), *Qualitative Research for the Social Sciences*, London: Sage.

Lupton, D. (2017), 'Towards design sociology', *Sociology Compass*, 12 (1): e12546.

Manning, N. (2015), *Political (dis)engagement: The Changing Nature of the 'Political'*, Bristol: Policy Press.

Mason, J. and Davies, K. (2011), 'Experimenting with qualitative methods: Researching family resemblance', in J. Mason and A. Dale (eds.), *Understanding Social Research: Thinking Creatively about Method*, 33–48, London: Sage.

Molesworth, M., Nixon, E. and Scullion, R. (2009), 'Having, being and higher education: The marketization of the university and the transformation of the student into consumer', *Teaching in Higher Education*, 14 (3): 227–287.

Morgan, J. (2011), '£6K must be ceiling, survey told Browne', *Times Higher Education*. Available online: https://www.timeshighereducation.com/news/6k-must-be-ceiling-survey-told-browne/415358.article (accessed 19 June 2019).

Morrissey, J. (2013), 'Governing the academic subject: Foucault, governmentality and the performing university', *Oxford Review of Education*, 39 (6): 797–810.

O'Leary, M. and Cui, V. (2020), 'Reconceptualising Teaching and learning in higher education: challenging neoliberal narratives of teaching excellence through collaborative observation', *Teaching in Higher education*, 25 (5): 141–156.

Olssen, M. and Peters, M.A. (2005), 'Neoliberalism, higher education and the knowledge economy: From the free market to knowledge capitalism', *Journal of Education Policy*, 20 (3): 313–345.

Outhwaite, W. (1996), *The Habermas Reader*, Cambridge: Polity Press.

Solomon, C. and Palmieri, T. (2011), *Springtime: The New Student Rebellions*, London: Verso.

Sombatpoonsiri, J. (2015), *Humour and Nonviolent Struggle in Serbia*, New York: Syracuse University Press.

't Hart, M. (2007), 'Humour and social protest: An introduction', *International Review of Social History*, 52 (S15): 1–20.

Tomlinson, M. (2017), 'Student perceptions of themselves as "consumers" of higher education', *British Journal of Sociological Education*, 38 (4): 450–467.

Visagie, J. (2005), 'Deconstructing the discourse of community service and academic entrepreneurship: The ideological colonisation of the university', *Acta Academica*, 37 (1): 222–237.

Vitis, L. and Gilmour, F. (2016), 'Dick pics on blast: A woman's resistance to online sexual harassment using humour, art and Instagram', *Crime Media Culture*, 13 (3): 335–355.

Yoels, W.C. and Clair, J.M. (1995), 'Laughter in the clinic: Humour as social organization', *Symbolic Interaction*, 18 (1): 39–58.

14

Neoliberal Governmentality in Higher Education in Peru: An Example of Students' Unions' Resistance and Conflict

Diego A. Salazar-Morales

Introduction

In 1991, Peru's autocratic leader Alberto Fujimori ordered the military to intervene in public universities, claiming that the Maoist organisation Shining Path had long been encouraging students' ideological radicalisation. Together with this measure, Fujimori also introduced an aggressive privatisation scheme for Peru's higher education system consisting of tax exemptions, consultancies for private universities, and a lack of general regulatory oversight.

After ten years of military intervention and in the wake of Fujimori's regime (1990–2000), a dual system was established: a system of well-funded private universities, connected to international academic centres, serving the Peruvian elites; and another system of underfunded public universities, with few international connections, and peripheral to the global academic debate. However, this divide has not only led to marked differences in education quality and access to the job market, it has also created a stigma around public university students and their organised attempts to resist budgetary reductions, governmental manipulation of their programmes, police intervention and, ultimately, privatisation (Jave et al. 2014; Nureña 2016). Since then, every students' union mobilisation has been automatically labelled by the media, public officials and private university consortiums as 'Shining Path resurgences', threats to democracy and even 'pro-terrorist', thus effectively silencing reformist agendas while promoting constant police intervention in university campuses.

In light of the Peruvian experience, this chapter looks to the Foucauldian concept of governmentality to cast light on the dynamics of university governance in Peru. Through a detailed 'genealogical' analysis that simultaneously combines documentary evidence, official speeches of Peruvian government functionaries, and in-depth interviews with students' union leaders, this chapter presents three different mini case studies that illustrate how the country's predominant neoliberal governmentality has racially segmented its entire higher education system. I demonstrate how racial categorisations produce a hegemonic discourse that associates whiteness, social capital and power with the private higher education system, while in the case of the public system, it conveys concepts of indigeneity, marginality and radicalism. This chapter also describes the power mechanisms sustaining the application of such governmentality.

The chapter proceeds as follows: first, I revise the theoretical elements that construct the concept 'governmentality' and its neoliberal version in Peru; next, I provide a detailed historical revision of how higher education has been segmented in Peru since the 1990s; then, I reflect theoretically on the 'genealogical' method and its applicability to mini case studies; finally, I present three distinct cases on how Peruvian neoliberal governmentality and, more specifically, its power technologies interact with students' unions.

Governmentality in Peru: Neoliberalism and racism

Governance and governmentality studies have grown in number since the publication of Foucault's lectures at the Collège de France in 1978–1979 (Foucault 2008). The concept 'governmentality', broadly speaking, refers to the institutional ensemble, and the practices that emerged in the eighteenth century in Western Europe that forged a way to understand government as being concerned with the 'population', its economic management, and related strategies to foster its prosperity (Foucault 1994: 218). Foucault also argues that governmentality has its roots in Western European societies and their historically structured apparatuses of power (disciplines, new societal and 'self' power technologies), which, at the same time, have emerged as by-products of novel ways of knowing, classifying and deciphering the presences and absences of a certain population (Townley 1993; Lemke 2019: 129–130). For Foucault, government is not only a set of tangible institutions and regulations (taxes, police, health institutions, etc.) but the logics that support their reproduction and maintenance over time (Dean 2010: 17).

Arguably, Foucault's 'governmentality' can be applied to multiple settings, including the logics, apparatuses and technologies of power that neoliberalism has developed since its incursion into world politics. In his lectures of 1978–1979, known as the *Birth of Biopolitics* (1997: 73–79), Foucault sheds light onto neoliberalism as a novel 'way of governing' based on (1) the expansion of the economical 'cost-benefit' logic to the whole of society (Dean 2010: 175) and (2) the consideration that markets are society's only 'organising and regulative' principle (Lemke 2019: 135). Yet, multiple scholars still recognise that the most salient aspect of neoliberal governmentality is the reification of 'the entrepreneurial nature of individuals' (Lemke 2001: 200). They – the individual entrepreneurs – are 'responsible' for their own government (McNay 2009: 61), and they function independently of 'state support' (Lemke 2001: 201). In this context, state pastoral functions and apparatuses are confined to a regulatory role (Lemke 2001: 201).

Applied to the Peruvian context, Foucault's analysis of neoliberal governmentality collides with a fundamental post-colonial racist society against indigenous peoples. In Peru, as multiple scholars have discussed (Ferrari 1984; Drinot 2006; Sandoval and Toche 2004; Arrunategui 2010), the value of indigenous peoples – who happen to be among the poorest sectors of society – have been historically determined by their capacity to 'adapt' and renounce their culture in favour of 'modernisation' projects. There have been multiple historical attempts to introduce indigenous peoples to modernity (through 'blood mixing' – *mestizaje* – alphabetisation, rural development projects, and/or through 'agricultural technification' during the 1960s) (Burns 1998; Contreras and Oliart 2014; Pribilsky 2009). Currently, neoliberals adopt the novel conception of the 'self-made' entrepreneur responsible for their life choices and opposer of state support (Drinot 2014) to transform the 'Indian' into a subject 'worthy' of governmental concern.

Notably, Old and New governmental rationalities in Peru have distinguished two sectors of the population: one associated with backwardness and 'not amenable to governmentalisation', the other a contributor to progress and thus malleable, productive and commensurable to 'national progress' (Drinot 2014: 178). These divisions extend to every corner of Peruvians' interactions in the economic, political and social spheres, which have been 'fed' by a programmed classification of who is 'in' (white, privately educated individuals) and who is 'out' (the communist threat, ungovernable indigenous people, or radical students attending national universities) (Burga 2008).

In this context, the object of governmental concern, for Peruvian neoliberals, is not the population as a whole, but only certain sectors of it (Drinot 2014). Sectors that are traditionally considered white, or close to whiteness (see

Seshadri-Crooks 2002), non-indigenous and even based '...on [their] ontological capacity ... to contribute to, and indeed be subjects of, projects of "improvement" and national "progress" more generally' (Drinot 2011: 186). Most importantly, as Drinot (2014) recognises, the dualisation of Peruvian governmentality invokes the implementation of different power technologies. Thus subjects who are 'in' are governed through formal state apparatuses and the law is adequately applied; for subjects considered 'out', the government prefers force and imposition – for them, the application of the rule of law is all but chimera (Burga 2008).

It is not a surprise, then, that such duality also applies to Peru's higher education dynamics. Neoliberal governmentality along with racism has contributed to the segmentation of the Peruvian higher education system. On the one hand, the private higher education system in Peru is 'connected', benefiting from tax exemptions, and is designed for Peruvian elites and/or for those who aspire to whiteness or look less indigenous (Nureña 2016). The public system, on the other hand, operates as the institution of last resort for those who cannot afford private education. It is also associated with radicalism, a 'lack of network and connections' (Nureña et al. 2014), indigeneity and 'backwardness' (Jave et al. 2014).

The two systems co-exist and interact under the same governmental umbrella, and their interaction has prompted public discussions (Burga 2008; Jave et al. 2014; Cuenca 2015; Nureña 2016), which discursively reveal the nature of their division, and the concepts associated with each of them.

Peruvian higher education in neoliberal times: Liberalisation by militarisation

Militarisation of higher education

By the end of the 1990s, universities had long been part of a political radicalisation pattern in Peru. Several left-oriented student organisations had flourished and emerged in response to the gradual abandonment of universities by the Peruvian state. After a period in the 1960s and 1970s when universities were integral to the Peruvian (and Latin American) state in the pursuit of industrialisation policies, they were suddenly left behind after regime change in 1980 and even more so after the economic crisis of 1987–1989 (CVR 2004: 603–649). This process, together with a tradition of pedagogical dogmatism (Sandoval

2004), severe cuts in funding for public universities (CVR 2004; British Council 2016), and the war policy on the part of the Peruvian government directed at the emerging guerrilla movements (Shining Path and the Tupac Amaru Revolutionary Movement – the MRTA in Spanish), contributed to the stigma felt by the public universities and their students: they were considered 'no go' areas, and the continual politicisation of the student body fed into the hands of the government 'who wanted to ensure control of the student movement' (CVR 2004).

Moreover, this situation worsened when the Shining Path and the MRTA began recruiting their *cuadros* ('strongmen') from the *dirigentes* (the leaders of university political organisations) who were known for their political skills (Jave et al. 2014). However, despite their efforts, the Truth and Reconciliation Commission (CVR 2004) and several scholars (Jave et al. 2014; Ramírez Zapata and Nureña, 2012; Nureña 2016) have documented that the university *dirigentes* not only rebuffed the Shining Path and MRTA but also challenged them politically and prevented students from joining the ranks of the guerrillas.

Despite the efforts of the *dirigentes* to retain control of public universities, in May 1991 Alberto Fujimori, together with members of the military and the police, entered the Universidad Nacional Mayor de San Marcos – an emblematic Peruvian university, founded in 1551 to educate the Spanish colonial elite – claiming that he wanted 'a university without terrorists', and that his only aim was to maintain the 'social order' (CVR 2004: 633; *Latina* 2007). Other important public universities in Peru were then occupied by the military who began patrolling their campuses,[1] monitoring classrooms and prohibiting any mention of or classes delivering 'terrorist ideology' – namely, Marxism-related courses (*El Comercio* 2016)

Moraña (2012) and Jave et al. (2014) argue that military intervention led to a general depoliticisation of the university. In practice, the CVR (2004) found that during this time, the *dirigentes* were afraid of being associated with any 'guerrilla organisation' and that some students were 'disappeared' as part of the military strategy to instil fear into the student body and prevent them from joining Shining Path. As a result, most student organisations – including the Federation of Peruvian Students (FEP), the emblematic Federation of the Universidad Nacional Mayor de San Marcos (FUSM), as well as other regional students' unions – all but disappeared during the 1990s before reorganising in 2015. This, as Nureña (2016) claims, was the response of the state to the long-term 'stigma' felt by students from public universities when airing their grievances (e.g. free education for everyone, an increase in budgets, corruption and clientelism in public universities, and respect for university transport fees) (FEP 2016).

Liberalisation of the higher education market

Yet Fujimori's policies did not only involve military intervention, he also resorted to administrative control. He created a Reorganisation Commission (CORE in Spanish) to appoint faculty, administrative and other staff happy to pledge allegiance to his regime while at the same time preventing 'the articulation of political opposition movements' (CVR 2004: 638). In addition, his crusade included advocating for 'private participation in education affairs in Peru' (Puiggrós 1996). Thus in 1996 Legislative Decree (D.L.) 882 was passed into law, which facilitated profit-making within private education. This decree exempted private universities from paying rent-related taxes in all its activities, and established tax credits to be used for reinvestment in other ventures – not necessarily linked to educative purposes – as well as other tax breaks.

Consequently, by 2014, the number of private universities had more than trebled: in 1990, there were 24 private institutions, but in 2014 when President Ollanta Humala (SUNEDU 2019a) finally annulled Decree 882, the number had grown to 92. In line with this, the National Superintendence of Higher Education of Peru (SUNEDU) reported that since the mid-1990s, the number of students applying to higher education had increased from 68,000 to 173,000 (SUNEDU 2019b).

Also, these new private universities resorted to 'cheap' degrees to attract young members of the population. In the main, they provided programmes in the Social Sciences, Law and Administration at the expense of Engineering, the Natural Sciences and Medicine, because of the high price of delivery of the latter (Castro and Yamada 2013). Moreover, some private universities served as platforms for the political entities that funded them, including offering scholarships and other positions to supporters (Barrenechea 2014). Others operated successful businesses on the side unrelated to their academic activities, including football teams, airlines and restaurant chains, among others; these universities were also apt to appoint cronies to the academic structures of their university ventures (Collyns 2019).

Interestingly, since the 1990s, public universities have also grown in number. Pressured by local citizens, who found in universities a route to social mobility, the government has opened 24 new universities in the last 30 years. Currently, there are 51 public universities in the country – yet in financial terms, the budget per student is 20 per cent less than it was in the 1970s (around $1000 per student) (British Council 2016).

Critical reflections on theory and methodology

Many scholars agree that Foucault's *oeuvre* in the 1970s experienced a shift from 'archaeology' to 'genealogy'. Arguably, his early works (*Madness and Civilization* [1961] 1965; *The Birth of the Clinic* [1963] 1973; *The Archaeology of Knowledge* [1969] 1972, etc.) explored the association between specific types of scientific discourses and how they change over time by analysing what is – and what is not – 'logical and rational' in society. Yet it was not until *Discipline and Punish: The Birth of the Prison* ([1975] 1991) that he juxtaposed the notion of 'power' with discursive formations and how they impact on disciplining the subject. It was then that the idea of a 'genealogy' emerged (Lemke 2019: 49)

'Genealogy', as a method, not only involves the analysis of the ensemble of historical discursive formations and the 'knowledges' that sustain them (Lemke 2019: 50), but also explains how 'power relations' ensure the construction of discourses that discipline the subject (Foucault 1998: 98). Specifically, the 'genealogical' approach demands the identification of the 'discourse' that sustains the logics, knowledges and apparatuses of power of a state in more or less three basic elements: (1) the logics and justifications of the exercise of power of a determined discourse, (2) the historical period in which it was born, and (3) the 'aims and objectives' of power (Foucault 1998: 95). For Foucault, these elements help to unpack the 'history of the present' of a governmental phenomenon. It should illustrate 'contingency' and 'discontinuity' of power dynamics, meaning that attention should be paid to 'the small causes that generate massive effects' (Biebricher 2008: 367).

Based on these characteristics, the genealogical approach has important implications for this chapter. First, its application requires the identification of the 'discursive formation' sustaining the conflict within higher education in Peru. This task starts by identifying the conflicts in higher education in 'the present' so as to uncover its rationalities as materialised in institutions and state apparatuses (Mahon 1992: 105). In practice, this process translates into a reconsideration of the documents, official speeches, laws and public appearances that defended or advanced a neoliberal ideology.

Second, a 'genealogy' involves a 'history' – a sequence of events that together illustrate in practice the associations between 'power-knowledge' and discourse (Biebricher 2008: 369). This history should depict the practicalities, conflicts and distinctive arrangements involved in how, in our case, the Peruvian neoliberal governmentality has shaped its higher education. Arguably, this task requires a timeline identifying the decisions, and their implications, based on the empirical.

Yet these events can only be read if put in the larger context of Foucault's theory (Lemke 2019: 50). Thus, the third implication of the genealogical approach for this study is theoretical. Genealogy, together with governmentality, invokes the utilisation of theory, its elements and practicalities to form a narrative describing higher education politics. The assessment of the evidence to illustrate the Peruvian neoliberal governmentality is not detached from its historical context, and it definitely cannot be processed without a proper theoretical iteration.

Thus, by drawing on Foucault's genealogy, I address the dual nature of Peruvian neoliberal governmentality in the practical realm. My 'analysis of the present' of Peruvian higher education has led me to identify the different responses of the Peruvian government, and specifically, how it reacted to resist students' demands for improvements in higher education.

I chose to use three mini case studies. Yin (1981) and others (Feagin et al. 1991; Yazan 2015) define a case study approach as a technique that employs various data sources (e.g. reports, verbal, video records, interviews, etc.) and research strategies to analyse a contemporary phenomenon in its 'real-life context' (Yin 1981: 60). Accordingly, I collected data from sources reproducing and contesting discourses related to Peruvian neoliberalism in the higher education sector. These sources included documentary evidence, reports and interviews with student organisations ($n = 20$) intermittently collected between 2017 and 2019. Interview evidence is noted as 'Int. #'; similar sentiments on the part of different interviewees are also noted. Together, this evidence is employed to identify a sequence of events whereby power dynamics, discursive ensembles and concrete actions reflect 'encounters' between Peruvian neoliberal governmentality and the challenges posed by students' unions. Two of the mini case studies involve a national debate about radicalism, viability and presumed 'privileges' that students from public universities have because they 'study for free' (Macera 2017). The third case study shows how compliant the police and Peruvian authorities are with the interests of private universities' student unions.

Encounters between public and private higher education

Case study 1: Repression in the Andes

During the government of Alejandro Toledo (2001–2006), any promises to reform Fujimori's neoliberal economic policies rapidly lost support. Thus, in

May 2003, a general strike was called by the Unique Syndicate of Peruvian Teachers (SUTEP in Spanish) in support of their demands for improved pay and conditions. Many others, including health professionals, members of the judiciary, agricultural workers and university students joined them, including the FEP. Students' unions of various universities blocked the entrances to their campuses as a sign of support for the general strike – a collective action known as '*toma de universidad*' (*El Universo* 2003).

'*Las Tomas*' – as students colloquially refer to them – are seen as the epitome of university protests and have a longstanding tradition within the university movement (Int. #3, similar in #2 and #4). 'It means pressuring into action other students and making the authorities aware of our problems . . .' (Int. #6, similar in #10). Yet '*tomas*', once popular with the elites when they received their education from public universities (de la Fuente 2017), are in neoliberal Peru portrayed as 'resurgences of terrorism' (Int. #6, similar in #19).

In this context, public university students' support for SUTEP's national mobilisation in 2003 was considered 'subversive' (LUM 2016). In May, students of the Universidad Nacional del Altiplano (UNA) in the city of Puno – in a region sharing a border with Bolivia, mainly composed of Aymara indigenous peoples – blockaded their university campus, a '*toma*'. With a disapproval rating that peaked at 82.9% of the population (*El Universo* 2003), Toledo declared a state of national emergency, which included suspending certain constitutional rights, such as the rights to collective action and free movement.

As a result of this measure, the military and police stormed the university campus on 29 May to free the blockade that had been in place for almost a month. The military successfully ambushed the students and took control of the UNA campus. One student was shot dead, and another 40 were badly injured (*La Republica* 2003).

Despite the terrible outcome, and widespread opposition to the brutal use of military force, the then Minister of Defence, Loret de Mola, argued that '. . . [the military responded] to the provocations of students, and other people who were Shining Path militants . . . the military heard subversive [Shining Path] chanting, and they shot, first into the air, and then at the students to save their lives' (*La Republica* 2003). A day after the events, the National TV institute broadcast (*Television Nacional del Peru*, TNP in Spanish) the government's version of events, with members of the military declaring they heard 'Shining Path chanting, and were attacked by the students' (LUM 2016).

Case study 2: Repression in the capital

In 2008, there was another significant uprising, this time in Lima, Peru's capital. Student organisations at the Universidad Nacional Mayor de San Marcos (UNMSM) (which previously saw military intervention in 1991) fiercely opposed the construction of a new bypass sponsored by the city council. The Ministry of Transport, which had not consulted with university representatives regarding the project, proposed it would improve transit in the city – however, it would also mean the destruction of the university's campus (Int. #11, similar in #15, #19, #20).

UNMSM has constantly struggled to find space to secure its operations. Since its foundation in 1551, the university has been moved physically far away from important government buildings. In the 1960s, it was confined to the city boundaries, so that protesting students could not reach the Parliament building or the Government Palace (Burga 2008). This trend has continued over the years, and further attempts to reduce university spaces have followed, the most notorious being the construction of the bypass which would mean the loss of 9000 square metres of the university's campus. One of the *dirigentes* interviewed said: '. . . the city council project [the bypass] will destroy the university . . . there is noise from the passing cars, insecurity will grow . . . we have to consider that [both the university] and municipal authorities have not consulted with anyone'. Another said: '. . .we live in a state of abandonment; there is no money, no teachers, no internet. . .' (Int. #10).

Paradoxically, while the government championed the construction of a new road, at the same time destroying one of its public university campuses and putting the students under stress and in danger, they also moved to stigmatise the students and their complaints. The mayor of Lima, Luis Castaneda (2003–2010), is recorded as saying: '. . . every project we implement has generated protests, its okay for us and with the students that is no different, the problem is that with every protest there are subversive groups – only 200 of them' (*Gestión* 2019).

Despite the opposition of the *dirigentes*, in June 2008 the city council began demolishing parts of the university and planned to begin construction of the bypass. The students immediately called for a general strike and performed another '*toma*'. At the time of my interviews, most *dirigentes* considered these events to be one of the reasons for the reconstruction of the university federation in 2015 (*Gestión* 2019). In fact, for a long time after the *fujimorista* intervention, organic student representation remained low profile. This external event put student representatives, as the voice of the university's concerns, at the forefront of the public debate. As one of them, now graduated and an attorney, revealed: '...the university walls had been destroyed over the weekend, without dialogue ...and we wanted the media to know that our actions were intended to defend our public university...' (Int. #13).

In practice, however, the students were displayed in the media as 'terrorists' and 'masked vandals', rejecting any city development (Int. #8, similar in #9). On 8 May 2008, a planned march from the university campus to the city council offices was forcefully repressed by the police. Despite claims that the march 'was pacifist in nature, and intended to let society know that we want development of the city but with respect for our campus' (*La Republica* 2008), the police used tear gas and opened fire against the students, later entering the university campus. As a result, 17 students were injured and 24 arrested, mainly student *dirigentes* (*Gestión* 2019).

Despite the actions of the authorities, subsequent media portrayals of the students as 'terrorists' and the city council being adamant they would not withdraw the project, the students effectively managed to halt construction by constantly occupying the area where the road should have been built. However, those parts of the university demolished in June 2008 would not be rebuilt either by the university authorities or the council (Durand Guevera 2019).

Most recently, in April 2019, there was another clash between the students and the police: student demands for the reconstruction of their university and an announcement by the city council that they were to pursue the building of the bypass triggered new protests. In September 2019, backed by a reconstructed federation (the FUSM) and the support of the national students' organisation (FEP), the students once more occupied the campus, as in 2008. The media portrayed the student protest as a 'terrorist resurgence'. For the *dirigentes* of the UNMSM, this is a common organised response that reflects how civil society, the media and government view public universities. One said: 'This is a recurrent theme when students from public universities protest' (Int. #17). Another stated: '...the media, authorities and government actively lie about the public universities ...they only report about us when there is a conflict, but all the time we have no regular faculty and no infrastructure ... and then they want to build a bypass over our heads' (Int. #14). A third added: '...we come to public universities full of expectations...but what we have is this' (Int. #20). The '*toma*' continued until 19 September 2019 when the police stormed the university campus firing tear gas to disperse the students, detaining 17 of them – again mostly *dirigentes* (*La Republica* 2019).

Case study 3: A different treatment

The government response, however, is notably different when private university students protest. One notable case is the conflict between the Pontificia Universidad Catolica del Peru (PUCP) and the Archbishop of Lima in 2011. This conflict, despite being regulated by the Canonical Law, and thus a private matter, attracted public and media attention and a call for the central government to intervene in favour of the university (BBC 2011). Accordingly, the PUCP student federation (FEPUC) – the only student federation in the private sector – called for action to 'save' the university from the archbishop's 'intervention' (Perú21 2012). The conflict spilled over into the media, where student representatives voiced their concerns and journalists presented the conflict as an attempt by a 'far-right archbishop, Juan Luis Cipriani' to launch an attack 'on academic freedom' (Neuman and Zarate 2012).

Unlike the response to protests in the public system, that by the students of PUCP was not portrayed as a 'terrorist resurgence' or the students as 'vandals' – instead, the 'pacifist' nature of their collective action was constantly emphasised. Despite the students blocking roads on 23 September, there was no police intervention or repression. Yet, this was not the first conflict the university's students were involved in. Repeatedly, FEPUC together with other students' representatives have called for action against the governing board of the university because of rises in student fees (RPP 2011). For instance, on 17 August 2018 students blocked the entrance to the campus, closing public roads in front of the university, protesting for '. . . more transparent economic management of their institution and a real cost determination of the semester fees' (*La Republica* 2011). But again, there was no police intervention.

Later in 2018, the National Institute of Intellectual Property and Competence (INDECOPI) found that since 2011, the university had been illegally levying fines for delays in the payment of students' fees and ordered the repayment of monies held by the university (Perú21 2018). Accordingly, FEPUC also called for the occupation of the university's buildings, effectively blocking its campus entrance. On 4 December 2018, a '*toma*' was declared, and in an official communication FEPUC claimed that the illegal fines not only revealed that there was an 'abuse of authority', but also a long-term lack of transparency as regards the management of the university's accounts (*Wayka.pe* 2018). As a result of these actions, the governing board of the university resigned, but only after its president, Marcial Rubio, admitted publicly that the university resorted to illegal charges because of 'their flawed economic position . . . [after years] of struggle against the Archbishop of Lima' (RPP 2018). Again, at no time did the police intervene.

Discussion and conclusion

The cases analysed here illustrate that Peru's governmentality operates through the purposeful segmentation of its population based on their presumed value to society. Throughout history, this differentiation has existed, yet under the Peruvian 'neoliberal' governmentality, the mechanism appears more subtle and hard to identify. Previous studies have portrayed the deep divide in public/private higher education in the country in terms of under-employment (Lavado et al. 2014), a general lack of capacity (Yamada and Oviedo 2016) and the radicalism (Jave et al. 2014) of public university students, yet 'governmentality' helps us to see beyond such stereotypical portrayals. This concept helps us to disentangle the underlying reasons for the divide – that is, the *raison d'état* (racialisation), the mechanism of operation (segmentation of the population) and power technologies (responsibilisation/sovereignty) responsible for dualising the Peruvian higher education system. In doing so, this chapter has adopted Foucault's genealogical approach. This method allows the identification of discursive changes, which, when viewed in a specific historical period, shape a certain governmentality. Specifically, the genealogical approach has guided my search for discursive change in Peru since the 1990s, when the higher education narrative shifted towards neoliberal principles. But also, it guided me further: to realise the racialised narratives predominant in almost every aspect of the country's political sphere.

In this context, this chapter shows that Peruvian higher education institutions are subject to different power technologies. While repression is actively used as a mechanism to stigmatise public university students, private universities benefit from a variety of financial exemptions and political favours. But the divide is even more profound, in that public universities are considered 'no go areas', a latent 'terrorist' threat and in need of 'ascetic cleansing' (Jave et al. 2014). Theorised as 'potential threats', then, public university students are a population that require sovereign control. This is manifested in the power of taking students' life, repressing the existence of the abnormal in a way that is conducive to defend society – to everyone– '. . . for the purpose of wholesale slaughter in the name of life necessity' (Foucault [1976] 1978: 137). This is not the case for private higher education institutions in Peru.

As a final reflection, the use of governmentality – and genealogy – also requires us to make use of multiple data sources (primary and secondary) to help reconstruct how certain discourses (neoliberalism in this case) underlie the politics of higher education movements. Together, the data shed light on the 'unspoken' mechanisms governing the duality of the higher education system in Peru and the particular racial connotations that sustain it (Foucault [1975] 1991: 30).

Note

1   Universidad 'La Cantuta', Universidad Nacional del Centro, and the Universidad Nacional San Cristobal de Huamanga.

References

ABC (2003), 'Toledo declara el Estado de Emergencia para frenar a los sectores huelguistas', *ABC*. Available online: https://www.abc.es/internacional/abci-toledo-declara-estado-emergencia-para-frenar-sectores-huelguistas-200305290300-184125_noticia.html (accessed 16 October 2019).

Arrunategui, C. (2010), 'El racismo en la prensa escrita peruana. Un estudio de la representación del Otro amazónico desde el Análisis Crítico del Discurso', *Discurso & Sociedad*, 4 (3): 428–470.

Barrenechea, R. (2014), *Becas, bases y votos. Alianza para el Progreso y la política subnacional en el Peru*, Lima: Instituto de Estudios Peruanos.

BBC (2003), 'Perú: más protestas y marchas de duelo', *BBC*. Available online: http://news.bbc.co.uk/hi/spanish/latin_america/newsid_2954000/2954032.stm (accessed 16 October 2019).

BBC (2011), 'Perú: la pulseada entre la Universidad Católica y la Iglesia', *BBC*. Available online: https://www.bbc.com/mundo/noticias/2011/09/110927_peru_conflicto_universidad_catolica_arzobispo_lima_jp (accessed 16 October 2019).

Biebricher, T. (2008), 'Genealogy and governmentality', *Journal of the Philosophy of History*, 2 (3): 363–396.

British Council (2016), *'La reforma del sistema universitario peruano: internacionalización, avance, retos y oportunidades'*, Lima: British Council. Available online: https://www.britishcouncil.pe/sites/default/files/la_reforma_del_sistema_universitario_peruano_-_internacionalizacion_avance_retos_y_oportunidades.pdf.

Burga, M. (2008), *La reforma silenciosa. Descentralización, desarrollo y universidad pública en el Perú*, Lima: Red para el Desarrollo de las Ciencias en el Perú.

Burns, K. (1998), 'Gender and the politics of mestizaje: The convent of Santa Clara in Cuzco, Peru', *The Hispanic American Historical Review*, 78 (1): 5–44.

Castro, J. and Yamada, G. (2013), *Calidad y acreditación de la educación superior: retos urgentes para el Perú*, vol. 1, Lima: Fondo Editorial, Universidad del Pacífico.

Collyns, D. (2019), 'Telesup school's fake facade called "a symbol of Peruvian university system"', *The Guardian*, 8 July. Available online: https://www.theguardian.com/world/2019/jun/08/telesup-schools-fake-facade-called-a-symbol-of-peruvian-university-system.

Congress of Peru (1996), 'Ley de Promoción de la Inversión en la Educación', *El Peruano: Normas Legales*. Available online: http://www.leyes.congreso.gob.pe/Documentos/DecretosLegislativos/00882.pdf.

Contreras, C. and Oliart, P. (2014), *Modernidad y Educación en el Perú*, Serie Diversidad Cultural 8, Lima: Ministerio de Cultura. Available online : https://centroderecursos.cultura.pe/sites/default/files/rb/pdf/ModernidadyeducacionenelPeru.pdf.

Cuenca, R. (ed.) (2015), *La educación universitaria en el Perú: democracia, expansión y desigualdades*, Lima: Instituto de Estudios Peruanos. Available online: http://repositorio.iep.org.pe/bitstream/IEP/603/2/estudiossobredesigualdad10.pdf.

CVR (2004), 'Informe Final de la Comision de la Verdad y Reconciliacion. Capitulo: Las Universidades. Lima: Comision de la Verdad', in CVR, *Informe Final de la Comision de la Verdad y Reconciliacion*. Available online: http://cverdad.org.pe/ifinal/.

de la Fuente, J.R. (2017), 'Las universidades latinoamericanas en el siglo XXI: globalización y calidad', in *Hacia dónde va la universidad latinoamericana? Experiencias de gestión, 2000–2010*, 63–68, Lima: Consejo Nacional de Educación. Available online: http://www.cne.gob.pe/uploads/libro-hacia-do-nde-va-la-universidad-latinoamericana.pdf.

Dean, M. (2010), *Governmentality: Power and Rule in Modern Society*, London: Sage.

Drinot, P. (2006), 'Construcción de nación, racismo y desigualdad: una perspectiva histórica del desarrollo institucional en el Perú', in J. Crabtree (ed.), *Construir instituciones: democracia, desarrollo y desigualdad en el Perú desde 1980*, 11–33, Lima: Instituto de Estudios Peruanos. Available online: online: https://core.ac.uk/download/pdf/51208985.pdf↑ge=11.

Drinot, P. (2011), 'The meaning of Alan García: Sovereignty and governmentality in neoliberal Peru', *Journal of Latin American Cultural Studies*, 20 (2): 179–195.

Drinot, P. (ed.) (2014), *Peru in Theory*, London: Springer.

Durand Guevera, A. (2019), 'Cien años de la reforma universitaria: un itinerario inconcluso', *Revista Quehacer*. Available online: http://revistaquehacer.pe/n3 (accessed 16 October 2019).

El Comercio (2016), 'Cuando el Ejército entró a San Marcos y La Cantuta hace 25 años', *El Comercio*. Available online: https://elcomercio.pe/huellas-digitales/archivo/ejercito-entro-san-marcos-cantuta-25-anos-207690-noticia/ (accessed 16 October 2019).

El Universo (2003), 'Toledo con 9.2% de aprobación, según sondeo', *El Universo*. Available online: https://www.eluniverso.com/2003/07/21/0001/14/808AF7630E464 09E9EBEB0001BBC0CC8.html (accessed 16 October 2019).

Feagin, J.R., Orum, A.M. and Sjoberg, G. (eds.) (1991), *A Case for the Case Study*, Chapel Hill, NC: University of North Carolina Press.

FEP (2016), 'Boletin de la Federacion de Estudiantes del Peru', *Autonomía*. Available online: https://issuu.com/mmjjaagg/docs/i_bolet__n_de_la_fep (accessed 16 October 2019).

Ferrari, A. (1984), 'El concepto de indio y la cuestión racial en el Perú en los "Siete ensayos", de José Carlos Mariátegui', *Revista Iberoamericana*, 50 (127): 395–409.

Foucault, M. ([1961] 1965), *Madness and Civilization: A History of Insanity in the Age of Reason*, trans. R. Howard, New York: Vintage Books.

Foucault, M. ([1963] 1973), *The Birth of the Clinic: An Archaeology of Medical Perception*, trans. A.M. Sheridan, New York: Pantheon Books.

Foucault, M. ([1969] 1972), *The Archaeology of Knowledge*, trans. A.M. Sheridan, New York: Pantheon Books.

Foucault, M. ([1975] 1991), *Discipline and Punish: The Birth of the Prison*, trans. A.M. Sheridan, London: Penguin.

Foucault, M. ([1976] 1978), *The History of Sexuality*, trans. R. Hurley, New York: Pantheon Books.

Foucault, M. (1994), *Power: The Essential Works of Foucault 1954–1984*, ed. J.D. Faubion, London: Penguin.

Foucault, M. (1997), *Ethics: The Essential Works of Foucault 1954–1984*, ed. J.D. Faubion, London: Penguin.

Foucault, M. (1998), *The Will to Knowledge: The History of Sexuality*, vol. 1, trans. R. Hurley, London: Penguin.

Foucault, M. (2008), *The Birth of Biopolitics: Lectures at the Collège de France, 1978– 1979*, ed. M. Senellart, trans. G. Burchell, London: Palgrave Macmillan.

Gestión (2019), 'Estudiantes toman universidad San Marcos: seis claves para entender el conflicto por el "by-pass"', *Gestión*. Available online: https://gestion.pe/peru/ estudiantes-toman-universidad-de-san-marcos-seis-claves-para-entender-el-conflicto-por-el-by-pass-fotos-nndc-noticia/ (accessed 16 October 2019).

Jave, I., Cépeda Cáceres, M. and Uchuypoma, D. (2014), *Entre el estigma y el silencio: Memoria de la violencia entre estudiantes de la UNMSM y la UNSCH*, Lima: Pontificia Universidad Católica del Perú, Instituto de Democracia y Derechos Humanos.

Jessop, B. (2011), 'Constituting another Foucault effect: Foucault on states and statecraft', in U. Bröckling, S. Krasman and T. Lemke (eds.), *Governmentality: Current Issues and Future Challenges*, 56–73, London: Routledge.

La Republica (2003), 'Loret de Mola exculpa a militares por muerte de estudiante en Puno', *La Republica*. Available online: https://larepublica.pe/politica/357350-loret-de-mola-exculpa-a-militares-por-muerte-de-estudiante-en-puno/ (accessed 16 October 2019).

La Republica (2008), 'Dura represión a sanmarquinos deja 17 heridos y 24 detenidos', *La Republica*. Available online: https://larepublica.pe/politica/224265-dura-represion-a-sanmarquinos-deja-17-heridos-y-24-detenidos/ (accessed 16 October 2019).

La Republica (2011), 'Alumnos de la PUCP realizan plantón en defensa de las escalas de pago', *La Republica*. Available online: https://larepublica.pe/sociedad/565546-alumnos-de-la-pucp-realizan-planton-en-defensa-de-las-escalas-de-pago/ (accessed 16 October 2019).

La Republica (2019), 'Alumnos de San Marcos levantan toma de campus tras lograr acuerdos con rector', *La Republica*. Available online: https://larepublica.pe/sociedad/2019/09/22/protestas-en-san-marcos-alumnos-de-la-unmsm-levantan-toma-de-ciudad-universitaria-tras-acuerdos-con-rector-orestes-cachay/ (accessed 16 October 2019).

Latina (2007), *Documentary: Fujimori: La guerra clandestina*, part 2 of 2, *YouTube*. Available online: https://www.youtube.com/watch?v=UonuJ_IIeW8 (accessed 16 October 2019).

Lavado, P., Martinez, J. and Yamada, P. (2014), 'Una promesa incumplida? La calidad de la educación superior universitaria y el subempleo profesional en el Peru', Working Paper Series 2014, Banco Central de Reserva del Peru.

Lemke, T. (2001), 'The birth of bio-politics': Michel Foucault's lecture at the Collège de France on neo-liberal governmentality', *Economy and Society*, 30 (2): 190–207.

Lemke, T. (2019), *A Critique of Political Reason: Foucault's Analysis of Modern Governmentality*, trans. E. Butler, London: Verso.

LUM (2016), 'Enfrentamiento entre estudiantes y militares en Puno. Centro de Investigacion y Documentacion', Lima: Ministerio de Cultura. Available online: https://lum.cultura.pe/cdi/video/enfrentamientos-entre-estudiantes-y-militares-en-puno.

Macera, D. (2017), 'San Marcos el suertudo, por Diego Macera', *El Comercio*. Available online: https://elcomercio.pe/opinion/columnistas/san-marcos-suertudo-diego-macera-412776-noticia/ (accessed 16 October 2019).

Mahon, M. (1992), *Foucault's Nietzschean Genealogy: Truth, Power, and the Subject*, New York: SUNY Press.

McNay, L. (2009), 'Self as enterprise: Dilemmas of control and resistance in Foucault's *The Birth of Biopolitics*', *Theory, Culture and Society*, 26 (6): 55–77.

Moraña, M. (2012), 'El Ojo que Llora: biopolítica, nudos de la memoria y arte público en el Perú de hoy', *Latinoamérica. Revista de estudios Latinoamericanos*, 54: 183–216.

Neuman, W. and Zarate, A. (2012), 'Catholic Church and university in Peru fight over name', *The New York Times*, 1 August. Available online: https://www.nytimes.com/2012/08/02/world/americas/catholic-church-and-university-in-peru-fight-over-name.html?pagewanted=1&_r=4&ref=world (accessed 16 October 2019).

Nureña, C.R. (2016), 'El estigma genera despolitización?: participación, estigmatización por la violencia política y rechazo a Sendero Luminoso en la Universidad Nacional Mayor de San Marcos', *Revista Andina de Estudios Políticos*, 6 (2): 117–133.

Nureña, C.R., Ramírez, I. and Salazar-Morales, D. (2014), *Jóvenes, universidad y política: una aproximación a la cultura política juvenil desde las perspectivas de los estudiantes de la Universidad Nacional Mayor de San Marcos*, Lima: Senaju.

Perú21 (2012), 'El conflicto no es con Cipriani', *Perú21*. Available online: https://peru21. pe/lima/conflicto-cipriani-17998-noticia/ (accessed 16 October 2019).

Perú21 (2018), 'Conoce por qué la PUCP está devolviendo dinero a sus alumnos', *Perú21*. Available online: https://peru21.pe/peru/atencion-pucp-realizo-cobros-ilegales-alumnos-devolviendo-fotos-443289-noticia/ (accessed 16 October 2019).

Peters, M.A. (2007), 'Foucault, biopolitics and the birth of neoliberalism', *Critical Studies in Education*, 48 (2): 165–178.

Pribilsky, J. (2009), 'Development and the "Indian Problem" in the Cold War Andes: *Indigenismo*, science, and modernization in the making of the Cornell-Peru Project at Vicos', *Diplomatic History*, 33 (3): 405–426.

Puiggrós, A. (1996), 'Educación neoliberal y quiebre educativo', *Nueva Sociedad*, 146: 90–101.

Ramírez Zapata, I. and Nureña, C.R. (2012), El pensamiento Gonzalo: la violencia hecha dogma político, Lima: Secretaría Nacional de la Juventud.

RPP (2011), 'Estudiantes de la PUCP realizaron protesta en las afueras de su campus', *RPP*. Available online: https://rpp.pe/lima/actualidad/estudiantes-de-la-pucp-realizaron-protesta-en-las-afueras-de-su-campus-noticia-406652 (accessed 16 October 2019).

RPP (2018), 'PUCP: el escándalo de los cobros indebidos que derivo en la renuncia del rector Marcial Rubio', *RPP*. Available online: https://rpp.pe/peru/actualidad/pucp-el-escandalo-de-cobros-indebidos-que-derivo-en-la-renuncia-del-rector-marcial-rubio-noticia-1169033 (accessed 16 October 2019).

Sandoval, P. (2004), *Educación, ciudadanía y violencia en el Perú: una lectura del informe de la CVR*, Lima: Tarea and Instituto de Estudios Peruanos. Available online: http:// repositorio.minedu.gob.pe/bitstream/handle/123456789/479/268.%20 Educaci%C3%B3n%2C%20ciudadan%C3%ADa%20y%20violencia%20en%20el%20 Per%C3%BA%20una%20lectura%20del%20informe%20de%20la%20CVR. pdf?sequence=1&isAllowed=y.

Sandoval, P. and Toche, E. (2004), 'Las universidades después del conflicto: notas para un debate', in F. Reátegui Carrillo (ed.), *Realidades de posguerra en el Perú: omisiones, negaciones y sus consecuencias*, 51–62, Lima: PUCP.

Seshadri-Crooks, K. (2002), *Desiring Whiteness: A Lacanian Analysis of Race*, London: Routledge.

Springer, S. (2012), 'Neoliberalism as discourse: Between Foucauldian political economy and Marxian poststructuralism', *Critical Discourse Studies*, 9 (2): 133–147.

SUNEDU (2019a), 'Universidades Peru'. Available online: https://www.sunedu.gob.pe/ lista-universidades/ (accessed 16 October 2019).

SUNEDU (2019b), 'Estadísticas de Universidades por Programa de Estudios'. Available online: https://www.sunedu.gob.pe/sibe/ (accessed 16 October 2019).

Townley, B. (1993), 'Foucault, power/knowledge, and its relevance for human resource management', *Academy of Management Review*, 18 (3): 518–545.

Vargas, J. (2015), 'Navegando en aguas porcelanosas: una mirada al sistema universitario peruano', in R. Cuenca (ed.), *La educación universitaria en el Perú: Democracia, expansión y desigualdades*, 19–58, Lima: Instituto de Estudios Peruanos. Available online: http://repositorio.iep.org.pe/bitstream/IEP/603/2/estudiossobredesigualdad10.pdf.

Wayka.pe (2018), 'Alumnos de la PUCP anuncian plantón por cobros irregulares', *Wayka.pe*. Available online: https://wayka.pe/alumnos-de-la-pucp-anuncian-planton-por-cobros-irregulares/.

Yamada, G. and Oviedo, N. (2016), 'Educación superior y subempleo profesional: ¿Una creciente burbuja mundial?', *Documento de Discusión CIUP DD1609*, Diciembre. Available online: http://repositorio.up.edu.pe/bitstream/handle/11354/1428/DD1609.pdf?sequence=1.

Yazan, B. (2015), 'Three approaches to case study methods in education: Yin, Merriam, and Stake', *The Qualitative Report*, 20 (2): 134–152.

Yin, R.K. (1981), 'The case study crisis: Some answers', *Administrative Science Quarterly*, 26 (1): 58–65.

15

The Space of Authoring in Constructing Student and Graduate Career Identities

Fiona Christie, James Rattenbury and Fiona Creaby

Introduction

This chapter illustrates the application of Figured Worlds[1] theory (Holland et al. 1998) in exploring student and graduate identities. It argues that Figured Worlds offers a novel lens to explore contemporary identity in a context in which a competitive graduate labour market puts added pressure on individuals' sense of who they are and want to become. Figured Worlds is a socio-cultural theory that seeks to create a model for analysis and interpretation of social worlds that engages with how individuals and collectives respond to their cultural and material circumstances. Although the theory has been used within the social sciences for nearly twenty years, it has had limited reach amongst researchers of higher education. In their seminal book, *Identity and Agency in Cultural Worlds*, Holland et al. (1998) address a central paradox that humans are products of context and yet producers of remarkable improvisation. Predominantly, they hybridise Bakhtinian, Bourdieusian and Vygotskian ideas to argue for a social perspective that frames identity as a dialogical performance of multiple selves, continually developed through social engagement. We argue that the theory's blend of the traditions of Soviet philosophy and social psychology, American empirical anthropology and French sociology offers a valuable lens for analysis of individual subjectivities in contemporary contexts in which neoliberal ideas appear to have hegemonic influence over society, the economy as well as individual psychology. Such hybrid theory can serve to make us pause and reflect upon how we make sense of and resist social worlds, in which engines of control exist in dispersed ways. Notably, some of Holland and her co-authors' writing is being recently re-published, which is an indicator of its renewed appeal (Holland and Lave 2019).

Figured Worlds is a social practice theory, and it places emphasis on activity and the interaction of actors in specific contexts. It shares characteristics with social theory and theorists,(e.g. Archer 2007) who explore issues of the reflective self, and the role of structure and agency for individuals and collectives. In our view, a key marker of difference in Figured Worlds theory is its anthropological focus on culture in its micro-sociological analysis. It also gives priority to the relationship between theory and method. Perhaps owing to their American scholarly heritage, Holland et al. (1998) present theory using empirical data, resonating with the Chicago School's theoretically informed empiricism and symbolic interactionist approach (Blumer 1986; Mead 1934), which sought to uncover how individuals confer meaning on themselves, rather than how it is attributed by others.

We argue that there are implications for researching higher education based on application of the theory. A consideration of how Figured Worlds' tools are applied across different students/graduates offers a way to highlight and discuss how identity develops and how this can support individuals when constructing meaning and developing agency in uncertain circumstances. It allows for a critical review of contemporary higher education contexts, arguing that individual subjectivities are ignored when concepts such as the 'Student Voice' are co-opted as part of extended feedback collection, rather than exploring the complexity of student and graduate identities, and the normal multiplicity of voices therein. Particular strengths of the theory lie in tools such as a consideration of 'voice' and how people orchestrate dialogically competing 'voices' and 'narratives' ('heteroglossia') (Holland et al. 1998: 170). Notions of 'multi-voicedness' or 'heteroglossia' allow for a focus on dynamic individual subjectivities, which serve to firmly distance Holland and her co-authors' approach (1998: 45) from a classic Bourdieusian analysis, which argues that enduring habitus transformation can only occur across generations. We acknowledge that newer scholars of Bourdieu would take issue with their depiction of Bourdieusian theory and defend his work, arguing that it does allow for examples of shorter-term habitus evolution (e.g. Choudry and Williams 2016; Ingram and Abrahams 2015). However, we contend that Figured Worlds allows for a deeper exploration of how individuals/collectives make their own meaning, giving scope for small transformations.

Qualitative data from one of the authors' research with recent graduates in the north of England (Christie 2018) will illustrate the theory's application. The data presented will focus on imagined ideas of being a graduate and the career possibilities that may follow. Two exemplars are used to illustrate Figured Worlds' thinking tools. Presentation of data follows an in-depth analysis, giving close attention to interview data, which has been the predominant way that Figured Worlds has been applied. The integration of the theory's tools with contemporary literature about careers and employability informs the analysis outlined in this chapter. Figured Worlds broadly adopts a textual/narrative analytical approach, with priority given to elements of language, such as the imagery, tropes, repetitions, and new words that are used by participants.

Figured Worlds theory – underlying principles

Holland et al. (1998) synthesise ideas from a range of twentieth-century thinkers. From Bourdieu (1977 and Bourdieu and Passeron (1977)) they reshape notions of habitus into what they call 'history-in-person' (Holland and Lave 2001), i.e. those embodied dispositions and characteristics which constrain people but may also give scope and allow for improvisation. They also draw on ideas of the field, which they call 'figured worlds' (Holland et al. 1998: 41), where a set of structured practices and objective relations exist and position people, which Holland et al. depict figuratively, as well as materially. They invoke Bourdieu's (1977 and Bourdieu and Passeron's (1977)) depiction of agency, which involves strategic improvisation within the limited choices that are available within a field, exploring in some detail what needs to be in place for such agency to be enacted.

From Vygotsky (1978, 1986) and Leont'ev (1978) they adopt a focus on semiotic mediation in activity, and the conception of a self that develops within a 'zone of proximal development' (Holland et al. 1998: 272) and is associated with 'scaffolding' (1998: 83) that allows for growth. Their 'figured worlds' (1998: 41) share this focus on the symbolic. Building upon Bourdieu's (1977) emphasis on power in the field through objective agents and institutions, the 'figures' (Holland et al. 1998: 51) that appear in the 'figured worlds' of Holland and her co-authors may be material/embodied subjects and/or objects but are also likely to be mediated semiotically through cultural models and signs. Such signs that are framed linguistically can enter the psyche and become incorporated into one's 'history-in-person' (1998: 65), which can contribute to future reflection, improvisation and action in a process they call 'symbolic bootstrapping' (1998: 267). Such signs, symbols or mediating devices/tools may include specific words, metaphors or phrases, but also emblematic 'narratives' (1998: 53). They describe such signs as 'identity tools' (1998: 41). We argue, for example, that words or phrases such as 'the graduate' or 'the unemployed graduate' have both material and symbolic meaning. Graduation itself is steeped in symbols – for example, caps, gowns, certificates and ceremony, all acting as markers of the cultural importance of this life event. Signs may be rooted in use of figurative language, but arguably can also be traced in how graduates depict their situation in 'narrative' terms, drawing on discourses and cultural models.

Extending this use of the symbolic, from Bakhtin (1981, 1986), Holland et al. (1998) adopt an emphasis on the uses of language. They adopt the notion of 'dialogism' (1998: 169) and that individual speech and action are always in dialogue and responsive to others and context. Thus, people 'self-author' (1998: 170) their identities using the cultural tools that their historical context gives them, speaking in different genres as they generate 'narratives' (1998: 53) about themselves. Arguably, dominant discourses of graduate employability and careers have certain 'narratives' which underscore how individuals construct meaning (Christie 2018; Pryor and Bright 2008). Major 'narratives' (or what they also refer to as 'standard plots') include the 'narrative' of mobility and transformation ('rags to riches'), which is associated with the 'public story of higher education' (Brooks and Waters 2017; Finn 2015; Loveday 2015). Additionally, the 'narrative' of adversity ('overcoming the monster') is associated with neoliberal ideas of 'grit' (Duckworth 2016) and more recently 'resilience' (Burke and Scurry 2019). In addition, we as authors have suggested elsewhere four 'voices' that capture societal perspectives on careers (Christie 2019). The idealistic 'voice' resonates with a values-based and subjective definition of career success exemplified by the protean career orientation (Hall 2004). The tactical 'voice' evokes a more competitive and strategic approach (e.g. D'Alessandro 2008). The self-critical 'voice' reflects a belief in meritocracy, so lack of success is based on individual shortcomings (Moreau and Leathwood 2006). And finally, the context-critical 'voice' can stem from both a view of higher education as a disappointed consumer and/or an awareness of a degraded labour market for graduates (Standing 2014; Tomlinson 2014).

In homage to Bakhtin, Holland et al. refer to the 'space of authoring' (1998: 170) that is complementary to Vygotsky's 'zone of proximal development'. They also draw together Bakhtin's notion of the 'carnivalesque' and Vygotsky's notion of 'serious play' (1998: 272) to explore how the 'space of authoring' may offer scope for challenging rules, and argue that individuals may create new ways of thinking and acting, by the orchestration of the different 'voices', 'narratives' and discourses available to them within 'figured worlds'.

Holland et al. define 'identity in practice', which is the core object they seek to illuminate in their theory:

We take identity to be a central means by which selves, and the sets of actions they organise, form and re-form over personal lifetimes and in the histories of social collectivities ... Identity is one way of naming the dense interconnections between the intimate and public venues of social practice ... Practiced identities are constructs that can be referenced to several contexts of activity.

1998: 270–271

They go on to summarise four constructs (1998: 271-272) that can be used by those using a Figured Worlds lens. An understanding of these constructs is pivotal in considering what improvisation an individual may make within a field or figured world.

1. Figured worlds – the field populated with embodied and symbolic figures, and cultural models.
2. Positionality – the position held in a field linked to power, status and rank.
3. Space of authoring – the resources available to author self and narratives utilised.
4. World-making – the imagining of a different social positioning and structure, through the orchestration of existing cultural resources/voices.

In this chapter, we will focus primarily on the constructs of 'space of authoring' and 'figured worlds', and mainly explore the thinking tool of 'figured identities' (Holland et al. 1998: 141), and how these develop through the use of different 'voices' and 'narratives'.

Figured identities – on being and becoming a graduate

'Figures' that graduates author themselves in relation to can represent the idealised 'could be' or 'should be' models that individuals measure themselves against. Holland et al. (1998: 51) use examples of 'figures' within the domestic political world of Nepali women (e.g. a good woman or a good daughter). Others have applied Holland and her co-authors' theoretical notion of 'figures' – for example, in relation to competing 'figures' of being a 'caring' or 'competent' doctor (Bennett et al. 2017). In this tradition, it is possible to argue that 'figures' associated with being a graduate are embedded in cultural ideas of what it represents and how this relates to having a career that befits a graduate. A notion of what 'could be' or 'should be' influences how individuals explain their situation and what language they use. Such 'figures' are associated with the identity-making that graduates invest in and the liminality that is commonplace (Holmes 2015) for recent graduates' identity formation. This is called 'figured identity'.

The rite of passage of becoming a graduate has a long history, and was evocatively illustrated in the 1960s film *The Graduate* (director, Mike Nichols 1967), in which the lead character, who has just completed his degree and returns home to a party celebrating his graduation at his parents' house, is uncomfortable as his parents deliver accolades and neighbourhood friends ask him about his future plans. Despite the lead character's own ambivalence to his homecoming, such a depiction epitomises the 'figure' of a graduate as one of expectancy and hope, on the brink of a new life. This depiction is not just a private one but is also social; collectively graduates and their destinies act as a touchstone for what the future may be like for us all. Much of society invests considerable hope in graduates; the word itself invokes a certain status that is not accorded to other leavers of cycles of education/training such as school leavers or completing apprentices. The co-opting of the status of the word graduate has been attempted in other contexts, such as in the enactment of graduation ceremonies for nursery children. More recent depictions of the 'figure' of the graduate in contemporary literature are increasingly ambivalent (e.g. Bissett 2011; Killeen 2015), but retain hope and expectation at their core. Even hip-hop musicians write about what it is to be a graduate or conversely to be a 'college drop-out', illustrating the enduring cultural resonance of becoming or not becoming a university graduate (e.g. West 2004).

Labour market literature substantiates the ambivalence of such cultural evocations, illustrating how the definition of a graduate job has evolved (Elias and Purcell 2013), while the spectre of graduate unemployment/under-employment attracts media attention and fears of both economic and societal failure (CIPD 2015; Tholen 2014). Within this context of engrained but uncertain notions of what a graduate is, government-led employability policy drivers have contributed to defined notions of what being a successful graduate is as measured by positive outcomes in the guise of further study and graduate level employment (HESA 2016). Universities focus attention on skills, attributes, scholarship and citizenship (Barrie 2012; Dacre Pool and Sewell 2007; Yorke 2006) in outlining what characterises a graduate. Holmes (2015) has led criticism of prevailing ideas of measuring 'graduateness' in terms of skills/attributes, preferring to foreground a graduate identity approach; he argues that for individuals, it can be an uncomfortable journey to feel worthy to call themselves a graduate and being in a work/career situation that allows them to do this. Normative implications surrounding public policy and graduate career prospects are increasing, as it is suggested that funding for courses should follow likelihood of success in the labour market (Augar 2019).

'Figured identities' intersect with 'positional or relational identities', the latter giving more emphasis to issues of positioning, power and inequality that may impact on the ability to claim a 'figured identity'. Holland et al. describe this in their own empirical work on a university campus:

> They were gaining a sense of their position vis-à-vis others, noting their relative lack of privilege and power. They were developing relational identities along with the figured identities.

> 1998: 220

An exploration of 'positional identity' is a useful tool in contemporary society where there is considerable inequality, which impacts on graduate outcomes, as well as individual confidence to enter certain career fields. Inequalities are a preoccupation of sociological writing as well as policy-makers (Social Mobility Commission 2019; Bathmaker et al. 2016).

In using the construct 'space of authoring', Figured Worlds seeks to illuminate how individuals construct meaning dialogically around their 'figured' and 'positional identities'. In so doing, individuals draw upon different 'voices' and 'narratives' about careers and may begin to orchestrate these critically. We go on to present exemplars of the 'self-authoring' (Holland et al. 1998: 170) of two research participants, both of whom are young women from working-class backgrounds who graduated (2014) from the same mid-ranking university in northern England. Methods in the study blended semi-structured interviews and a biographical approach. They contrast in terms of subject studied (i.e. Accountancy and Performing Arts), as well as ethnicity (British Asian and Mixed). Their disciplines of study contrast in imagined ideas of being a graduate. Performing Arts subjects do not tend to promise normative possibilities of career success, whereas Accountancy offers clearer structured career pathways. The exemplars serve to bring alive the individual subjectivities that these young women engage with as they find their way in the world.

Applying theoretical tools

The Performing Arts graduate

Sophia is a Performing Arts graduate and can be observed explicitly comparing herself to notions of how a graduate of her subject might be viewed, as well as how this contests with wanting to call herself an actor, which is what she desires to become. At the time of participation in the project, she had graduated about eighteen months previously and had recently moved to France for a two-year programme at an acting school, uneasily making use of an inheritance from her late father.

Her 'self-authoring' is dialogic (Holland et al. 1998: 170) as she articulates her own story to the researcher but also with an eye on how the multitude of characters within society may view her. She navigates different 'figured worlds' (1998: 41) as she tells her story, from that of being a successful undergraduate, to being an unemployed actor, to moving to France to study acting. Hope and expectancy underpin how she talks about herself and she draws upon emblematic 'narratives' (and narrativised characters within these) (1998: 53) in explaining her positioning. She clearly reflects upon how society-at-large may position her as a Performing Arts graduate and answers (and resists) this with evocative language that traces her dialogic engagement with making sense of who she is. For her, having a degree has been about her creative development as a performer. She feels that society-at-large positions Performing Arts degrees negatively and she defends her degree, framing this politically by commenting on government policy.

> Leaving university with a Performing Arts degree can sometimes feel like you shouldn't have done it at all. It's very difficult to shake off the stereotype of being this showbiz, jazz hands, tokenistic, high energy team member. It can be demeaning at times: 'oh, you did performing arts, can I have a latte please'. I bet no one said that to Rik Mayall or Alan Rickman when they were studying. Performing Arts degrees have a bad rep for being doss degrees, and, of course, this stems from the governments lack of interest in Arts and Culture. Overall, I've learnt a lot from being at university, academically and personally (cliché I know).

Her view of her degree is coloured by the labour market reality that a degree is not necessary to become an actor. When asked about her career goals, she seeks clarification of what is meant by career, and whether acting is counted as a 'normal career' or 'something you just do'. The 'figure' of an actor has a strong pull for her, but it is a precarious 'figure' that she cannot claim just because she is a graduate in a suitable subject: 'I'm sort of determined to prove that I am worthy to be an actor'. Being a Performing Arts graduate and doing her degree in the face of detractors (notably she recounts how her late father dismissed her ambitions) is evidence of this personal commitment and sacrifice to become an actor. She believes that in France there is a more positive attitude to being an actor and the education associated with this, which is good for her own self-worth: 'being in the arts is very, very highly regarded, not like it is in the UK where it's just you work unpaid for as long as possible'.

Her experience at the acting school promises to be a transformative one and in telling this story she describes the leader of the school symbolically in heroic terms. She is 'mesmerised' by the experience and her commitment to the school is a sign of her commitment to be a 'worthy' actor. She chose the school over 'big dreams in London' of studying an MA at a specialist drama school. For her, 'acting is my life'.

> He [the school's lead teacher] will strip you down ... and then he's able to sort of push you in the right direction to show your beauty as an actor ... I'm having this sort of emotional sort of existential change, I'm still really in the same place as I was financially possibly, you know a year and a half ago ... another twenty something year old cliché, which is what we all are.

Being a performer appears to have been a therapeutic experience for her; drama was the only thing she liked at school and eventually excelled. Her attitude to her current programme of study follows in this tradition and she invests considerable hope in the school's lead teacher, whose methods are extremely tough. She talks about a low period soon after she graduated when she felt adrift. During this time, she describes her clichéd experience of an actor signing on the dole to the bewilderment of Job Centre staff. Pragmatic concerns continue to lurk behind her idealism about her acting career.

In her authoring of self, it is possible to observe 'heteroglossia' (Holland et al 1998: 170) as she switches 'narratives' and 'voices'/discourses – for example, Sophia's story shifts between adversity (relationship with family and school) and mobility (both geographically and personally) as she traces her path to becoming a 'worthy' actor. Interestingly, her use of these 'narratives' reflects her self-actualisation and transformation as she describes her experience at the French acting school which contrasts with conventional career advancement. In so doing, she captures a more idealistic 'voice' (Christie 2019), one that evokes a values-based orientation and a subjective measure of success (Hall 2004). We observe that by using the tool of 'heteroglossia', it is also possible to explore the tensions and contradictions in her story, such as the juxtaposed and narrativised 'father figures' of the father she rebelled against (and guiltily used an inheritance from) compared to her teacher who she eulogises. It is possible to see glimmers of what Holland et al. call 'world-making' (1998: 272) in how Sophia orchestrates these 'voices' and 'narratives' in order to develop her identity as a 'worthy actor' in 'newly imagined communities', which are far from her original family roots in an English town.

The Accountancy graduate

Our second exemplar is from Farzana who also participated in the research eighteen months after graduation. She took a four-year sandwich degree in Accounting and Finance with a placement in the third year. At the time of the interview, she was working as a trainee accountant and studying for the final stage of professional accounting exams. Like Sophia, she moves between different 'figured worlds' (Holland et al. 1998: 41), including that of being a successful undergraduate, a trainee accountant as well as that of her family context. She also draws upon mobility and adversity as 'narratives' (1998: 53), although in distinctly different ways to Sophia.

Although on a path that could be considered traditional in terms of a graduate career (i.e. with the scope for structured career advancement), Farzana reflects upon challenging experiences along the way. These depict her choices as illustrating her independence and her desire to break certain gender stereotypes. She describes a growing belief in her ability drawn from experiences at university such as being a student ambassador, to the discomfort of moving into professional accountancy. She balances this independence with a strong connection and loyalty to family, who are presented as important supporters and challengers. As such, she searches for her own subjective sense of identity across different 'figured worlds' and orchestrates different 'voices' (Holland et al 1998: 170) as she manages her desire to become a professional accountant while remaining a dutiful daughter.

Farzana recounts dialogically (Holland et al. 1998: 170) an early experience that stimulated her to explore accountancy. She describes a careers talk given at her all-girl's secondary school by the 'college careers guy', the content of which her form tutor clearly disagreed with.

> ... he was literally telling us about nursing careers, midwifery careers ... so quite a bit of a stereotype going on ... and our tutor at the time was like, 'hey you know ... cut everything that the college guy said, cos you girls, it doesn't mean you've got to limit yourself to those sorts of careers. You can go into business, you know, accounting' and then her exact words were, 'well if you want to be an astronaut tomorrow then go out and be it'.

This incident in which Farzana became aware of contrasting perspectives upon what women's careers should be, leads her to be more determined to build her own career in a non-stereotyped way. Arguably, in the 'figured world' of an all-girls school, there may well be greater attunement to old-fashioned though still-enduring stereotypes of female careers, although notably the form tutor also expresses their own bias in terms of idealised suitable careers for more academic girls. Farzana has responded to the idealism of her tutor though picking a more realistic career path (accountant rather than astronaut), but during the course of her interview does present an idealistic 'voice' (Christie 2019) of someone who is highly motivated in her occupation. This 'voice' may contradict clichéd notions of careers in accountancy being a pragmatic and lucrative choice for many.

Farzana utilises both mobility and adversity 'narratives' (Holland et al. 1998: 53) as she depicts her quest to become a chartered accountant. This requires her to develop the resources to imagine herself as one. This potential grows through her successful university career, though she also reflects on the adjustment from university to work environments. Although manifest differently to Sophia, Farzana also employs the 'narrative' of adversity when describing the 'sacrifice' she needs to make to qualify as an accountant, requiring considerable study for exams outside her working hours. The 'figure' (1998: 51) of a chartered accountant has a powerful draw for her.

> . . . my long-term aim was to be a professional chartered accountant . . . So yeh, you sacrifice your weekends, which has been the hard part, but it has to be worth it. It's a short-term sacrifice for the long gain . . . it's just determination and patience as well, cos I did fail one of them (exams) in between and I had to retake it and I passed it, so it's picking myself up and having the courage to take on such a hard task . . .

This adversity 'narrative' of bouncing back from failure is associated with neoliberal ideas about grit and resilience (Burke and Scurry 2019). Farzana is putting her own spin on this and 'self-authoring' (Holland et al. 1998: 170), with the implication that she is making sense of the tensions between failure and quitting, together with the importance of using her support network in keeping going.

Farzana presents as aware of how her identity must change in order to be seen as a nascent finance professional. She recounts the significance of important mentors and senior colleagues as role models. These individuals do not have the heroic depiction that Sophia presents, however, they appear as valuable gatekeepers for her. In fostering these relationships that can give her the insider knowledge that her family cannot, she demonstrates a tactical 'voice' (Christie 2019) in relation to employability, enacting the development of useful networks.

> . . . I like sort of talking to people that have 'been there done that' sort of thing and I do gain quite a lot of insight into their careers . . . I do like to sort of, maintain those kind of relationships. I've got a lot from it. They do kind of push me on quite a lot and that's the reason why I'm working so hard as I am today.

Notably, Farzana positions her family as a significant influence upon her and giving her the support and motivation she craves. She articulates her 'family mantra' that education is pivotal to occupational and social mobility. She expresses considerable loyalty and obligation to her family having lived at home throughout university and beyond, with no desire to live independently from them. As the youngest of six sisters, she considers family as important to her in paving the way for female independence.

> ... my father sort of pushes us into education, you know has that sort of mantra that without education you won't really go far ... I am a family sort of girl and I didn't really want to move out, they [parents] didn't get to go to university so that's why we sort of appreciate the fact that we've got the opportunity and that's why as I say, we've all pushed on so much ...

She talks about saving for a deposit on a house and moving in with her partner in the near future, indicating that she is ready for financial and domestic independence. Her negotiation of her 'positionality' as a young woman (managing social and familial expectations) alongside a figuring of her identity as a graduate and professional accountant illustrate a weaving of 'positional' and 'figured identities' (Holland et al. 1998: 220).

Farzana's story has firmly contradicted stereotypes of what someone like her should do while also fulfilling familial obligations. Although she is in what is deemed a very traditional graduate career, her story of reaching this position is not an ordinary one. Mobility and adversity 'narratives' underpin her story. She draws upon an idealistic 'voice' in which she claims a career in which she can harness her skills and knowledge fully, while also expressing a tactical 'voice' through which she has carefully employed additional resources, networks and sacrifices in order to get ahead. Like Sophia, in her heteroglossic orchestration of voices and narratives (Holland et al. 1998: 170), we can observe glimmers of her own 'world-making' (1998: 272) as she develops her own identity.

Critical reflection on theory and methodology

To facilitate a deep exploration and gain rich insights into 'identity in practice' (Holland et al. 1998: 271), Figured Worlds broadly adopts a narrative and textual analytical approach. Ethnographic, narrative and biographical approaches are often utilised depending on the research focus and context. A key aspect of Figured Worlds is the relationship between its four constructs and how an analytical focus on different constructs can facilitate methodological choice in ways that can best illuminate and explore 'identity in practice'. Holland et al. (1998) use data collected from different methods to explore each of the four constructs in-depth as they build towards the importance of each construct when understanding 'identity in practice'. Hence, a range of qualitative methods could be employed singularly or in tandem in Figured Worlds research, including: participant observation; interviews; stories, biographies and autobiographies; conversations and focus groups; journals and diaries; digital media; songs, poetry, video/film. However, some methods may be more appropriate in certain contexts than in others, such as observation when exploring children's identities through play (Barron 2014) or cultural rituals, dress and the use of artefacts and symbols (Holland et al. 1998), or interviews in life-history approaches (Creaby 2016; Solomon 2012).

Our interest in student and graduate 'voice' influenced our choice to work with in-depth interviews as the most useful tool in allowing for a detailed exploration of dialogical tensions each participant experienced via analysis of the 'space of authoring' construct. Indeed, the potential for making sense of single stories is a strength of a Figured Worlds approach due to the richness this can bring to exploring identity in context and thus also influenced our participant numbers. Although the focus on individual cases can be problematic in generating recommendations for policy-makers, we argue that a focus on individual subjectivities is useful in highlighting complexity and that there are no 'one size fits all' recommendations to emerge from our analysis. However, it is striking to observe commonality in the deep personal engagement of both Sophia and Farzana in consideration of their careers. This reflects dominant individualistic discourses, which lead individuals to measure their own worth as people in whether they are successful or not. However, in both cases their orchestrations of different 'voices' and 'narratives' gives them scope to begin to evaluate such norms. We conclude that profound insights can be gained from individual cases, so that it is not necessary to become preoccupied with the unit of analysis when engaging with Figured Worlds.

In considering the challenges we faced in bridging the theory/method relationship, we reflect that Figured Worlds is a valuable and rich, yet complex framework. Underpinned by a social constructionist ontology and requiring a thorough understanding of socio-cultural perspectives, philosophical issues are integral to the research process as they constitute what researchers silently think about research (Scott and Usher 2010). As Braathe and Solomon (2014) and Creaby (2016) argue, a researcher's own position, bias, assumptions and subjectivities, along with matters of trustworthiness and multi-vocality, are important considerations in Figured Worlds research. In conducting analysis in this research project, an exploration of researcher 'positionality' as a careers professional at the participants' university and thus an 'insider' researcher (Mercer 2007) was helpful in being alert to the nuances of power, position and privilege within the higher education context. A consideration of the researcher's own role (with multiple identities as careers adviser, educator, scholar) in the dialogic social construction of participants' realities served to facilitate a deeper and more nuanced understanding.

We also recognise how using a Figured Worlds lens encourages academic knowledge exchange, which led us in writing this chapter together towards richer insights into our own understanding of student and graduate identities, as well as of each other as colleagues, which is important to us as higher education practitioners. Indeed, we argue that Figured Worlds requires reflexivity and is helpful in enriching practitioner understanding of the student experience. Thus, we feel that a researcher must anticipate the various nuances and challenges that are involved in engaging with a Figured Worlds lens, especially in practitioner inquiry and matters that relate to one's own professional identity.

In conclusion, we argue that Figured Worlds offers a valuable lens through which to explore the multiplicity of student and graduate identities and illuminate the space for possibility and agency. It can help to go beyond the dominant ways in which 'Student Voice' and 'Graduate Outcomes' are constructed and facilitate a deeper understanding of student and graduate journeys and our own roles as educators within learning communities.

Note

1   Figured Worlds in upper case refers to the theory as a whole; figured worlds in lower case is one of four constructs within the whole theory.

References

Archer, M.S. (2007), *Making Our Way through the World*, Cambridge: Cambridge University Press.

Augar, P. (2019), *Independent panel report to the Review of Post-18 Education and Funding*, CP 117, London: DfE. Available online: https://assets.publishing.service.

gov.uk/government/uploads/system/uploads/attachment_data/file/805127/
Review_of_post_18_education_and_funding.pdf.

Bakhtin, M. (1981), *The Dialogic Imagination: Four Essays*, Austin, TX: University of
Texas Press.

Bakhtin, M. (1986), *Speech Genres and Other Late Essays*, Austin, TX: University of
Texas Press.

Barrie, S.C. (2012), 'A research-based approach to generic graduate attributes policy',
Higher Education Research and Development, 31(1): 79–92.

Barron, I. (2014), 'Finding a voice: A figured worlds approach to theorising young
children's identities', *Journal of Early Childhood Research*, 12(3): 251–263.

Bathmaker, A.-M., Ingram, N.A., Abrahams, J., Hoare, T., Waller, R. and Bradley, H.
(2016), *Higher Education, Social Class and Social Mobility: The Degree Generation*,
Basingstoke: Palgrave Macmillan.

Bennett, D., Solomon, Y., Bergin, C., Horgan, M. and Dornan, T. (2017), 'Possibility and
agency in Figured Worlds: Becoming a "good doctor"', *Medical Education*, 51(3):
248–257.

Bissett, A. (2011), *Pack Men*, London: Hachette Books.

Blumer, H. (1986), *Symbolic Interactionism: Perspective and Method*, Berkeley, CA:
University of California Press.

Bourdieu, P. (1977), *Outline of a Theory of Practice*, trans. R. Nice, Cambridge Studies in
Social and Cultural Anthropology, vol. 16, Cambridge: Cambridge University Press.

Bourdieu, P. and Passeron, J-C. (1977), *Reproduction in Education, Society and Culture*,
London: Sage.

Braathe, H.J. and Solomon, Y. (2014), 'Choosing mathematics: The narrative of the self as
a site of agency', *Educational Studies in Mathematics*, 89 (2): 151–166.

Brooks, R. and Waters, J. (2017), *Materialities and Mobilities in Education*, Abingdon:
Routledge.

Burke, C. and Scurry, T. (2019), *Graduate resilience: A review of the literature and future
research agenda*, London: SRHE. Available online: https://www.srhe.ac.uk/
downloads/reports-2017/CBurke-TScurry-SRHE-Research-Report.pdf (accessed
23 September 2019).

Choudry, S. and Williams, J. (2016), 'Figured Worlds in the field of power', *Mind, Culture,
and Activity*, 24 (3): 247–257.

Christie, F. (2018), *Constructing early graduate careers: Navigating uncertainty in
transition*, PhD dissertation, Lancaster University.

Christie, F. (2019), 'Competing voices: A Figured Worlds approach to theorising
graduate perspectives on career success', *International Studies in Sociology of
Education*, 28 (3/4): 326–344.

CIPD (2015), *Over-qualification and skills mismatch in the graduate labour market*,
CIPD Policy report. Available online: www.cipd.co.uk/Images/over-qualification-
and-skills-mismatch-graduate-labour-market_tcm18-10231.pdf (accessed 23
September 2019).

Creaby, F. (2016), *Identity in practice: A sociocultural exploration of leadership learning and development*, EdD thesis, Manchester Metropolitan University.

Dacre Pool, L. and Sewell, P. (2007), 'The key to employability: Developing a practical model of graduate employability', *Education + Training*, 49 (4): 277–289.

D'Alessandro, D. (2008), *Career Warfare: 10 Rules for Building a Successful Personal Brand on the Business Battlefield*, New York: McGraw Hill Professional.

Duckworth, A. (2016), *Grit: The Power of Passion and Perseverance*, New York: Simon & Schuster.

Elias, P. and Purcell, K. (2013), *Classifying graduate occupations for the knowledge society*, Futuretrack Working Paper no. 5, Warwick: IER. Available online: www2.warwick. ac.uk/fac/soc/ier/futuretrack/findings/elias_purcell_soche_final.pdf (accessed 23 September 2019).

Finn, K. (2015), *Personal Life, Young Women and Higher Education: A Relational Approach to Student and Graduate Experiences*, Basingstoke: Palgrave Macmillan.

The Graduate (1967), [Film] Dir. M. Nichols, USA. Turnam Productions.

Hall, D.T. (2004), 'The protean career: A quarter-century journey', *Journal of Vocational Behavior*, 65 (1): 1–13.

HESA (2016), *Consultation on principles and future requirements for the UK's public interest data about graduates*, Cheltenham: HESA. Available online: https://www. hesa.ac.uk/innovation/records/reviews/newdlhe/consultation (accessed 23 September 2019).

Holland, D. and Lave, J. (eds.) (2001), *History in Person: Enduring Struggles, Contentious Practice, Intimate Identities*, Santa Fe, NM: School of American Research Press / Oxford: James Currey.

Holland, D., and Lave, J. (2019), 'Social practice theory and the historical production of persons', in *Cultural-Historical Approaches to Studying Learning and Development*, 235–248, Dordrecht: Springer.

Holland, D., Lachicotte, W., Skinner, D. and Cain, C. (1998), *Identity and Agency in Cultural Worlds*, Cambridge, MA: Harvard University Press.

Holmes, L. (2015), 'Becoming a graduate: The warranting of an emergent identity', *Education and Training*, 57 (2): 219–238.

Ingram, N. and Abrahams, J. (2015), 'Stepping outside of oneself: How a cleft-habitus can lead to greater reflexivity through occupying "the third space"', in J. Thatcher, N. Ingram, C. Burke, and J. Abrahams (eds.), *Bourdieu: The Next Generation: The Development of Bourdieu's Intellectual Heritage in Contemporary UK Sociology*, 140–156, Abingdon: Routledge.

Killeen, C. (2015), *In Real Life*, Edinburgh: Canongate Books.

Leont'ev, A.N. (1978), *Activity, Consciousness, and Personality*, trans. M.J. Hall, Englewood Cliffs, NJ: Prentice-Hall.

Loveday, V. (2015), 'Working-class participation, middle-class aspiration? Value, upward mobility and symbolic indebtedness in higher education', *The Sociological Review*, 63 (3): 570–588.

Mead, G.H. (1934), *Mind, Self and Society*, Chicago, IL: University of Chicago Press.

Mercer, J. (2007), 'The challenges of insider research in educational institutions: Wielding a double-edged sword and resolving delicate dilemmas', *Oxford Review of Education*, 33 (1): 1–17.

Moreau, M.P. and Leathwood, C. (2006), 'Graduates and employment and the discourse of employability: A critical analysis', *Journal of Education and Work*, 19 (4): 305–324.

Pryor, R. and Bright, J. (2008), 'Archetypal narratives in career counselling: A chaos theory application', *International Journal Educational Vocational Guidance*, 8 (2): 71–82.

Scott, D. and Usher, R. (2010), *Researching Education: Data, Methods and Theory in Educational Enquiry*, London: Bloomsbury.

Social Mobility Commission (SMC) (2019), *State of the Nation 2018–19: Social Mobility in Great Britain*, London: SMC. Available online: https://assets.publishing.service. gov.uk/government/uploads/system/uploads/attachment_data/file/798404/SMC_ State_of_the_Nation_Report_2018-19.pdf. UK Government.

Solomon, Y. (2012), 'Finding a voice? Narrating the female self in mathematics', *Educational Studies in Mathematics*, 80 (1/2): 171–183.

Standing, G. (2014), *The Precariat: The New Dangerous Class*, Londonk: Bloomsbury.

Tholen, G. (2014), *The Changing Nature of the Graduate Labour Market: Media, Policy and Political Discourses in the UK*, Dordrecht: Springer.

Tomlinson, M. (2014), *Exploring the impacts of policy changes on students' attitudes and approaches to learning in higher education*, York: HEA. Available online: https://www. heacademy.ac.uk/system/files/resources/exploring_the_impact_of_policy_changes_ student_experience.pdf (accessed 23 September 2019).

Vygotsky, L.S. (1978), *Mind in Society: The Development of Higher Mental Process*, Cambridge, MA: Harvard University Press.

Vygotsky, L.S. (1986), *Thought and language*, revised edition, Cambridge, MA: MIT Press.

West, K. (2004), *The College Dropout* [Album], USA, Def Jam Recordings.

Yorke, M. (2006), *Employability in Higher Education: What it is and what it is not*, York: HEA.

.

Index

9 781350 141551